Myths, Games and Conflict

Myths, Games and Conflict

Exploring the landscapes of Greek Gods and Heroes

Allan Brooks

Typeset by the author in Times New Roman 11pt

Maps and plans drawn by the author

All photographs are by the author

Cover design by the author

ISBN 978-1-4092-2232-3

Contents

Figures

Maps

Outline maps are based on those freely available from the Central Intelligence Agency. Site and town plans are sketch maps prepared by the author from observation and are only approximately to scale.

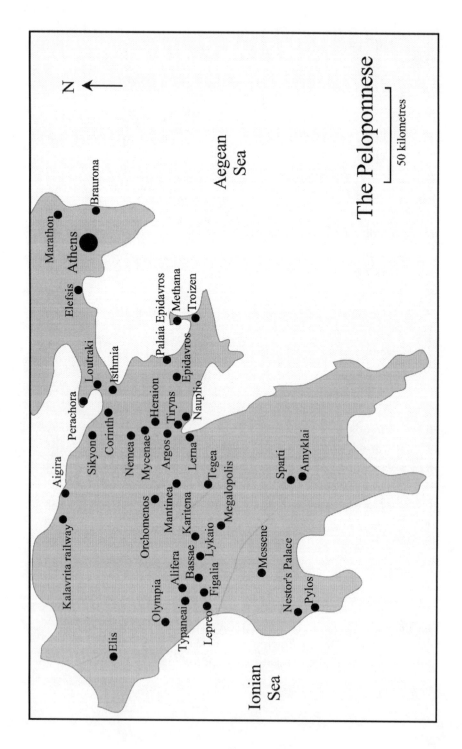

The Peloponnese

N

50 kilometres

Aegean Sea

Ionian Sea

Braurona
Marathon
Athens
Elefsis
Palaia Epidavros
Methana
Troizen
Loutraki
Isthmia
Epidavros
Perachora
Heraion
Corinth
Tiryns
Nauplio
Sikyon
Mycenae
Argos
Nemea
Lerna
Aigira
Tegea
Kalavrita railway
Orchomenos
Sparti
Mantinea
Amyklai
Karitena
Megalopolis
Olympia
Alifera
Lykaio
Bassae
Typaneai
Figalia
Messene
Lepreo
Elis
Nestor's Palace
Pylos

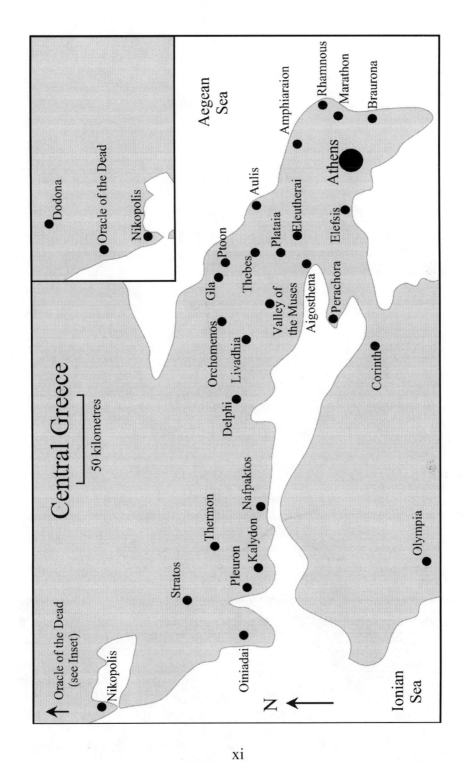

xi

Preface

The Greek Myths described what the ancient Greeks believed about their history, their ancestry and their gods. The myths were rooted in a real world, a compact physical environment of inhospitable, rugged mountains separating small agricultural plains, that occupy what is now southern and central Greece. This book is an exploration of that landscape and of the myths themselves.

The Greek pantheon was large and complex. The subject matter of the myths covers the gods' origins, their lives, and their relationships with humanity. There is a vast body of myth concerned with society itself: justifications for the form of social order, rites of passage from childhood into the adult world and the foundation of the communities themselves. Features in the landscape often have myths to explain their creation. There are also stories of the heroes, superhuman figures who, as a group, lie somewhere between gods and men. Their myths are often pan-hellenic but there are also local heroes venerated only within their own community.

With such a huge range of material any book describing the Myths must be selective. In this work selection is achieved by following a journey through the landscape of mainland Greece in a logical progression from sanctuary to sanctuary. Emphasis is placed on more isolated and remote locations. Whenever possible a god is introduced at the place where he was first known or where his cult was first celebrated, for example Dionysus is discussed at Eleutherai on the border between the territories of Thebes and Athens. The intention is to describe not just the roles of the major Greek gods but also regional variations of cult practice and examples of minor deities of importance only within their own locality. The well-known sites, Mycenae, Epidauros, Delphi and Olympia, are explored, but primarily from the perspective of their foundation myths and religious significance. Equal attention is given to examples of hero cults, for example the sanctuaries of Hippolytus at Troizen and Trophonios at Livadhia. The myths themselves are told, as far as possible, in their simplest form, omitting later embellishments.

Practical Notes

This book is a topographical guide to the Greek Myths. Its purpose is to relate the myths in their original settings: either the location in which the principal events were thought to have occurred, or the places in which they were celebrated. As such it aims to be a practical guide. The format therefore describes a set of logical itineraries that the visitor may follow. A hire car is the most convenient method of exploration. Chapters two, three and four follow a route that begins in Athens and leads via Thebes and Delphi to the famous sanctuary of Dodona in Epiros. Chapters five, six and seven describe various routes from Athens to Olympia and the western Peloponnese. Chapters eight and nine deal with the Argolid and the south and complete the journey around the Peloponnese. Many of the important sanctuaries described are in quite remote locations and detailed directions are given wherever necessary. For more basic practical information it is assumed that the reader will have access to one of the standard travel guides to Greece.

Budget airlines, inexpensive car hire and mobile phones have transformed travel in Greece but the country still suffers from a lack of good maps. One of the best available is the GeoCenter Euromap sheet, 'Greece and the Islands' at 1:300000. A good alternative, published in Athens, is the Road Editions series, which covers the entire mainland in five sheets at 1:250000. Number five, the Peloponnese, and Number four, Central Greece, cover the greater part of the routes in this book. They are sporadically available in UK bookshops, but are found everywhere in Greece, especially in any shop catering for foreign tourists. However, the following caveats apply. On the GeoCenter map passable rural tracks may not appear, while the Road Editions maps often show local roads in rural areas which may be little more than footpaths. Road Editions are much better at indicating archaeological sites, although they have lapses. The ideal solution is to have both maps and compare.

Another problem for the visitor is the vexed question of site opening hours. Archaeological sites in Greece fall into three main groups. The first are the most famous, Delphi, Olympia, Mycenae and Epidavros. These are enclosed, have prescribed opening times, usually longer than

Practical notes

average, and ticket offices. The second group includes a number of secondary Classical sites, also enclosed, some with ticket offices, some without, but with more limited opening hours subject to local variations. Those of the third group, the most numerous, and the subject of the greater part of this book, lie unenclosed and unvisited because of the seclusion of their locations.

Standard opening times are published, and can be found via alphabetical lists of archaeological sites and monuments at **www.culture.gr.** Winter opening hours should apply between November and March and are usually 8.30 to 15.00. Summer hours extend this to 17.00 or 18.00. Sites are often closed on Mondays, even if the published schedule states open daily. However these times are subject to frequent local variation. It is possible to find a site locked at 14.00 when stated hours are 8.30 to 15.00. Equally sites due to close at 15.00 may remain open into the evening. On public holidays sites are either closed, or occasionally, open and free. Unfortunately, the exact arrangements change from year to year. Places that were unfenced become fenced; fences become rusty and broken. Sites that appear fenced have unlocked gates, or gates only locked at dusk. Conversely, someone has to remember to unlock them each morning.

On a positive note there has been a dramatic improvement in road signs giving directions to the monuments of Greece. These signs, almost always brown, sometimes refer to the place by name, but more often simply by the ubiquitous phrase "Archaeological Site". They are now provided for virtually every known location in the country. Finding a site is therefore much easier and throughout this book these are simply referred to as 'brown signs'.

1

Introduction

Myth and religion in ancient Greek society

The monuments of Greece that can be seen today fall into three categories. Firstly, there are those of ancient Greek religion. Shrines, sanctuaries and temples clearly come under this heading, but there are also the theatres, gymnasia and stadia that were essential to Greek religious festivals and games. Secondly, there are the civic buildings, the fountains, stoas and meeting houses that surrounded and formed the Greek agora (usually translated, rather misleadingly, as the market place). Thirdly, there are the city defences, the cyclopean walls of the Bronze Age kingdoms and the lengthy circuits from the Classical and Hellenistic city-states that have survived all over rural Greece.

The title of the book reflects the facets of Greek culture and history that have shaped these monuments. The use of the word 'Myth' rather than religion is deliberate. Religion immediately brings to mind an organised Church with a priesthood, a creed or body of belief, and the notions of sin and an afterlife. All these ideas must be discarded to understand the way in which religion for the Greeks was embedded within their society. There was simply no division at all between the secular and the religious life. Other concepts alien to Greek religion, were those of Heaven and Hell in the later, Christian, sense. The heavens were for the gods alone. The underworld was not a place of punishment, but the dwelling place of the "shades of the dead". The souls of the dead were thought to dwell there as mere shadows with no real existence. A place of punishment, known as Tartarus did exist, but only a very few, guilty of the most terrible crimes, were imprisoned within. Tantalos, who cooked his own son and served him as a meal for the gods, was punished there for eternity (see Chapter 7). Sanctuaries had their priests but there was no hierarchy equivalent to the Christian Church. The organi-

1

sation of religious events, the great festivals and games, was in the hands of the civil authorities and, under democracy, the general assembly. With no centralised church and no single creed there could be no meaning to the idea of heresy. In fact, the only real religious crime possible was sacrilege, but this would be seen as breaking the rules of society rather than a separate religious offence.

The Greeks' conception of their gods was expressed in the tales we now call the Greek Myths. The word myth originally simply meant story and did not have the modern connotation of something fictitious. The myths had no definitive form. There was no single sacred text and they were often inconsistent. It was this very adaptability that allowed them to stay relevant as society and culture changed. Only the coming of Christianity ended over a thousand years of belief. The myths are primarily concerned with the interaction between men and gods in a past golden age when the gods sired children of mortal women. However this golden age was not in an unknown dateless past. It was thought to be a period of just a few generations that came to an end shortly after the events of the Trojan War. The great heroes of that time were the sons of gods but were not themselves immortal. The greatest of them all was Herakles, better known as Hercules. Although a flawed character capable of great cruelty (see Hercules the nose-slicer, Chapter 3), he did achieve immortality and a place on Mount Olympus. There are myths legitimising the founding of a city or colony, myths providing a ruling family with a genealogy linking it to a hero or god, myths designed to explain natural events, myths describing the intervention of the gods on behalf of the Greeks in battle, and myths that are the shadow of a genuine early history. There are also the creation myths that provide a link between the earlier worship of Mother Earth and the Olympian gods. There are examples of all of these in later chapters.

The Greek pantheon was already largely in existence by Mycenaean times. In its fully established form there were twelve principal gods; Zeus, Hera, Athena, Artemis, Apollo, Poseidon, Demeter, Dionysus, Aphrodite, Hephaistos, Hermes and Ares, perceived as dwelling on Mount Olympus. They were in fact the third generation of deities. The primary myth of the birth of the gods begins with Mother Earth, Gaia or Ge, emerging from Chaos, the empty and infinite space that existed before creation. She gave birth to her son Uranus (Ouranos), and by him she bore the Titans, the Cyclopes and the Hecatonkheries, the hundred-handed giants. Uranus was deposed by Kronos, one of the Titans. Kronos in his turn was deposed by his son Zeus (see Chapter 2). Zeus and his two brothers, Hades and Poseidon, then divided control of the world by lot. Zeus obtained the heavens, Poseidon the sea and Hades the underworld. The earth was to be shared by all three.

The Olympian gods were thought to have human form and many human attributes, both virtues and vices. They were born, had relationships and produced children. There is therefore a long list of minor gods from this extended family, often with important roles (for example see Nemesis, Chapter 2). This anthropomorphism extended to physical frailties; Hephaistos was born lame. Each of the major gods also had various powers, or spheres of influence, indicated by the various epithets attached to their names. For example Apollo is worshipped at Bassae (Chapter 7), as Apollo Epikourios, the Helper, and in Argos (Chapter 8), as Apollo Lykios, the Wolf-god. Often the epithet refers to a place, for example Apollo Ptoios, that is Apollo of Mount Ptoon (Chapter 3), and may simply reflect a community's need to differentiate their god from their neighbour's. However while the complete world of minor deities, heroes and sundry mythological creatures is incredibly complicated, this complexity does not prevent an understanding of the relationships between the Greeks and their gods.

Greeks paid respect to their gods by observing their cult. Animal sacrifice was the central ritual of cult practice. All that was necessary to create a shrine was to dedicate a place or an object to the god and to mark out the sacred area with boundary stones or a wall. For regular sacrifice an altar would be required, but shrines varied from the simple to the elaborate. Most shrines would have no temple. Although the temple seems to us the ultimate symbol of Greek religion, it was not a place of worship as such, but simply the building that housed the cult statue of the god. The centre of cult activity was the altar standing in the open air. Animal sacrifice was not the gory spectacle we might imagine, as the animal was slaughtered primarily to provide meat for the human participants. The sacrifice to the gods was simply the inedible parts of the beast, the bones and skin, burnt as an offering on the altar, a very pragmatic division. (See chapter 6 for the myth explaining the origin of this practice).

Although cult observance was essential to procure divine favour, the Greeks had limited expectations of the gods' influence on human behaviour. With no concept of original sin and no devil luring man from the correct path, they had no doubt that men were responsible for their own misfortunes. The gods might protect men from themselves and they might punish hubris, but their principal role was to reinforce social morality. What the Greeks hoped for from their gods above all else were the gifts of healing and prophecy. However the Greeks did not think of prophecy as fortune telling. The need to discover the will of the gods was an essential part of decision-making, whether the decision was personal, political or military. The Spartans notoriously delayed marching to battle until the omens were favourable. There are examples of healing sanctuaries and oracles throughout the book.

The Greeks also had shrines to the great heroes and venerated their tombs. They believed that the heroes were blessed with superhuman strength and something of this power persisted beyond the grave. The heroes were not restricted to figures from a mythical past. Any individual who performed great deeds could acquire this status and be venerated after his death. The 192 Athenians who died in the Battle of Marathon in 490 BC became heroes and their cult persisted for several hundred years.

The second element of this book's title refers to the Games and festivals that were such a fundamental part of Greek culture. Our perception of ancient Greek competition is dominated by images of the Olympic games, which are now thought of as athletic contests. But all the great games were religious events. Each of the four pan-Hellenic games was dedicated to a major deity, Zeus at Olympia and Nemea, Apollo at Delphi and Poseidon at Isthmia. There were numerous other subsidiary games and every city would have had its gymnasia and training ground. The games also usually included, and at Delphi began with, musical contests and the performance of tragedies and comedies. In fact, in Athens, drama festivals were always both competitions and religious events, the most famous being the Great Dionysia honouring the god Dionysus.

Conflict was a persistent element in Ancient Greek society and is a recurring theme in the myths. Many of the tales of the age of heroes are concerned with dynastic or territorial disputes. Battles between brothers over their inheritance are common. This is the basic theme of the war of the Seven against Thebes. One of Hercules's lesser known roles was as a sacker of cities. These myths must have reflected real conflicts between the Mycenaean states in the Bronze Age. The Greeks' anthropomorphic view of their gods means that they are often shown as interfering or meddling in human affairs. Jealousy is a frequent motive for their actions and they also show favouritism. Hera's jealousy over Zeus's affairs is the theme of many of the most potent myths. It was her actions that denied Hercules the kingdom of Mycenae. Conflict was certainly the most frequent condition in Classical times. The city-states were in constant dispute with each other, either individually or in short-lived alliances. Athens for example, fought two out of every three years throughout the 5C BC. In addition the Greek mainland as a whole was periodically threatened by external invaders. It was at these times that the cities would attempt to behave as a nation. Over the centuries alliances of Greeks fought against the Persians, the Macedonians, the Gauls and the Roman Empire. The gods were believed to have appeared and influenced the outcome of all the battles of the Persian War.

The history of Greece did not end with its absorption into the Roman Empire. Sacred sites were taken over by Christianity and many early sanctuaries have churches in their precincts to this day. If anything, the impact of conflict on the landscape intensified as the Empire began to collapse. The endless struggles between the Byzantines, the various marauding groups of opportunists collectively known as the Franks, the Venetians and the Turks in the following centuries, have left the coasts and strategic hilltops of Greece littered with forts and castles, often built with materials looted from classical ruins.

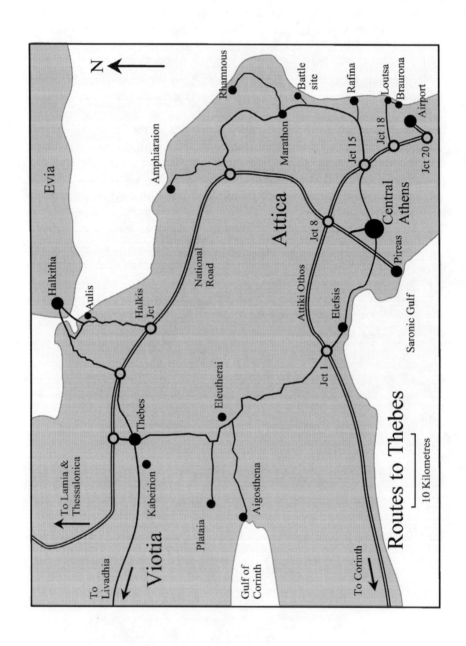

N

Rhamnous

Battle site

Rafina

Loutsa

Braurona

Airport

Jct 18

Jct 20

Jct 15

Marathon

Amphiaraion

Evia

Attica

Central Athens

Jct 8

Pireas

Halkitha

Aulis

National Road

Attiki Othos

Elefsis

Halkis Jct

Saronic Gulf

Eleutherai

Jct 1

To Lamia & Thessalonica

Thebes

Kabeirion

Aigosthena

Viotia

Plataia

To Livadhia

Gulf of Corinth

To Corinth

Routes to Thebes

10 Kilometres

2

Athens to Thebes

Rural Attica beyond Athens sees very few tourists. Two itineraries are described below. The first follows a coastal route from Athens to Thebes via Marathon, visiting the important sanctuaries of Artemis, Nemesis and Amphiaraos, as well as the site of Iphigenia's sacrifice at Aulis before the Greek fleet embarked for Troy. The second takes the old road to Thebes via Elefsis. Along this route there are remote and little visited sanctuaries, ancient cities, major battle sites and the locations of some of the most powerful of the Greek myths, those of Oedipus, Hercules and Dionysus.

A. Via the Coast

Braurona (Vravrona, Βραβρωνα)
Sanctuary of Artemis. Iphigenia and her brother, Orestes, brought the famous image of Artemis here from Tauris. The myth of Callisto.

Braurona lies on the coast due west of Athens and 7km south of the seaside resort of Loutsa. Here stand the remains of the Sanctuary of Artemis Brauronia, reputedly the site of the tomb of Iphigenia.

Artemis, Diana to the Romans, daughter of Zeus and Leto, was the virgin goddess of hunting and childbirth, and the protector of children. She was the twin sister of Apollo and shares many of his attributes. Like Apollo she was armed with a bow, and her arrows could send sudden death to women. Her mother, Leto, was the daughter of Coeus and Phoebe, two of the Titans, the children of Ouranos (Uranus) and Gaia. Zeus is said to have consummated his extra marital affair by changing himself and Leto into quails. Hera, Zeus's wife, was consumed with jealousy by the affair. She sent the serpent, Python, to pursue Leto

7

across the world. Leto fled to the island of Delos, originally called Or-
tygia, Quail Island, where the twins were born. Artemis was born of
Leto painlessly and, for this reason, she subsequently became the goddess of childbirth. After his birth, Apollo was to slay Python, his
mother's persecutor (see Chapter 3, Delphi).

The founding of the sanctuary at Braurona is related to the myths of
Iphigenia and her brother, Orestes. They are said to have brought the
statue of Artemis from Tauris, a city on the Black Sea coast, to
Braurona. The story began with the Greek fleet assembled at Aulis (see
below) in preparation for the expedition against Troy. The fleet was be-
calmed because Agamemnon, their leader, had offended Artemis by
killing one of her sacred animals. She had withheld the winds in retribution. Calchas, said to be the wisest seer of the Greeks, advised that
Agamemnon must sacrifice his daughter, Iphigenia, to placate Artemis.
Iphigenia was brought from Mycenae, believing she was to be married
to Achilles. Agamemnon accepted that the sacrifice must proceed, but
at the moment the knife descended, Artemis intervened and transported
Iphigenia to Tauris, putting a hart in her place on the altar.

At Tauris, Iphigenia became the priestess of Artemis. Her brother,
Orestes, came to Tauris at the bidding of the Delphic oracle to steal the
statue of Artemis and atone for his matricide. (The full story of Orestes,
in which he avenges the murder of his father by killing his mother,
Clytemnestra, is told in Chapter 8). The Taurians, who still practised
human sacrifice, captured Orestes and intended to sacrifice him to Artemis. However, Iphigenia recognised her brother. The two escaped to
Greece with the cult statue, landing at Braurona where the sanctuary
was subsequently established. This is the bare outline of the myth.

The sanctuary lies on the coast road, 14km due south of Rafina and
is easy to find. It lies in a marshy valley on the seaward side of the road
from Loutsa to Porto Rafti. The site is fully enclosed. The entrance and
ticket office are next to the road. The published opening hours are 8.30
to 15.00 daily, but the site is likely to be closed on Mondays. The small
hill to the right of the entrance has traces of occupation from 3500 BC
to 1300 BC, when it was abandoned. It is possible that this abandonment represents evidence for the myth of Theseus's unification of
Attica. The sanctuary appears to have been founded in the 8C BC but
was abandoned again in the 3C BC after flooding.

The most striking part of the site is the huge stoa, built in the 5C BC,
with three wings. A substantial part of the colonnade of the north wing
has been re-erected. The pillars and entablature that, from a distance,
appear to be part of a temple, come into view immediately on entering

the site. Behind the colonnade is a range of rooms that contained couches and stone tables. These are thought to have been examples of the ritual dining rooms often associated with Classical sanctuaries. The temple of Artemis, which lies between the stoa and the Byzantine chapel of St. George, now only exists as foundations. The best preserved element is the retaining wall. The altar may have stood on the site of the church. Just above the church are the remains of another shrine in front of more remains, buried by boulders. These are believed to be the collapsed roof of a cave and the site of the Tomb of Iphigenia.

The stoa has been identified by an inscription as the parthenon of the bears (arktoi). Here, young girls performed rituals and a dance, possibly in imitation of bears, during the festival known as the Brauronia, held every four years. These rites are not fully understood, but the clearest connection between Artemis and bears is found in the legend of Callisto, one of the followers of Artemis, who hunted with her in the mountains of Arcadia.

Callisto was the daughter of Lykaon (see Chapter 6, Lykosoura). She became a devoted follower of Artemis, taking part in the hunt and keeping a vow of chastity. Zeus fell in love with her and she became pregnant, either by seduction or rape. Callisto attempted to keep her pregnancy hidden from Artemis. However, her secret was revealed when the goddess and her followers came to bathe in a spring and Callisto was expelled for breaking her vow. Hera's jealousy and desire for revenge caused her to transform Callisto into a bear. Her fate was to be killed by Artemis herself during the hunt. Zeus then intervened by sending Hermes to rescue his unborn son, Arkas, who later to give his name to the Arcadians and became their king. Callisto was transformed by Zeus into the constellation of the Great Bear.

To reach Braurona follow Ave. Marathonas (Λ.Μαραδονας) from junction 15 of the Athens ring road (Attiki Othos, Αττική Οδός) to Rafina (Ραφήνα). The centre of Loutsa (Λούτσα) is 7km to the south and Braurona is a further 7km on the coast road. Alternatively leave the ring road at junction 18 and take the minor road to Loutsa via Spata. On weekdays there is a strong chance that you will have this interesting site to yourself.

Marathon (Μαραθώνας):
The defeat of the Persians at the battle of Marathon and the athletic feats of Pheidippides.

Today the name of Marathon is known throughout the world as an Olympic event. The modern race is run over approximately 26 miles, the distance from Marathon to Athens. It was introduced to the first modern Olympics in 1896 and has been included ever since. Yet it commemorates an event that almost certainly never happened. This latter day myth first appeared 500 years after the heroic battle between Greeks and Persians. The story, in which Pheidippides, also known as Philippides, ran the 26 miles from Marathon to Athens to proclaim the Greek victory before collapsing and dying in the agora, may well be a confusion of the two great feats of endurance connected with the battle and recounted by Herodotus, the 5C BC historian.

The battle that took place in September 490 BC was caused by Persian expansion westwards. The Persian king, Darius, intended to punish Athens for the assistance she had given to the coastal Greek cities of Asia Minor when they had revolted against his authority. Bringing their army by sea, with horses for the cavalry in special horse transports, the Persians' punitive expedition landed first on the island of Euboia (Evia). They sacked Eretria and then crossed to the mainland, landing in the Bay of Marathon. When news of this reached the Athenians, they realised they were likely to be outnumbered by the Persians and sent Pheidippides, a professional runner, to Sparta to seek help against the common enemy. The distance from Athens to Sparta is about 220km. Pheidippides is reported to have reached Sparta in two days, a feat of endurance many times greater than the legend of the run from Marathon to Athens. The Spartans, though willing to assist, held to their religious law that prevented them marching to battle before the full moon. Their delay was a genuine religious scruple, for once the full moon had passed, an army two thousand strong set off, and by a forced march reached Attica in three days. However, by then, the carnage was over and all they were able to do was view the Persian dead and offer praise to the Athenians for their victory. On his way to Sparta, Pheidippides is said to have met Pan on the mountainside near Tegea. The god asked him why the Athenians had ceased to worship him when he had helped them in the past and would do so again. This story led the Athenians to believe that their victory had divine assistance. Thereafter, there was a revival of the worship of Pan and a sanctuary to him was created beneath the Acropolis in Athens.

Figure 1 Marathon: The tomb of the Athenians

Figure 2 Marathon: The replica Victory Monument

While the Spartans were waiting for the full moon to pass, the Athenian army marched to Marathon and made camp in the Sanctuary of Heracles (Hercules) on the southern edge of the plain, blocking the route to Athens. They were joined by one thousand men from Plataia who, having sought Athens's aid against Thebes in the past, now stood by their ally. There was a stand-off between the two armies for several days, the Persians being unwilling to attack the strong position of the Athenians, who in turn were unwilling to attack without Spartan reinforcement. It is now believed that Darius's commander, Datis, having failed to draw out the Greek forces, decided to reload his cavalry onto some of his ships and send them around the coast to a now undefended Athens. This was the impetus for the Greek attack, for they now had to defeat the army still in front of them and get back to protect their city. Their attack fortunately became a Persian rout. Datis's army was pursued across the marsh that formed the north-eastern part of the plain and over 6000 of them were cut down. Greek losses were, incredibly, only 192 dead. The magnitude of the Greek victory was attributed to divine help. As well as assistance from Pan it was believed by the Greeks that the ghost of Theseus had been seen fighting amongst them.

The greater part of the Persian forces escaped in their ships and set sail for Athens. Then came the Athenian race to get back to the city. This was not the race of one individual, but of an entire army, and one presumably already exhausted by the day's fighting. They reached the outskirts of Athens in time. The Persians abandoned their plans and returned home. The Athenians buried their dead beneath a great earth mound. Under another are the graves of the Plataians.

It is unfortunate that the topography of the plain has changed substantially over the millennia. It is now difficult to visualise the battle scene as it was. The level of the land has risen as alluvial material from the hills has been deposited. As a result, the streams that cross the plain run in gullies that did not exist at the time of the battle. The modern Olympic rowing centre has now changed the coastline beyond recognition. Of course battles themselves leave little for future visitors to see. Here, the main monuments are the two mounds covering the graves of the dead Athenians and Plataians and the site of the original victory monument. The Athenian mound is 10M high and 80M in diameter. In the centuries after the battle it became the site of an important hero cult and is still much visited today. To reach the battle site follow Ave. Marathonas (Λ.Μαραδονας) from junction 15 of the Athens ring road. Continue north past the turning for Rafina. Beyond Nea Makri, the main road enters the Marathon plain and a right turn signposted "Marathon

Tomb" leads to the Athenian burial mound. Further along the main road towards Marathon village, a signposted left turn leads to the museum and another mound, the Tomb of the Plataians. This has been partially excavated but is now overgrown and easy to miss. It lies to the right of the road 200M before the museum. The well organised museum displays finds of every era from the locality including reconstructed fragments of the victory monument. The original site has been located and a replica has been erected close by. To visit it return to the main road towards Marathon. Take the right turn towards the Olympic rowing centre and Rhamnous. After a kilometre a sign points down a minor road on the right. The monument is a further 800M and stands close to the foundations of the original.

Rhamnous (Ραμνούς)
The Temple of Nemesis and Themis. Nemesis's role in the battle of Marathon. The myth of Leda and the swan.

Just a few miles north of Marathon lies the principal Sanctuary of the goddess Nemesis, here called Nemesis Ramnousia, identifying her directly with the site. Nemesis was the goddess of indignation and retribution for evil deeds, or undeserved good fortune. She was the daughter of Night, Nyx, and granddaughter of Khaos, one of the Protogenoi, Khaos, Gaia, Tartaros and Eros, the first elemental gods. It is a common human feeling that those who are blessed with too many gifts deserve some compensating misfortune. Nemesis was the goddess who dispensed this compensation to those who overstep the boundaries. Her job was to balance the extravagance of her sister Tykhe, also known as Fortune.

Pausanias, the Greek traveller who wrote his Guide to Greece in the 2C AD, believed that Nemesis was responsible for the fate of the Persians at Marathon. They had been so sure of success in battle with the Athenians that they had brought with them a block of Parian marble from which to carve their victory monument. Such presumption showed that the Persians believed they controlled their own destiny. This denial of the gods' power to intervene in human affairs risked divine wrath.

As well as the temple of Nemesis, this sanctuary has a smaller temple to the goddess Themis who is often associated with the worship of Nemesis. Themis was the second wife of Zeus, the daughter of Gaia, and the goddess of custom and order. Themis, Nemesis and Dike, the goddess of justice, were the principal assistants of Zeus in his role as

13

founder of law and order.

To reach the sanctuary, drive to the outskirts of the modern village of Marathon, where there is a right turning, signposted to Rhamnous. Near Kato Souli (Κάτω Σούλι) take care to follow the road around to the left. In this area the Road Editions map is substantially more accurate than the Geo-Center. A tarmac road rises steadily, and 3km after passing the right turn for Ayia Marina (Αγία Μαρίνα), the site entrance is reached. The site is fully enclosed. It should be open daily 8.30 – 15.00, but note earlier reservations about opening times. Entrance is free. From the ticket office a path climbs uphill to the sanctuary built on a large, artificial platform faced with marble blocks. It overlooks the fortified headland below. An ancient road connects the two. The walled headland was both a town and a fortress, one of a series of coastal and border forts of Attica built to command a road or, as in this case, a stretch of coastline. As the 5C BC and the Peloponnesian War drew to a close, and Sparta began to blockade the land routes into Attica, Rhamnous became strategically important as the port through which Athens imported grain from Euboia.

The ancient road descends past the remains of Classical grave enclosures. The fortification circuit is about 1km long and the south gate and various towers are visible. Within the walls stood public buildings including a theatre. The remains of the sanctuary now consist of the lower courses of the small temple of Themis and the larger Doric temple of Nemesis, built side by side on an artificial platform. There are also foundations of the essential altar and of a long stoa. The temple of Nemesis was rebuilt in the 5C BC after the Persians destroyed the original during their second invasion of Greece, ten years after Marathon. The temple held the cult statue of the goddess. The head still exists and is now in the British Museum. According to Pausanias, the statue was carved by Pheidias from the very block of Parian marble the Persians brought to Marathon for their victory monument, although in reality, the statue is of a different type of marble. The base of the statue, now thought to have been made by Pheidias's pupil Agorakritos, has been reconstructed from fragments. It shows Helen of Troy being presented to her real mother, Nemesis, by Leda.

The legend of Leda, the swan and the birth of Helen is well known but complex. It is one of the myths linking the gods to the genealogy of ancient kings. Leda was the daughter of Thestius, the son of the god Ares, and the wife of Tyndareus, king of Sparta. Zeus saw her bathing in the river Evrotas (Sparta is in the Evrotas valley) and was captivated by her beauty. He disguised himself as a white swan and commanded

Aphrodite to pursue him in the form of an eagle. The swan took refuge in Leda's arms. The resulting union produced not children but a pair of eggs. From one egg came Helen and her brother Polydeuces (Pollux) and from the other Clytemnestra and Castor. Versions of the legend differ as to how many of the four were fathered by Zeus and how many by Tyndareus. Helen and Clytemnestra were ultimately to marry Menelaus and Agamemnon, respectively kings of Sparta and Mycenae.

Later, the legend grew that Helen's mother was really Nemesis and it was she who produced the mythical egg. One version has Leda finding the egg in a marsh, another has Hermes carrying the egg from Nemesis and throwing it into Leda's lap. In both tales Leda brings up Helen as her own child. This later story may be an Athenian appropriation of the original Spartan myth and the inspiration for the carving.

Although the area of the sanctuary is well maintained and there are now excellent site-plans on display, at the time of writing, the area of the headland below is unfortunately fenced off and closed, as is the new building housing the reconstructed statue base. It is to be hoped that this policy will soon be reversed.

Amphiaraion (Αμφιάρειον)
Sanctuary and healing centre dedicated to Amphiaraos, one of the Seven against Thebes

The Amphiaraion lies a few miles to the north of Rhamnous in a secluded wooded valley. It was the centre of the cult of Amphiaraos, the healing god. The story of his death and deification introduces the events that followed the exile of Oedipus and the further tragedies that befell those connected with the ensuing civil war. Again, the complex myths surrounding Oedipus may be part legend from the age of heroes and part Mycenaean history. However, like all sanctuaries, the Amphiaraion was a religious centre and the legend is an example of how the Greeks believed a mortal could achieve divine status through the intervention of Zeus.

After Oedipus's exile from Thebes, his two sons, Eteocles and Polyneices, agreed to share the kingship, reigning in alternate years. They hoped to avoid their father's curse that they would never resolve the issue of the succession (see Thebes below). Eteocles took the kingship for the first year, but refused to give it up and drove his brother into exile. Polyneices fled to the court of Adrastus, king of Argos. As a result of a prophecy by the oracle at Delphi, the king gave Polyneices his daughter in marriage and his support in reclaiming the throne. The expedition to restore Polyneices was to become known as the war of the Seven against Thebes. The Seven were Polyneices himself, Adrastus, Hippomedon, Parthenopaios, Capaneus, Tydeus and Amphiaraos, who was both a famous warrior and had gifts of prophecy and healing. This allowed him to foresee that the expedition would fail and all except Adrastus would die fighting. At first Amphiaraos refused to take part, but his wife, Eriphyle, was bribed by Polyneices with the famous necklace of Harmonia that he had brought with him from Thebes. Accepting this bribe, Eriphyle persuaded her husband to go to war. In one version of the legend Amphiaraos's anger that his wife could be bribed caused him to make his son, Alcmaeon, swear that he would avenge his father by killing his mother. Each of the Seven led a section of the army against one of Thebes's seven gates. Each was repulsed after fierce fighting. Eteocles then led the Theban army out of the city to fight the Argives on the plain and there was great slaughter. Polyneices offered to resolve the issue in single combat with his brother, who accepted. Each mortally wounded the other, thus fulfilling their father's curse that they would never resolve the issue. Their uncle, Kreon, took command of the Theban forces, the Argives were routed, and of the seven commanders, only Adrastus escaped. Amphiaraos fled from the battle along the bank of the Ismenos, pursued by Periklymenos. Just as he was about to receive a spear between his shoulders, Zeus saved him from his fate by splitting open the earth, which engulfed him, together with his chariot. He became an Immortal. The sons of the Seven, known as the Epigoni, were to avenge their fathers ten years later when they razed Thebes to the ground. On his return home, Alcmaeon fulfilled his father's command and slew his mother. He in turn, was to lose his life and be avenged by his sons (see Chapter 4, Akarnania).

To reach the Amphiaraion from Rhamnous take the road back towards Marathon village for three kilometres where a right turn leads to Grammatiko (Γραμματικό). In the village turn right for Varnanas (Βαρνάνας) and Kapandriti (Καπανδρίτι). Here, take another right turn signposted to Kalamos (Κάλαμος). From Kalamos a road with a brown sign descends through a wooded valley. The site entrance is on the right, immediately after the road crosses the stream. The Sanctuary of Amphiaraos lies below the road on either side of the stream in an attractive location among the trees. The site is fenced and the published opening hours are 8.30 to 15.00, closed on Mondays.

In the centre of the sanctuary is the sacred spring where it was believed Amphiaraos rose up as a god from within the earth. The cult was established in the 5C BC. Its popularity continued into the Roman period with a festival every 4 years. The sanctuary was both an oracle and a healing centre. An oracle was primarily a place, rather than an individual. Although at Delphi the prophecy was received by the priestess from the divine source (see Chapter 3), another common method, and the one used here, was for the prophecy to be delivered as a dream. Those seeking help would sacrifice a ram and then spend the night in the sanctuary, sleeping on the fleece, a process known as incubation. Prophecies would be revealed in dreams or healing would be received from the god. However, cures did not depend entirely on divine intervention, as the waters were believed to have medicinal properties and baths were provided for treatment. At this practical level, the place strongly resembles a 19C spa. Walking down from the gate, the temple of Amphiaraos is on the right. The sacrificial altar with the sacred spring is below it. Pausanias describes how the altar was divided into sections, each sacred to a group of deities or divine heroes, including Hercules and Jason as well as Amphiaraos. To the left, is a long line of Roman statue bases, then a long stoa, the Enkoimeterion, with marble benches where the suppliants slept on the ram's fleece. The claw feet supporting the benches are still visible. Immediately behind is the theatre, with carved seats or thrones in place. The baths were beyond the stoa further downstream. On the other side of the stream are the extensive, but overgrown, remains of the buildings designed to provide accommodation for the visitors and patients.

This is a secluded and beautiful place, which you should have completely to yourself.

Aulis (Αυλις)
Temple of Artemis

The site of Iphigenia's sacrifice can still be seen and visited as a detour from the route north to Thebes on the National road (effectively a motorway). It lies off the road to Halkitha (Χαλκιδα, ΧΑΛΚΙΔΑ, or Halkis, Chalcis) about 15km from the motorway junction. A small temple to Artemis stood on the site. Unfortunately what remains is now in rather unattractive surroundings. As the road nears the coast, beyond the village of Vathi (Βαθύ), the Halkis shipyard can be seen across the channel to the right. A brown sign points right to the temple of Artemis. A minor road first crosses the railway line and then runs parallel to the main road after passing through an area of factories. After 2km there are white signs for the Archaeological site on either side of the road. The site is fenced, but the temple can clearly be seen as the road cuts across the eastern corner of the foundations. There is a site plan and a description in Greek. The area has been inhabited since Mycenaean times. The visible remains are of the temple built in the 5C BC on top of an earlier building. To the south are remains of workshops and a pottery kiln from the 3C and 2C BC. On the other side of the road, directly opposite the temple, is a 5C spring (KPHNH on the site plan), said to have been built originally by Agamemnon. The sanctuary flourished under the Romans but was destroyed by the Goths in 396 AD. The fields to the east of the sanctuary now occupy the silted up inlet that would have formed the harbour in Mycenaean times (ΑΡΧΑΙΟΣ ΛΙΜΗΝ on the site plan). Unfortunately to visualise the scene of the sacrifice with the Greek fleet in the background it is necessary not just to imagine that the fields are flooded, but also to remove the cement works that dominates the horizon.

From the Halkitha junction it is 30 kilometres to Thebes via the National Road (see below).

Figure 3 Aulis: The Temple of Artemis

B. The Old road to Thebes

This route first follows the line of the Sacred Way that ran westwards for twenty kilometres from the centre of Athens to ancient Elefsis on the coast at the bay of Salamis. It then turns north, inland, to Thebes. Although the route is not scenically attractive, it passes some of the finest extant classical fortifications of mainland Greece. It skirts the eastern flank of Mount Kithaeron (Kitheronas, Κιθαιρονας) where Oedipus was left to die as an infant. It then drops to the plain of Viotia and the sites of the great battlefields of Leuktra and Plataia before reaching Thebes.

Elefsis or Elefsina (Ελευσίς, Ελευσίνα)
The site of the great Sanctuary of Demeter. The home of the Mysteries.

Ancient Elefsis has a reputation as a difficult site to understand. This, combined with its urban surroundings, means that it is little visited and there is a good chance of having it almost to yourself. It is certainly true that the excavations at the site are complex. Given that it was in use for the best part of two thousand years and continually expanded, it could hardly be otherwise. However the sanctuary is a superb example of modern archaeological excavation, and the many phases of development have been carefully revealed. The first settlement at Elefsis dates from the 18-17C BC and the worship of Demeter dates from Mycenaean times. The city was independent until the first half of the 6C BC when it came under the control of Athens. From this point, the cult of Demeter grew in importance and the continual enlargement of the sanctuary reflects this. Embellishment continued until after the annexation of Greece by the Roman Empire. The mysteries were performed until the end of the 4C AD.

Demeter was the sister of Zeus and the daughter of Kronos (Cronus) and Rhea. After Kronos had castrated and dethroned his father Ouranos, Gaia prophesied that he in turn would be replaced by one of his sons. Kronos attempted to avoid his fate by swallowing each of the children he had by Rhea. After he had swallowed Hestia, Demeter, Hera, Hades, and Poseidon, Rhea was determined to conceal the birth of her next child. On the advice of her parents, she went to Crete to give birth to Zeus. She deceived Kronos with a stone wrapped in swaddling clothes, which he swallowed, believing it to be her child. (In another version of this myth, Zeus is born on Mount Lykaion in Arcadia, see Chapter 6).

19

When Zeus had grown to manhood, Gaia tricked Kronos into vomiting up the children he had swallowed, preceded by the stone, which Zeus set up at Delphi. The supposed stone was still there in the 2C AD when Pausanias saw it near the tomb of Neoptolemus. Zeus then led his siblings in a war against Kronos and the other Titans who were defeated and confined in Tartarus. The era of the Olympian gods began.

Demeter was the goddess of agriculture and the bringer of the seasons. By her brother Zeus, she was the mother of Persephone and Iacchos, the name of Dionysus in the Eleusinian mysteries. In the Arcadian myth she also had a daughter by Poseidon. To escape from his lust, she had changed into a mare and hidden among a herd of other mares grazing in Arcadia. Poseidon transformed himself into a stallion and caught her. The product of their union was the Arcadian deity Despoina and the horse Arion. This famous animal was given to Adrastus, king of Argos, by Hercules, and on it he won the horse race of the first Nemean Games. Later it carried him to safety after the defeat of the Seven against Thebes. (For the Sanctuary of Despoina see Lykosoura, Chapter 6. For Nemea, see Chapter 8. For Adrastus, see above).

The foundation myth of Elefsis begins when Persephone, often known as Kore (Κορή), the Maiden, was gathering flowers in a meadow near Elefsis. The earth split open and Hades (Pluto) rode out from the Underworld in a golden chariot pulled by his immortal horses. He seized Persephone and carried her back to his kingdom. Only Hecate, and Helios the god who sees and hears everything, heard her cries of distress. For nine days Demeter wandered the earth seeking her daughter, neither eating nor drinking. On tenth day, Hecate came to her and told her she had heard Persephone's cries but had not seen her abductor. Together they went to Helios who told Demeter that Zeus had given Persephone to his brother Hades. She had been carried down into the underworld in his chariot. Helios attempted to convince Demeter that Hades was a fitting husband for her daughter, as he was her own brother. But Demeter was inconsolable and wandered the earth in disguise, avoiding Olympus and the other gods. In her wanderings she came to Elefsis and the house of king Keleos. The king's daughters found her sitting by the Maiden well disguised as an old woman. They invited her to their house and there she sat for a long time in her sorrow. When Metaneira, the wife of Keleos, offered her red wine to drink, she refused. Instead she asked for a mixture of meal and water, flavoured with mint, to drink. Metaneira invited Demeter to be her young son's nurse. The goddess, who had told Metaneira her name was Doso, took care of the child, named Demophon. She attempted to repay the family's kindness by making him immortal. She fed him ambrosia and each night put him in the fire, so that his mortality would be burned away, and he would become immortal. However, one night Metaneira kept watch and saw Demophon in the fire. She cried out in great alarm. Demeter, in disgust that her gift was not understood, snatched the child from the fire. She revealed herself as a goddess, telling Metaneira that she had denied her son the gift of immortality. Demeter then gave instructions that a temple and altar be built. She taught the people of Elefsis the rites that they must perform there in order to regain her favour. Demeter then hid herself away in her temple. She vowed that she would neither return to Olympus, nor permit the grain to germinate, so that there was a famine across the earth for a year. If the crops would not grow, the gods would not receive their due sacrifices. Realising this, Zeus sent the gods, one after another, to Demeter with offers of gifts. Although they pleaded with her to return, she rejected all their entreaties. Finally, Zeus sent Hermes to the underworld to bring back Persephone. As long as she had not tasted food during her time there, she would be able to return to the world as before. Hades, however, had given her pomegranate seeds to eat. Consequently, she had to spend one third of each year in the underworld, returning to the world above when spring came. Demeter agreed to this arrangement and ended the famine. She then taught Keleos, his son Triptolemos, and the other leaders of Elefsis her rites and her mysteries.

This is the substance of the myth set out in the Homeric Hymn to Demeter, written perhaps, in the 7C BC. Later traditions expand the role of Triptolemos. He is depicted receiving seeds of wheat and the knowledge of agriculture from Demeter. He becomes a teacher of agriculture to the whole world, journeying from place to place on a winged chariot.

The exact nature of the mysteries remains elusive. The penalty for revealing the details of the experience was death. Pausanias, who was determined to include in his guide to Greece everything 'worth seeing' and who was himself an initiate at Elefsis, was unfortunately equally fastidious in his adherence to the prohibition. His description stops at the sanctuary wall. Nevertheless, the greater part of the elaborate annual celebrations, known as the Great Eleusinia, was held in public each September. This began when the sacred objects (what they were is unknown) were brought from Elefsis to Athens. The initiates, who had already been admitted to the Lesser Eleusinia earlier the same year, then purified themselves in the sea and sacrificed a piglet. On the fifth day, a great formal procession carried the sacred objects back to Elefsis along the Sacred Way, bearing also a statue of Iacchos, a god who either was, or later became identified with, Dionysus. The procession approached Elefsis in the evening. The initiates would then break the fast they had maintained, by drinking the kykeon, made from meal (possibly roasted barley) and water flavoured with mint, the same drink that Demeter requested from Metaneira. At this point, the initiates entered the sanctuary and the celebrations moved from the public display to the secret religious ceremonies.

Entire books have been written attempting to identify the nature of the mysteries. The fasting of the initiates, the fact that the events lasted nine days, and the role of the kykeon, show that the ceremonies were a representation of aspects of Demeter's search for Persephone. The Hymn to Demeter can give hints as to the subject matter of the mysteries, but not their actual form.

The site

The ancient city is built on a low, rocky hill between the modern town and the sea. The sanctuary lies directly below the highest point of the hill, which originally formed the acropolis.

The modern entrance gate opens onto the ancient paved surface of the Sacred Way leading, via the Great Forecourt, to the monumental gateway of the sanctuary. This gateway, or Great Propylaea, was a Roman copy of the Propylaea on the Athens Acropolis. A well can be seen just to the left of the six steps that lead to the entrance of the Propylaea. This has been tentatively identified as the Maiden well where Demeter was sitting when Metaneira's daughters first saw her. The way then leads via the Lesser Propylaea to a huge square platform, the site of the Telesterion, the hall of the mysteries.

It is immediately apparent that this enormous building has been accommodated on the sloping site by cutting into the rock on the northwest side, and terracing out over the slope to the southeast. The foundations seen today are from the enlargement at the time of Pericles. After this rebuilding, it formed a vast hypostyle hall supported by 42 internal columns. Eight tiers of seats were built around the inside of the walls. These can still be seen where they are cut into the rock. The Telesterion was further extended after 170 AD, with the addition of the massive Doric Portico of Philo. At the centre of the Telesterion stood the Anaktoron, the holy of holies. This building within a building was the core of the sanctuary. Its position was unchanged throughout the successive enlargements of the Telesterion. It was from this inner secret chamber that the Hierophant would bring the sacred objects.

From the 6C BC the sanctuary was enclosed by substantial walls. Beyond the Telesterion, turn left, southeast, to walk outside the precinct walls and gain the best impression of the height and scale of the construction. Virtually every type of Greek masonry is represented in the various sections of walling preserved. Uniquely, a section of dried mud brick wall remains from the wall built by Peisistratos in the 6C BC. It is now preserved by a corrugated iron roof. The Museum lies up the hill and has useful models of the site as it stood in its heyday.

Elefsina can be reached from the centre of Athens by the old main road through Dafnis and Skaramangas, or from the ring road (Attiki Odos) via junction 1. Follow signs for the town centre (Κεντρο). Ancient Elefsis occupies a large area two blocks south of Elefsina's main street. It is fully enclosed with a ticket office open 8.30 to 15.00 but closed on Mondays. Parking is possible directly in front of the site entrance. The leaflet issued with entrance tickets has an accurate site plan showing its historical development.

Eleutherai (Eleftherai, Eleftheres, Ελένθεραι)

The cult of Dionysus was introduced to Athens from here. A substantial 4C BC fort overlooks his temple.

From Elefsina the old road to Thebes heads inland. After twenty-six kilometres the road begins to climb the Gyphtokastro pass. In Classical times this was the border area between Athens and Viotia. Eleutherai was originally a Theban village but, at some point in the 6C BC, it transferred its loyalties to Athens. Today the few visitors who stop here, do so to admire the walls of the 4C BC border fort that still commands the pass. However, the area's real claim to fame is as the place from which the cult of Dionysus was introduced to Athens, and as the possible location of his home sanctuary.

Dionysus is a complex god and a latecomer to the Greek pantheon. He became one of the twelve gods dwelling on Mount Olympus only when Hestia, goddess of the hearth, relinquished her place in his favour. He had a dual nature that may well be the fusion of a Greek nature god and an eastern god imported from Anatolia. This is reflected in the different versions of the story of his birth, where he is said to be the son of Zeus and variously Semele, Demeter, Io, Persephone or Lethe. He is best known as the god of wine, fertility and agriculture, as well as the god of the theatre. However, the mystic nature of his rebirth, he is known as "twice-born", also makes him a god of the mystery religions.

Traditionally, his birthplace was Thebes. The most common story of his birth is yet another example of the recurring theme of Zeus's affairs with mortal women. Zeus fell in love with Semele, daughter of Cadmus, the founder of Thebes. Disguised as a mortal, Zeus became her lover. Hera, Zeus's wife, discovered the affair when Semele was already pregnant. Hera was extremely jealous of all her husband's many lovers, and would seek vengeance on both the unfortunate women and their offspring. She disguised herself as an old woman, befriended Semele and persuaded her to ask Zeus to come to her in his true form to prove his divine nature. As no mortal can perceive a god undisguised, Semele perished when he appeared as thunder and lightning. The unborn Dionysus was rescued from her dying body by Hermes, who sewed the foetus into Zeus's thigh to complete his term. His was thus born once of Semele and a second time from Zeus.

In the other important and gruesome version of the story, Dionysus is the son of Zeus and Demeter, or Persephone. After his birth, Hera sent the Titans to kill the baby Dionysus. They cut his throat and sliced him into pieces, which they boiled in a cauldron. However, his body was recreated by Zeus, or in other versions of the story by Rhea or Demeter, and again he can be said to have been twice-born.

Dionysus is credited with the discovery of winemaking. The many myths of his adult life describe his wanderings about the world, travelling as far as Egypt and India, and his battles against those who would not recognise his divinity. A recurring theme of these myths is the refusal of a local king to accept his worship, often with fatal consequences. For example, on his return to Thebes, Pentheus, the king, attempted to imprison Dionysus and his ecstatic female followers, the Maenads. The outcome was that Pentheus was driven mad by the god and was finally torn to pieces by the Maenads on Mount Kithaeron. These tales seem to reflect the introduction of viticulture into Greece and opposition to the use of wine in ritual.

When the cult of Dionysus actually spread throughout Greece is uncertain, although his name appears on Linear B tablets from the 13C BC. What is known, is that the cult was formally accepted in Athens in the 6C BC, when the festival of the Great Dionysia was introduced by Peisistratos. The wooden cult statue was brought from Eleutherai to Athens at this time and the Sanctuary of Dionysus Eleftherios was created on the slopes of the Acropolis. This event was commemorated annually in a procession held as a preliminary to the opening ceremony of the Great Dionysia. The statue was taken from his temple to a small shrine outside Athens on the road to Eleutherai, and then symbolically brought home, re-enacting the original event. The Athenian myth of Dionysus's first arrival in their city relates that the men of Athens refused to recognise him as a god. His response was to inflict upon them the curse of permanent erections, or satyriasis. The Delphic oracle told them that to be cured they must make wooden phalluses. Thereafter the phallus became part of Dionysian ritual. Huge phalluses symbolising fertility, were carried in the procession that took place on the first day of the Great Dionysia. The major events of the festival were the competitive performances of comedies and tragedies, performed in the other major component of the Athenian sanctuary of Dionysus, the theatre.

At the bottom of the Gyphtokastro pass is the left turn to Aigosthena. Beyond this the road begins to climb. The border fort at Eleutherai can be glimpsed as a line of walls and towers ahead on the crest of a hill. Below the curve of the hill, a brown sign appears abruptly on the right, immediately before a group of roadside tavernas where there is room to park. This sign points up a short dirt track that leads to the extremely well preserved northern section of the fort's circuit. The site is unenclosed and entry is via a path through a surviving postern gate. The towers retain their firing ports for archers and catapults. The doors onto the parapet still exist. Almost the full circuit can still be traced around the hill, a breeding ground for tortoises. To view the probable location of the original Sanctuary of Dionysus, walk to the far, eastern, end of the north wall. From here the view is back over the plain below. Directly below, under the line of the overhead power cables, the foundations of a temple can be seen. Pausanias says that the shrine of Dionysus lay in these fields. In his time, 2C AD, it still contained a copy of the wooden statue taken to Athens. Although it is possible to reach the temple on foot from the main road, the overgrown nature of the site means that its layout can be most clearly seen from above.

Aigosthena (Αιγόσθενα)
Sanctuary of Melampous, reputed to have brought the worship of Dionysus to Greece.

Aigosthena was known as the location of the Sanctuary of Melampous. He was the head of a family of great healers and prophets and was said to be the first mortal to be granted these gifts. His great grandson was Amphiaraos (see above). At Aigosthena, Melampous was worshipped as a god and an annual festival was held in his honour. Herodotus tells

25

Figure 4 View of the fortifications of Aigosthena

us that Melampous was responsible for introducing the worship of Dio-nysus to Greece from Egypt, an event supposed to have taken place before the war against Troy.

A visit to Aigosthena or Porto Germeno (Πόρτο Γερμένο) as it is now called, requires a detour of 20km from the main Elefsina -Thebes road. The route is straightforward, as clear signs exist for Πόρτο Γερμένο at the few junctions on the road. Now a small Greek seaside resort busy in summer, it lies at the mouth of an isolated and attractive valley, known today for its superb Classical fortifications.

Although of no great historical importance, the walls of Aigosthena are probably the best preserved and most photogenic in central Greece. The fortified acropolis forms a rectangle of walls and towers about 180M by 100M on a low rocky outcrop. Long walls reach 500M down to the sea. The good state of preservation and the great height of the east walls and towers is made all the more dramatic by their position on the ridge facing inland. This is the image that comes into view as the road curves back and forth down the steep descent to the village. The towers are still preserved to almost their full height and reach 10M above the level of the walls. Until earthquake damage in the 1980's, they were virtually intact. The Classical town belonged to Megara in the 4C but is little mentioned in contemporary sources, other than as the spot from which the Spartans retreated after their defeat at Leuktra (see below).

As the road approaches the village, a brown sign points to left. A gravel track leads through the olive groves to the foot of the eastern walls. The site is unenclosed and can be visited at any time. A rough path enters the acropolis by a postern gate in the shadow of a tower. Within is the small church of St. George and, built against the walls, the remains of Byzantine monastic cells. Further down the slope are the remains of a 5C AD basilican church. This building incorporated much ancient material and may be built on the site of the original sanctuary of Melampous. It is common for later Christian churches to be erected near the site of an earlier Classical sanctuary. The seaward side of the acropolis is less well preserved and of the long walls, only the northern leg survives. The remains can be approached just as easily from this side.

Plataia (Plataies, Πλαταιές)
Site of the final victory of the Greeks over the Persians. Remains of the ancient city include foundations of a temple of Hera and an altar to Zeus Eleftherios.

Beyond Eleutherai, the road crosses the summit of the pass and quickly descends to the broad Viotian plain. A bypass avoids Erithres making a great curve to the west the town. A byroad to the left leads, in 5km, to the modern village of Plataies, built just outside the walls of its ancient counterpart, overlooking the famous battle site.

After the Greek victory at Marathon in 490 BC, it was ten years before the Persians returned to avenge their defeat. The Persian king, Darius, had died in 486 BC. It was his son, Xerxes, who organised the invasion on a massive scale involving both a land army and a huge fleet. His elaborate preparations famously included a pontoon bridge across the Hellespont (the Dardanelles) for the army. He also cut a canal across the isthmus joining Mount Athos to the mainland so that the fleet could avoid the dangerous headland. Facing this onslaught at sea was the new Athenian fleet of triremes, built with the foresight of Themistokles and the proceeds of the Laurion silver mines (south of the modern airport). On land, an alliance of 31 city-states, dominated by Sparta and the Peloponnesian League, provided the army. Command of both army and navy was given to Sparta, a reflection of their pre-eminence as warriors among the Greeks.

It was to take two land battles and three battles at sea, before the Persians were finally driven from Greece. An initial attempt to stop the

Persian advance at the Vale of Tempe, in Thessaly, was unsuccessful. A stand was then made at the pass of Thermopylae. This was the scene of the famous sacrifice by the Spartan king Leonidas. He dismissed the bulk of his troops to fight another day, whilst he and his three hundred hand-picked Spartans, together with contingents from Thebes and Thespiai, fought to the last man. Paradoxically, Leonidas's death was seen as a good omen, because the Delphic oracle had told the Spartans that the defeat of the Persians would require the death of a king.

Meanwhile, the Greek fleet had assembled near Artemission, to the north of the island of Euboia, to face the Persian ships coming south. Although the ensuing naval battle was inconclusive, a substantial part of the Persian fleet was wrecked by storms and the Greek numerical disadvantage was eliminated. The Greek ships then retreated to the restricted waters between the island of Salamis and the mainland opposite Elefsina. Athens was evacuated to Salamis, Aegina and Troizen, where the population awaited the outcome of the conflict. The Persian army and fleet continued their progress south, sacking an empty Athens. The Persians now made their first serious mistake. Xerxes committed his ships to a full-scale naval battle in the narrow Salamis channel. The outcome was the destruction of a major part of the Persian fleet by the more manoeuvrable triremes. Xerxes then retreated with his remaining ships to Persia.

However, Attica and a large part of northern Greece were still in Persian hands. Xerxes had left his brother-in-law, Mardonios, in command of the still-intact army. It was at Plataia that the decisive land battle took place in the spring of the following year, 479 BC. In order to make maximum use of his cavalry, Mardonios had deliberately chosen the open countryside north of Mount Kithaeron for his encampment, enclosing it with a huge wooden stockade on the north bank of the river Asopos. With the death of Leonidas, the Greek forces were now commanded by the Spartan, Pausanias, the regent for Leonidas's under age son. The battle consisted of almost two weeks of skirmishes followed by one day of decisive fighting in which Mardonios was killed and those Persians who did not flee were slaughtered. The Persian occupation of Viotia had brought the Thebans over to the Persian side. The Thebans' reward was to see their city sacked and their leaders executed. At approximately the same time, the Greek fleet that had pursued Xerxes and his remaining ships, had a final, decisive victory at the Battle of Mycale off the coast of Asia Minor.

Just outside the modern village of Plataies, the road cuts through a line of ancient walls and runs through the southern half of the great cir-

cuit built by Philip II, when he refounded the city after his victory at
Chaironia, in 338 BC (see Chapter 3). The enclosed area slopes downhill to the north. The original, smaller settlement lay in the north west
corner of this circuit on a slight plateau. It was surrounded by its own
wall, still preserved to the south, and became an acropolis for the later
city. It had been destroyed by the Persians in 480 BC because Plataia
had remained loyal to the combined Greek cause, unlike the other
northern cities. The Spartans destroyed it in 427 BC. Finally, the traditional enemy, Thebes, sacked it in 373 BC. Today, only concealed
foundations remain within the circuit. The site of the battle between
Persians and Greeks lies to the north, with the action of the final day
taking place on the flat plain beyond the city's plateau.

The spoils of battle were used to cast a bronze column in the form of
three intertwined serpents. It was originally 8 M tall. The serpent heads
at the top carried a gold tripod. It was presented to the temple of Apollo
at Delphi in thanksgiving for the victory and was seen by Pausanias in
the 2C AD, although by then the gold had gone. The entire monument
was carried off by Constantine to embellish his new city of Constantinople. The remnants of the column, now only 5M tall, can still be seen
there on the site of the Hippodrome in the centre of Istanbul. At Plataia
itself an altar of Zeus Eleftherios, the Liberator, was erected and a festival was founded with games held every five years. These were still
taking place in 2C AD.

The site is extensive, unenclosed and overgrown with rough grass.
Although little visible survives from the 5C BC, the open fields in every
direction allow an uninterrupted view of the city area and the battle site
beyond.

Kabeirion
*Remains of the Sanctuary of the Kabeiroi to whom Demeter revealed
mysteries.*

Just outside of Thebes, about 3km along the Livadhia road, a brown
sign points left onto a dirt road to the seldom visited site of the
Kabeirion, or Sanctuary of the Kabeiroi. The worship of these little
known deities was an important local cult from the 6C BC until the late
Roman period. This was their most important sanctuary in mainland
Greece. Little is known of their origins, their names or even how many
Kabeiroi there were. Pausanias, who was very fastidious in religious
matters, refuses to name them or explain the rituals. From the various

29

accounts that exist, it appears that they were gods of fertility, metal-working and sailors, a curious combination. The names of two may have been Kabeiros and Pais. They may have been sons of Hephaistos. The Kabeiroi were entrusted with a secret gift from Demeter. The sanctuary was devoted to an unknown sacred rite, or mystery, attached to this gift. This rite was related in some way to the mysteries celebrated at Elefsis (see above). It was connected with the renewal of fertility and also with rites of passage from childhood to manhood. The museum in Thebes has examples of the style of pottery peculiar to the sanctuary, which typically show parodies of myths or Dionysian scenes.

The visible remains consist of a theatre with six rows of seats intact, directly facing the east end of a temple. Between the two was an altar, the centre of the sacred rites performed here. The unusual juxtaposition of theatre and temple appears to confirm the idea of rites involving public initiation. The complex included a stoa and was enclosed by a circuit wall. From the main highway the dirt road first takes a dog-leg course across a stream. After a few hundred metres, a sign at a fork indicates left. The road then heads due south towards the low hills. One kilometre from the main road, it swings left but a smaller, rougher track carries straight on. The site is concealed in a small valley directly ahead. The track climbs briefly around the shoulder of the hill and the site is revealed directly below on the right. Although they are enclosed by a wire fence and not routinely open, the remains lie at a lower level so that the layout is clearly revealed.

Thebes (Thiva, Θήβα)
The city founded by Cadmus. The myth of Oedipus and his sons. The birthplace of Dionysus and Hercules.

Thebes, more than any other Greek city, has a central place in myth. This begins with its legendary founding by Cadmus, who also reputedly brought the alphabet to Greece. It was the birthplace of Dionysus (see Eleutherai above) and Hercules (see Chapter 3), both born of Zeus's affairs with mortal women, and both suffering the jealousy of Hera, Zeus's wife. It was the home of the great seer, Teiresias. Above all, Thebes was the scene of the tragedy of Oedipus and the civil war between his sons. Traditionally, all the events portrayed in these stories take place before the Trojan War. To what extent they represent genuine dynastic battles between Mycenaean families, or attempts to legitimise a line of kingship by divine association, is unknown. What they do show is the central importance of prophecy to the Greeks. The use of oracles was not something that existed only in a mythological past, but was part of everyday life in Classical Greece. Establishing the will of the gods by consulting an oracle was considered essential before major decisions were taken.

The story of the founding of Thebes begins with the legend of Europa and the bull. Zeus fell in love with Europa, daughter of Agenor, king of Phoenicia. Disguised as a bull, he carried her away to Crete. Agenor sent his son Cadmus across the known world to search for his sister, commanding him not to return without her. Cadmus came to mainland Greece and eventually travelled to the oracle at Delphi. She advised him to abandon the search and follow a cow until it lay down from weariness. At this spot he should build a city. He followed the cow into Viotia until it sank to the ground. Here he was to found the city that became Thebes. His first task, however, was to sacrifice the cow to Athena. Cadmus sent his men to the nearby well of Ares to fetch water for the sacrifice, not knowing that it was guarded by a dragon. His men were killed and when he discovered this, he slew the beast by crushing its head with a rock. Athena ordered him to sow the dragon's teeth in the soil. Immediately armed men sprang up from the ground. These 'Sown men' began to fight amongst themselves, killing each other until only five were left. These five were the ancestors of the Thebans. With their help, Cadmus built the acropolis that he named the Cadmeia. Zeus gave Cadmus Harmonia, the daughter of Aphrodite and Ares, for his wife. The twelve Olympian gods attended the wedding in the Cadmeia. Their wedding presents included the golden necklace made by Hephaistos (see the legend of Amphiaraos above) and a golden robe given by Athena. After Cadmus, the legendary line of Theban kings passed from father to son, first to Polydorus, then to Labdacus, and then to Laios, the father of Oedipus.

The tragedy of Oedipus began when Laios consulted the oracle at Delphi to find out why he and his wife Jocasta were still childless after many years of marriage. The oracle told him that this was not a curse but a blessing, as he was doomed to perish at the hands of his own son. Laios refused to sleep with Jocasta again. But he lost his resolution when she made him drunk and she became pregnant. When the child was born, Laios snatched him away and left him to die on the slopes of Mount Kithaeron, just south of Plataia, having first pierced his feet with a nail and tied them together. The child was found by a Corinthian shepherd, who named him Oedipus, literally swollen-feet, from the injury he had suffered. He took him to Polybus, the king of Corinth, who with his wife Periboa, brought him up as their own child. Oedipus in turn, visited the Delphic oracle. He was horrified to be told that he was destined to kill his father and marry his mother. Convinced that Polybus and Periboa were his real parents, he resolved never to return to Corinth. On the road from Delphi to Daulis (see Chaironia below), Oedipus met Laios, who was on his way to Delphi to ask how the Thebans might be rid of the Sphinx. This famous monster had a woman's head, a lion's body, a serpent's tail and the wings of an eagle. There was a dispute over who should give way to the other on the road. Oedipus killed the unknown stranger, unaware that this was his real father.

Oedipus then made his way to Thebes. The Sphinx sat outside the city, asking each traveller the same riddle, which she was said to have learnt from the Muses. She devoured all those who could not answer. The riddle was, "What being has only one voice, sometimes four feet, sometimes two, and sometimes three, but is weakest when it has the most?" Oedipus correctly answered that it was man, who crawls on four limbs as an infant and leans on a stick in old age. The Sphinx then threw herself from a mountain and perished. The Thebans elected Oedipus king and he married Jocasta, still unaware of his true parentage. Oedipus and Jocasta had four children, two sons, Eteocles and Polyneices, whose subsequent history was described above, and two daughters, Antigone and Ismene. (Although Pausanias, referring to a lost epic poem called the Oidipodia, says that the gods exposed the incestuous nature of their marriage immediately and that the mother of Oedipus's children was really Euryganeia).

Plague came to Thebes. The oracle, when consulted yet again, said that relief could only come by expelling the murderer of Laios from Thebes. Oedipus at last learnt the truth about his parents from Teiresias, the seer. Jocasta hanged herself in shame, and Oedipus put out his own eyes. He left Thebes, with his daughter Antigone. After many years of wandering guided by Antigone, he finally came to Colonus, near Athens, where he was taken from the earth by the Eumenides or Furies. The civil war between his sons that followed Oedipus's death, led to the destruction of the city, and there is physical evidence of destruction twice in the Mycenaean period. Nevertheless, the city seems to have been continuously occupied and prosperous.

For much of its history Thebes was the enemy of Athens. The Thebans fought on the Persian side at the battle of Plataia in 479 BC and sided with Sparta in the Peloponnesian War. However, once Sparta became the dominant power in Greece, Theban and Athenian interests converged and they fought together in the Corinthian War, 395-386 BC.

The brief period of Theban primacy in Greece followed the battle of Leuktra in 371 BC, when Thebes alone, led by their greatest general Epaminondas, comprehensively defeated the Spartan army. Epaminondas then proceeded to break Spartan power permanently by his campaigns in the Peloponnese and the restoration of the state of Messenia (see Chapter 6, Mantinea and Chapter 9, Messene). Thebes again fought alongside Athens against Philip II and was defeated with her at the battle of Chaironia in 338 BC. The city was destroyed when it took part in the revolt against Alexander the Great, and although refounded twenty years later, it did not regain its former glory. The town prospered again in the Middle Ages, first under Byzantine rule and later under the Franks. After their conquest in 1204/5 AD, it became the capital of the Duchy of Athens. The largest extant monument in the town is the tower of the castle built by the St. Omer family, on a section of the ancient acropolis wall. It now stands in the garden of the museum. The town became a backwater when the Turks transferred the regional capital to Livadhia.

Approaching Thebes from the coast, the town lies 5km to the south of the Athens–Lamia National road. The route to the centre is signposted. The one-way streets of the central area are narrow and parking is difficult. The main street, Epaminondhou, is now pedestrianised. Despite the power of the myths and the city's pre-eminence in antiquity, a visit to Thebes is likely to be disappointing. There is virtually nothing of its history now visible. Each rebuilding of the city has occurred on top of the previous remains, right up to the present day. The centre of the modern town now sits exactly on the site of the ancient acropolis, the Cadmeia or Kadmeia. The modern suburbs occupy the area of the Classical city that surrounded the acropolis. This too, had walls, and another myth to account for their construction. Amphion and Zethus, sons of Zeus, are said to have built them. Amphion had a magic lyre given to him by Hermes. His playing caused the stones of the walls to move into position themselves. Nothing now remains. Nevertheless, the outline of the low hill of the Cadmeia is still clear and the positions of the seven gates have been reasonably established. Only the foundations of the circular towers of the Electra gate are actually visible. The remains of two Mycenaean palaces, one succeeding the other, have been found. Those with determination can spend an hour or two locating the fragmentary remains that rescue digs have revealed amongst the modern buildings. There is however one location that is still identified with Oedipus. This is the Spring or Fountain of Oedipus where he washed away his father's blood. It lies a few hundred metres due east of the

33

northern tip of the Cadmeia below the hill in a small park and is well signposted. The most rewarding visit is to the museum, located at the northern end of the Cadmeia. Its opening hours are normally 08.00 to 19.00, 12.30 to 19.00 on Mondays. It is possible to park outside. Here the archaeological work on the Cadmeia is very well documented, with plans of the rescue digs exhibited alongside examples of the finds, including the remarkable lapis lazuli cylinder seals from Mesopotamia. These give some credence to the myth of Cadmus's origins. There are also excellent exhibits from other sites nearby. These include the distinctive pottery from the Kabeirion (see above), Kouroi, stylised statues of young men, from the Sanctuary of Apollo at Ptoon (see Chapter 3), and statues of Artemis and Hecate from Aulis.

3

Central Greece

Thebes to Delphi

It is a little under 100km to Delphi taking the direct route from Thebes. The road is both reasonably good and, having bypassed Livadhia, has fine mountain scenery. However, there are numerous possible diversions along the way. The countryside to the north and west of Thebes was the scene of the exploits of Hercules in his youth, before he was exiled to Tiryns to perform his Twelve Labours. The Mycenaean citadel of Gla has a superb circuit of cyclopean walls that gives a clear idea of how Cadmus's acropolis at Thebes must have looked. Nearby, on Mount Ptoon there is a Sanctuary of Apollo with a famous oracle. Orchomenos, said to have been sacked by Hercules, is today an unpretentious modern town. It has an ancient history with remains from the Neolithic to the Mediaeval. Livadhia, home of the famous Oracle of Trophonios, is an exceptionally pleasant place worth visiting in its own right. It is also a very useful overnight base from which to explore the surrounding area. These sites are all unenclosed and can be visited at any time.

Hercules's mother was Alcmene, daughter of Electryon who was king of Mycenae and a son of Perseus (see Chapter 8). Alcmene was married to her cousin Amphitryon, king of Troizen, who became Hercules's stepfather. However, the birth myth of Hercules is set not in the Argolid, but in Thebes, because Amphitryon had been banished there after accidentally killing Electryon. Alcmene, although betrothed to Amphitryon, had refused to go ahead with the marriage until he had avenged the death of her eight brothers who had been killed in a cattle raid. While he was away from Thebes on this task, and on the very day of his success, Zeus disguised himself as Amphitryon and came to Alcmene describing how he had defeated the murderers of her brothers. Amphitryon himself came home the next day. Alcmene gave birth to

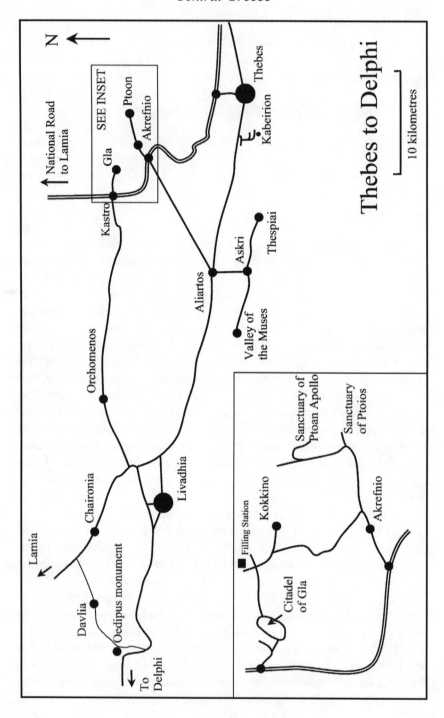

N

National Road
to Lamia

SEE INSET

Ptoon
Akrefnio

Gla

Kastro

Thebes

Kabeirion

Orchomenos

Aliartos

Askri

Thespiai

Valley of
the Muses

Chaironia

Lamia

Davlia

Oedipus monument

Livadhia

To
Delphi

Thebes to Delphi

10 kilometres

Sanctuary of
Ptoan Apollo

Sanctuary
of Ptoios

Kokkino

Filling Station

Akrefnio

Citadel
of Gla

two boys, one day apart. The first was Hercules, son of Zeus, and the second Iphicles, son of Amphitryon. On the day Alcmene was due to give birth, Zeus had boasted on Mount Olympus that he was about to become the father of a son who would rule over the house of Perseus, that is, Mycenae. Hera, in her jealousy, hatched a plan to prevent this. She made Zeus swear that the descendant of Perseus born that day would be the future ruler. In Mycenae, Sthenelos, Electryon's brother, was now king. Hera hastened to Mycenae and caused his wife Nicippe to give premature birth to their son, Eurystheus. At the same time she delayed the birth of Hercules so that it was Eurystheus who was to be favoured by Zeus's oath.

Thespiai (Θεσπιάι) and the Valley of the Muses
The myth of Narcissus and Echo. Hercules killed the lion of Kithaeron here. The Sanctuary of the Muses.

As he grew up, Hercules was given the best of education, receiving tuition in chariot driving, wrestling, archery and all the martial skills. He was also taught literature, singing and playing the lyre. It was while he was being instructed in the lyre that he killed his teacher Linus with a blow from the instrument when he was admonished for his technique. His stepfather, Amphitryon, sent him into the countryside around Thebes to look after his cattle, to avoid the risk of further accidents. When he was eighteen, he faced his first challenge when a huge lion began preying on the herds of his stepfather and those of Thespius, king of Thespiai. The mountains of Kithaeron and Helicon were the lion's territory. Hercules determined to kill the beast. Thespius had fifty daughters and wanted each to have a child by Hercules. He therefore made him his guest for the duration of the hunt. Hercules slept with all fifty daughters, some say on the same night, some say on consecutive nights. Finally, he killed the lion on Helicon using a club cut from a wild olive tree. From its skin he made his familiar cloak and he used its jaws for a helmet.

Modern Thespies (Θεσπίες) is a small farming village on the site of its ancient predecessor. Despite its relative obscurity it is the setting for some of the best known myths. As well as its connection with Hercules, it was the home of Narcissus. The great poet Hesiod lived nearby. His Theogony, written about 700 BC, is the source of much of our information about the origin of the gods. To the west lies the famous Valley of the Muses, now well signposted and easy to find.

Most people have heard of Narcissus, but few know that he was a native of Thespiai. There are several versions of the myth of Narcissus and Echo but they all relate the essential element, Narcissus falling in love with his own reflection. He was the son of the river-god, Cephissus, and the nymph, Liriope. He was known for his beauty, but was impervious to love, rejecting the advances of his many suitors. The most famous of these was the nymph Echo, who had distracted Hera with elaborate stories while Zeus was engaged with his mountain nymphs. Hera discovered the deception and she punished Echo by denying her the use of her own voice. All she could do was repeat the words of others. When Narcissus rejected her, she died of grief leaving only her voice behind. Nemesis punished Narcissus for his cruelty by causing him to fall in love with his reflection in the waters of a spring. Being unable to possess the object of his love, he too died of grief. In another version, he killed himself with a dagger and the narcissus flower sprang up from the earth where his blood had spilt. Pausanias, in the 2C AD, saw the spring identified with Narcissus near Thespiai, but is quite disparaging about the story. He tells of a lesser-known, more sympathetic version, in which Narcissus has an identical twin sister with whom he falls in love. When she dies he visits the spring to look at his reflection and see in it the memory of his sister's image.

The Muses dwelt on Mount Helicon, just to the west of Thespiai. An entire valley was dedicated to their worship. They were the goddesses of song and poetry and originally there were said to be three. However, by the time their cult had been established around Thespiai they were regarded as the nine daughters of Zeus and Mnemosyne, or Memory. Their names are; Kalliope, Kleio, Euterpe, Thalia, Melpomene, Terpsikhore, Erato, Polymnia and Ourania. Their role expanded to make them the patrons not just of song and poetry but also of the arts and sciences generally. There are no grand monuments in the Valley of the Muses, but the scenery is glorious and evocative. Curiously, most guidebooks still imply that the area is unattractive and difficult to find, but the valley now offers an easy route into the foothills of Helicon and the scene of Hercules's adventures.

To reach Thespiai and the Valley of the Muses take the Livadhia road from Thebes for 20km to Aliartos (Αλίαρτος). Approaching the outskirts of the village, a left turn south, signposted Thespiai, reaches the small village of Askri (Ασκρή, Ασκρά, Ασκραία) after 7km. A brown sign at a T-junction indicates right to the Valley of the Muses. Left leads to Thespiai. The road into the valley is well marked with a succession of brown signs. Leaving Askri it passes the football field, a shelter in the middle of the road and a cemetery on the right. After 1km, a brown sign points left down a good gravel road. Fork left at a second brown sign further on. Above, on the hill to the right, is a mediaeval tower. At yet another fork, this time without a sign, keep left again. The road can be seen ahead, climbing the valley towards a pass, with Mount Helikon to the left. At the foot of this pass a final brown sign on the left verge indicates, 'Valley of the Muses and ancient Askra'.

Below the road, on the opposite side of the stream, are the fragmentary ruins of the Sanctuary of the Muses. The foundations of a temple, or altar, can be clearly seen. A little above this are the hidden foundations of a long stoa. Higher up the slope you may be able to make out the outline of the theatre. This was used for the musical and poetic contests that constituted the Musean Games, held every four years. All these remains date from the 3C BC but the cult of the Muses is considerably older than this. In the opening verses of the Theogony, written about 700 BC, Hesiod describes the Muses singing and dancing on Helikon. They gave him a staff and breathed the gift of song into him when he met them on the mountain whilst he was shepherding his flocks. Askra was Hesiod's home. The ancient town lay on the slopes to the north of the valley. By Pausanias's time, all that was left was the solitary tower that still stands on the hill above the road.

Beyond the sanctuary, the road continues uphill to a higher plateau where there is a curious modern monument to the Muses in the form of nine white pillars. Here, the countryside becomes more remote, increasingly wooded, and the road deteriorates. Pausanias describes the slopes of Mount Helikon being covered in arbutus bushes, the strawberry tree named after its strawberry-like fruit, and the Muses' sanctuary standing in a grove. Whilst it is true that the immediate area of the temple is currently treeless, the valley as a whole is beginning to see noticeable reforestation and is re-acquiring its air of mystery.

Gla (Γλας)
The largest Mycenaean site in Greece. The ancient drainage works were said to have been blocked up by Hercules.

Thebes is surrounded by legend but has little in the way of visible remains today. In contrast the Mycenaean citadel of Gla is an enormous, magnificent ruin, but virtually nothing is known of its origins. The site lies close to the National road, fifteen minutes beyond the Thebes exit. Ten kilometres after passing Lake Iliki on the right is the junction for

Gla, signposted to Kastro (Κάστρο) and Orchomenos (Ορχομενός). Approaching the motorway junction across the bed of the drained Lake Kopais, the site of Gla is visible to the right of the road as a rocky mound in the flat landscape. Even at this distance the line of the great walls is visible. The site is signposted from the exit road.

Gla is many times larger than other Mycenaean sites and its function is uncertain. Its construction is thought to be connected with the massive drainage project undertaken by the Mycenaeans of Orchomenos, better known as the Minyans (see below), to convert the seasonal Lake Kopais into agricultural land. Originally the lake's outflow was through swallow holes. Permanent drainage has been achieved in modern times by construction of a tunnel to Lake Iliki and this has created the irrigated plain seen today. The Mycenaean solution was a system of dykes and canals to channel the waters more efficiently to the swallow holes. Completed by 1300 BC, it was destroyed or abandoned by 1200 BC. The lake returned to its previous state. It is possible that earthquakes partially blocked the swallow holes, but the mythical explanation is that Hercules blocked them up during his war against Orchomenos (see below). Gla is thought to have been an administrative centre and military fortification protecting the drainage system. It may also have been a place of refuge for the population living and working on the reclaimed land. Whether it was a joint project of the Mycenaean communities living around the lake, or under the direct control of Orchomenos, is unknown. The site is unenclosed and enjoys splendid isolation. In appearance it is now a low rocky hill, covered by wild flowers in spring, rising abruptly from the intensively farmed plain of square fields surrounded by irrigation ditches. The walls completely encircle the hill and are almost 3km in length. As the road approaches the hill, it becomes rougher. In front of the low cliffs it divides left and right, forming a complete circle around the hill. Turn right and drive around the site on the dirt road, to gain an overall impression of its size and the immensity of the walls. When parking on this road, be sure to leave room for passing tractors. Access can be gained either by the main gate on the south side, or, having almost completed the circuit, by the west gate above a derelict modern kiosk. This gate is closest to the most important building, the so-called palace, L-shaped and partially built into the northern section of the walls at the highest point of the hill. There are other structures in the centre of the site, sometimes referred to as the agora, but there are no remains indicating that the place was ever a conventional settlement. How much of it is visible will depend on the growth of the low, scrub vegetation at the time. From the walls, the view is of the low barren hills surrounding the plain with taller mountains to the north and west, snow capped to the end of April. The silence is disturbed only by the hum of insects and the intermittent sound of tractors working in the fields.

From Gla it is possible to drive directly to Orchomenos and Livadhia by retracing the route to the motorway and crossing over the highway to Kastro. The Orchomenos road is clearly signposted from here.

Mount Ptoon (Πτώον)
Sanctuaries of Ptoan Apollo and the hero Ptoios.

Hidden away on the slopes of Mount Ptoon to the east of Gla, is the important sanctuary and oracle of Ptoan Apollo. Here, the title of the god simply means Apollo of Mount Ptoon, but the mountain gets its name from the local hero Ptoios, who also has a sanctuary nearby. Ptoios had healing powers, but in spite of his obvious importance in antiquity is now an obscure figure. His father was Athamas, king of Orchomenos, who had a central role in the foundation myth of Isthmia (Chapter 5).

Apollo was in many ways the Greeks' most important god. He was the twin brother of Artemis and the story of his birth is described in Chapter 2, Braurona. He had many different roles. When he is represented with a bow and arrow he is a punishing god and his arrows brought sudden death. However, he is simultaneously the god who helps mankind if he is shown due respect. In this role, he is the father of Asklepios, the healing god (see Chapter 8, Epidavros). Often depicted leading the choir of the Muses, lyre in hand, Apollo is also the god of song and music. Above all however, he is the god of prophecy, with his most famous oracle at Delphi. His oracle here on Mount Ptoon was believed to be infallible.

The most direct approach to the site is by leaving the motorway at the junction before the Kastro (Gla) exit, signposted to Akrefnio (Ακραίφνιο). This village lies about 1km to the northeast of the motorway. Drive uphill to the square, where there are bars and tavernas. Continue straight on uphill on the Kokkino (Κόκκινο) road, passing a brown sign for the site. Where the road makes a sharp turn uphill to the left, a minor road goes straight on. Take this minor road as far as a fork, just by a large electricity pylon. The right fork is a dirt road. Above it, to the right, are the remains of the Sanctuary of the hero Ptoios, with altars and a temple on terraces hidden in the vegetation. However, as these cannot be seen from the road, it is better to take the left fork first up to the Sanctuary of Ptoon Apollo, because, from this road, views back down the valley reveal the terraces and will make subsequent location easier.

This left fork is signposted Ιερά Μονί Οσιάς Πελαγίας. After 1km uphill, a dirt road descends to the right, with a battered sign pointing to the church of Ayia Paraskevi (Αγια Παρασκευή). This small, white church is visible below on the other side of the narrow valley. The dirt road is passable. Just before the church, a brown sign on the left announces 'Ιερό Απόλλωνος Πτώου' – the sanctuary of Ptoan Apollo.

The site is on three terraces immediately above the track. A spring still flows down through the remains, so that the ground is wet and marshy in places. At the lowest level is an ancient water storage cistern with seven compartments. Above are two stoas, and the foundations of a 3C BC Doric temple. The original temple dated from the 7C BC. It shared the fate of Thebes in 336 BC when it was destroyed by Alexander as part of his reprisals for the revolt following the death of his father, Philip II. The temple was rebuilt after 316 BC when Kassander restored Thebes. The statues exhibited in the museum of Thebes (see Chapter 2) were found around this temple. Higher up again is cave that may have been the location of the oracle. In springtime the whole site is a riot of colourful flowers. The church, a little further along the track to the right, is restored and open. Its presence once again demonstrates the continuity of religious sites across the millennia.

There is an alternative route between the Ptoon sites and Gla. Return to the Kokkino road described above. Follow it over the hill and back towards Gla. Descend, skirting Kokkino, which lies on the hillside to the right. On reaching a crossroads, where there is a filling station, turn left. This road eventually meets the circular dirt road around Gla (see plan). To reach the Livadhia road, return through Akrefnio to the motorway and cross it, following the signs for Aliartos (Αλίαρτος). This road follows what was the east shore of Lake Kopais, and runs for much of its length under low cliffs pierced by caves.

Livadhia (Levadia, Livadhia, *Λειβαδειά, Λιβαδειά)*
The Oracle of Trophonios

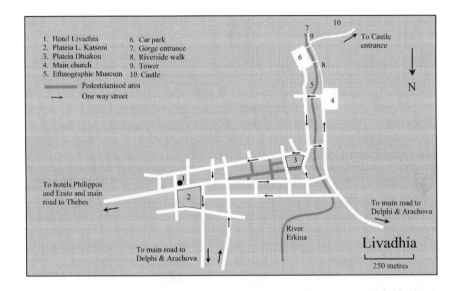

1. Hotel Livadhia	6. Car park
2. Plateia L. Katsoni	7. Gorge entrance
3. Plateia Dhiakou	8. Riverside walk
4. Main church	9. Tower
5. Ethnographic Museum	10. Castle

Pedestrianised area

One way street

To Castle entrance

N

To hotels Philippos and Erato and main road to Thebes

To main road to Delphi & Arachova

River Erkina

To main road to Delphi & Arachova

Livadhia

250 metres

The town has occupied its present site at the mouth of the Erkina gorge since Classical times, when it changed its name from Mideia to Livadhia, after Lebados of Athens. In modern Greek though, Livadhia means meadows. The river Erkina, or Herkyna, runs through the centre of the town. Its fame in antiquity was due to the Oracle of Trophonios, located above the gorge. In the Middle Ages Livadhia prospered. In the 13C it was assigned to the Duchy of Athens after the initial creation of the Frankish states. The period of occupation by the Catalans, 1311 to 1381, produced the castle seen today on its rock. The town continued to thrive during the Turkish occupation and is still the administrative capital of Viotia. Today much of the landscape of the Classical period has been preserved. Although there are now no visible remains of the oracular chamber, the springs and the riverside that formed an important part of the ceremonies, are still an impressive site. The gorge remains a dark and mysterious place.

Trophonios, and his brother Agamedes, were the sons of Erginos of Orchomenos, born after their father's defeat at the hands of Hercules (see below). The brothers were famous architects who built, amongst other things, an early temple to Apollo at Delphi. After his death, Tro-

43

phonios was worshipped as a hero. A temple was dedicated to him in Livadhia and the oracle was founded.

The legend of his death is very strange. It began when the two brothers built a treasury for king Hyreus, but constructed it in such a way that a stone could be removed secretly to give them access to the gold and silver inside. They began stealing from the hoard. Hyreus could not understand how the locks were being circumvented. He built a trap inside the treasury that ensnared Agamedes during the next robbery. Agamedes was unable to free himself and Trophonios cut off his head to make identification impossible. He escaped to the sacred grove at Livadhia where the earth split open and Trophonios was swallowed up.

Pausanias, who consulted the oracle and describes the experience, believed that Trophonios must have been the son of Apollo, the god of prophecy. Consulting the oracle was a complicated process that took several days. Pausanias calls it "going down to Trophonios".

First, there was a period of purification when the suppliant offered sacrifices to the gods, principally Zeus, Apollo, Hera and Demeter, and also to Trophonios himself. During this time he bathed only in the cold water of the river. A seer would inspect the entrails of the sacrifices to establish whether he would be well received by Trophonios. On the night he was to "go down", he would be taken to the river, anointed with olive oil and washed by young boys who had to be natives of Livadhia. He then had to drink first from the Spring of Forgetfulness, to empty his mind, and then from the Spring of Memory, so that he would be able to recall what was about to happen. Dressed in a linen tunic and stout boots and carrying honey cakes as an offering, he would climb the hill above the sacred grove to the oracle itself. This was a pit sunk in the ground, rather like a tholos tomb in shape. It was about 6M deep and could only be entered from above by a ladder carried up to the entrance.

Once inside, the suppliant would lie on the floor and push his feet and lower legs into an opening like a mouth at the base of the wall. Suddenly, he would be pulled through into a second chamber where he would receive the prophecy in some unidentified way, before being ejected back through the opening. The priests then took him to the seat of Memory, where he had to relate what had been revealed to him. According to Pausanias, he returned disorientated and in a state of terror. This procedure must have been a re-enactment of Trophonios's disappearance into the earth.

The gorge and springs can be reached from the town centre on foot. Alternatively it is possible to drive to the car park by the Ethnographic Museum. There are signs for both the Oracle and the Museum (see plan). The riverside walk, from the church up to the mouth of the gorge, has been transformed into a park shaded by majestic trees. The once derelict water mills have been renovated and now contain bars, cafes and exhibition galleries. The open area by the river is used every Easter Sunday for a public lamb roast. Large volumes of water issue from the base of the cliffs on either side of the stream at the gorge entrance. Here were the Springs of Memory and Forgetfulness from which those who wished to consult the oracle had to drink. Votive niches are cut in the rock on the right hand side. At the mouth of the gorge there is a massive tower on the right. This is the lower end of the main castle wall, and may be on the site of the temple of Trophonios with its sacred grove. In fact, it is easy to see that the base of the tower is built of re-used Classical blocks. The gorge is dark and bare in comparison to the attractive tree lined approach. A short walk leads past a modern theatre, and footpaths run high up to the left to two white painted chapels. The castle is hidden above the cliffs on the right. The site of the oracle itself is probably on the peak of Ayios Ilias that lies above the gorge beyond the castle hill. There are fragments of a temple of Zeus on this peak, but the traces of a later reconstruction of the oracle that have been found there are no longer visible.

The castle can be reached by a very steep lane running uphill from the tower at the gorge mouth. The cliffs of the gorge form the castle's main defences, the circuit being completed by the wall that can be seen on the left as you climb. Within the gate, the bailey is full of pine trees. There are some remains of the keep and a small church. The main reward of the climb is the view down into the gorge and to the towering snow capped mountains in the west.

To reach Livadhia from the direction of Thebes, take the signposted left turn 23km west of Aliartos. This leads in 6km to the centre. If approaching from Orchomenos, take the left turn from the main Delphi highway towards the town centre.

Orchomenos (Ορχομενός)

Byzantine church on the site of the temple of the Graces. Mycenaean tomb and palace. Hercules led a Theban sacking of the city.

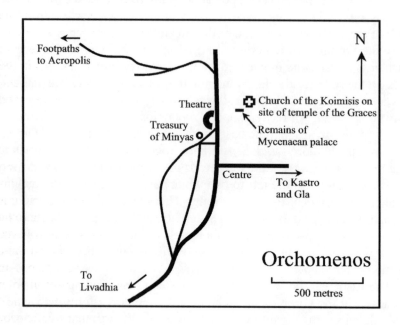

Orchomenos, first occupied in Neolithic times, has managed to preserve archaeological remains from every era down to the mediaeval period. These include the Mycenaean tholos tomb known as the Treasury of Minyas, well preserved remains of a 4C BC theatre, substantial sections of the Macedonian walls and a unique 9C AD Byzantine church, built on the site of the temple of the Graces. In the Mycenaean period, it dominated the area as the capital of the Minyans, a people named after the legendary King Minyas. His son, Orchomenos, gave his name to the town.

Minyan domination of the area apparently extended to Thebes and the conflict between the two cities is reflected in the myths of Hercules. Erginos, king of Orchomenos, had first marched against Thebes after his father, Klymenus, had been killed by Thebans at the festival of Poseidon at Onchestos, a town midway between Thebes and Orchomenos. The Thebans were defeated and forced to agree to the payment of an annual tribute in compensation for the murder. After he had killed the lion on Mount Helicon, Hercules returned to his home in Thebes. He happened to meet a group of heralds from Orchomenos on their way to demand the annual tribute. He is said to have sliced off their noses and sent them back. Pausanias actually describes a statue, called Hercules the Nose-slicer, standing outside one of the gates of Thebes. Erginos then marched on Thebes to avenge this outrage, but Hercules raised an army and the Minyans were defeated. With this great victory, Hercules's fame was assured. King Kreon, uncle of Oedipus, gave him Megara, his daughter, in marriage. The two cities were still rivals in the Classical period. Orchomenos was twice destroyed by Thebes in 364 and 349 BC. After the conquest of Greece by Philip II and Alexander, the Macedonians rebuilt the city.

Today it is a pleasant but unpretentious large village or small town, formed by the amalgamation of the two villages of Petromagoula and Skripou. It has re-adopted the ancient name Orchomenos. It makes no concessions to tourism at all, despite the importance of its several archaeological sites. It has the normal facilities of a working village, perhaps with slightly more emphasis on tractor parts. To reach the town from the centre of Livadhia, drive 1km north to the main Delphi road. Turn right and continue for 4km to the junction with the Thiva-Lamia highway. Turn left and, almost immediately, there is a right turn onto the Orchomenos road. Approaching the outskirts of the village after 7km, the ridge, crowned by the acropolis walls, can be seen on the left. The church, theatre and the visible Mycenaean remains, are all to be found at the opposite end of the village where the tail of the ridge meets the plain. In Mycenaean times this would have been the edge of Lake Kopais. At the entrance to the village the road splits into three. Take the main street, which is the right most of the three, and is signposted National Road (see plan). The centre of the village is a further half a kilometre. Keep straight on past the right turn for Kastro and Gla. There are brown signs at this junction. After 200M, the street enters an open area where, on the right, the Church of the Koimisis lies half hidden behind trees that provide a shady place to park.

The principal archaeological features are on either side of the road. To the right of the open space in front of the church are the excavated remains of a Mycenaean palace. On the opposite side of the road is the 4C BC theatre and beyond is the impressive Mycenaean tholos tomb known as the Treasury of Minyas. The tomb is the only part of the site subject to opening times, 8.30 to 15.00, and an entrance fee. It is well worth visiting this first to receive with the ticket one of the Greek Archaeological Service's excellent leaflets. This has a good plan of the area and the main sights.

The Treasury of Minyas is comparable with the tholos tombs of Mycenae, particularly the Treasury of Atreus. They were referred to as treasuries by Pausanias in the 2C AD when the knowledge of their original purpose had been lost, and the names persist to this day. The tomb is now roofless and, as a result, it lacks some of the dark grandeur of the tombs at Mycenae. In compensation, however, daylight allows a much better appreciation of the fineness of the construction and the skill of the stonemasons. The massive squared blocks, from which the tholos is constructed, have been cut to a subtle curve so that the walls form a true circle. The huge lintel of grey marble is cut to the same curve. The floor is carefully trimmed flat from the bedrock. A side chamber has a roof of slabs of green schist finely carved with spirals and rosettes. Unlike Mycenae, there will be nobody else there.

The Byzantine church of the Koimisis is built with re-used material from the theatre and the temple of the Graces that previously stood on the site. The entire west wall, above the level of the main door, is made of column drums from the temple. It is known to have been built in 874 AD from an inscription recording the event. The Graces, Charites or Kharites, were goddesses of grace and beauty, attendants of Aphrodite and companions of the Muses. There is uncertainty over their precise number and names, but according to Hesiod, who incidentally was said to be buried in the market place at Orchomenos, their parents were Zeus and Eurynome. Their names were Euphosyne, Aglaia and Thalia. Their worship at Orchomenos was very old. Eteocles, son of Oedipus, was said to be the first man to have offered sacrifice to them.

On the ridge above the theatre and the Treasury, have been found the remains of the successive phases of settlement. Prehistoric remains have been found immediately above the Treasury, the Classical city lay above this and on the highest terraces lay the Macedonian city.

From below, little can be seen of the city walls that enclosed the ridge. However, if you have the time and the inclination, a rewarding climb can be made to the keep that forms the acropolis. A sign by the church points left to 'The citadel of Orchomenos'. It is possible to drive about 500M up the ridge. After 200M the road forks. Take the right fork and drive through the houses until the tarmac road becomes a dirt surface that ends in a meadow on the lower terrace of the ancient city. From here it is a 30-45 minute walk up to the top. Vague paths thread their way through the low vegetation. Shorts are not recommended and carrying some water is a good idea. Eventually the remains of walls appear to the left and right and, ahead, the tower of the acropolis rises above an almost vertical cliff.

The final ascent, which is not apparent from a distance, is via a stepped corridor cut into the cliff at a slope of forty-five degrees. Eighty two rock-cut steps lead to the summit, from where there are views of the entire area of ancient Lake Kopais. The layout of the city walls is clearly seen below. The 4C BC walls of the acropolis were built on only two sides of the summit, as the cliffs formed sufficient defence on the other two sides. The purpose of the structure was probably to defend the city from attack from the ridge beyond. The acropolis is separated from the slopes beyond by a gully that may be partly man made.

Chaironia (Chaironeia, Χαιρώνεια)
Here Philip of Macedon, with the young Alexander, defeated the forces of Athens and Thebes. A massive stone lion stands as a memorial to the Theban dead. Remains of a rock cut theatre.

Even for those in a hurry, the minor diversion to see the massive Lion of Chaironia has to be worthwhile. The monument marks the site of the tomb of the Theban Sacred Band killed in the battle of Chaironia. The victory of Philip II and the young Alexander over the combined forces of Athens and Thebes in 338 BC marked the beginning of Macedonian hegemony over the whole of Greece.

Tension had been building between Athens and Macedon for two decades. Events came to a head in 339 BC when Amphissa was accused by the Amphictyonic League of cultivating the Krisaean plain. This League or "association of neighbours" was composed of the states and cities surrounding the temple of Apollo at Delphi. Its job was to control the affairs of the shrine. The Krisaean plain was dedicated to Apollo. Its use for agriculture or even grazing was prohibited. Philip II of Macedon had already become a leading figure in the League, following his inter- vention in the Sacred War against Phokis, which had seized Delphi in 356 BC. The League sought his help again against Amphissa and Philip promptly marched on the city. The threat of his presence, so close to Athenian territory, led directly to the battle at Chaironia. Although Ath- ens appealed to the other Greek states for help, only Thebes joined them in force on the battlefield. Sparta refused to get involved.

The site lies on the Thebes – Lamia road, 8km north of the Or- chomenos junction, on the outskirts of the modern village of Chaironia. The Lion stands to the left of the road on a massive stone plinth set be- low modern ground level. There is space to park immediately opposite. The statue is large and impressive, but curiously unlike a lion. It was discovered half buried in 1818 and was restored on its original plinth early in the 20C.

Driving on through the village, a sign points left to 'Ancient Theatre'. Turn left and the asphalt quickly becomes a track that leads to the theatre, ending directly in front of the orchestra. This is a remnant of Classical Chaironia, a city famous in Pausanias's time for the distillation of perfumes from the flowers of the lily, rose, narcissus and iris. It was also the home of Plutarch who was born here in 45 AD. The theatre is completely cut from the rock of the hillside and consequently the seating is well preserved. Directly above are quite substantial remains of the acropolis walls. The hill above the acropolis is one of the many places said to be where Rhea tricked Kronos into swallowing a stone instead of the infant Zeus (see Chapter 5, Elefsis).

The theatre seats look out directly over the battlefield. The opposing forces faced each other in lines extending from the foot of the acropolis across the plain to the river, where the Sacred Band fought to the death. Today it is an excellent place for a picnic.

To reach Delphi, carry on in the direction of Lamia for 6km. Take a left turn signposted to Davlia (Δαύλεια). It is 8km to this village, and then another 10km to the junction with the Livadhia – Arachova road. Three kilometres before this junction, where a steep valley leads off to the right, a stone monument was erected in 1996 by the side of the road, to mark the spot where Oedipus killed his father. The ancient road to Delphi led up this side valley. On the monument are carved lines, in ancient Greek, from Sophocles's Oedipus Rex.

Davlia (Daulis, Δαύλεια)
The myth of Tereus, Prokne and Philomela

Ancient Davlia lies close to the modern village of the same name. Pausanias tells us that the city was named either after the nymph Daulis, a daughter of Kephisos, or more prosaically from daula, the word for wooded thickets in ancient Greek. This was the location of the macabre myth of Tereus, Prokne and Philomela.

Pandion, king of Athens, made a strategic alliance with Tereus, a king of the Thracians in Davlia. Pandion had two daughters, Prokne and Philomela. He gave Tereus Prokne's hand in marriage to cement the alliance. In due course Prokne gave birth to a son Itys. Missing her sister, Prokne persuaded Tereus to bring Philomela from Athens to keep her company. However Philomela's fate on reaching Dauvlia was to be raped by Tereus. To prevent her revealing what had happened, he cut out her tongue and imprisoned her, telling Prokne she had died on the journey. For a year Philomela was kept imprisoned but she spent this time weaving a peplos or robe. She was able to incorporate into the fabric a few words that told of her fate and by signs she persuaded a slave to take the robe to her sister. Prokne deciphered the message and found and released Philomela. In her rage at her sister's disfigurement Prokne determined to wreak a terrible vengeance on Tereus and the reunited women killed the child Itys and butchered his body. Prokne then served up the flesh to Tereus at dinner and after he had eaten revealed the truth of the meal. The sisters fled, pursued by Tereus with an axe. Before he could cut them down, all three were transformed into birds by the gods. Tereus became a hoppoe, Prokne a nightingale and Philomela a swallow. The call of the nightingale is said to be a lament for the dead Itys.

The site stands on a conspicuous wooded hill to the south of the Delphi road a short distance west of the village. A modern concrete road (signposted) leads to the entrance gate. The city dates from the Mycenaean era and appears in Homer's Catalogue of Ships, the list of the cities participating in the Trojan War. The events of the myth of Prokne and Philomela, if they have any historical foundation, would date from just a few generations before the Trojan War. The Hellenistic walls of the acropolis, built on earlier foundations, are well preserved and the modern entrance is still through the original gate. Hidden within the trees that now cover the acropolis are the ruins of the church of St. Theodore built on the site and incorporating material from the temple of Athena mentioned by Pausanias.

Arachova (Αράχοβα)
Mount Parnassos and the Corycian Cave

The mountain town of Arachova straddles the main road from Livadhia 10km to the east of Delphi. It is the starting point for exploring Mount Parnassos, sacred to Dionysus and the Maenads, and the location of the Greek version of the Great Flood.

The Deucalion flood as it is known, is named after Deucalion, son of Prometheus (see Chapter 6, Sikyon). Zeus had become disgusted by the degeneracy of mankind. He sent a tremendous flood to wash away man and his works. Deucalion was given warning of the flood by his father. He built a ship on which he and his wife Pyrrha survived for nine days. The retreating waters deposited the ship on Mount Parnassos. From there the pair went to the Sanctuary of Themis to pray for the restoration of mankind. Themis appeared to them, instructed them to cover their heads and throw the bones of their mother behind them. They realised that the goddess was referring to the stones of Mother Earth. The stones that Deucalion threw behind him became men. Those that Pyrrha threw became women. Later, Deucalion and Pyrrha had a son, Hellen. He was the mythical ancestor of all the Hellenes, that is, the Greeks.

It is possible to explore the slopes of Parnassos by car, as a good road climbs to the ski centre below the main ridge. This road also provides access to the Corycian cave above Delphi, a site sacred to Pan. At the Delphi end of Arachova take the road signposted to the Ski Centre of Parnassos. This climbs steeply for 7km, eventually reaching a saddle. Spread out below, on an extensive plateau or alp, is a surprisingly large amount of new ski-chalet development, around the original village of Kalivia (Καλύβια). The upper slopes of Parnassos rise beyond the plateau. The cave is on a wooded hillside on the far side of the alp. Drive on, through the scattered houses, for 2km. Where the new development ends, a reasonable gravel road leads off to the left into the woods by a battered sign that reads, 'Ayia Triada, Chat Tours, KOPYKION ANTPON, Corycian Cave, Grotte Corycienne'. After half a kilometre, turn right at a junction where a sign points left to Ayia Triadha and a much smaller one indicates Korykian cave right. One kilometre further on, take another road that turns sharply uphill to the left. There is no sign at this junction, but 50M up the track, a battered sign on the right, 'KOPYKIAN ANTPON', confirms the direction. The road climbs steadily uphill for 2km, ending abruptly on a small platform where there is room to turn around.

The cave is 20M above on a higher terrace. The large entrance admits sufficient light to see the interior. The main chamber is about 90M deep and 60M wide. Archaeological evidence has shown that the cave was used in the Neolithic period and in the late Bronze Age as well as in Classical times. There are tremendous views to the south across the Gulf of Corinth where the peaks of Helmos and Killini rise into the clouds. To the north, the ski runs and lifts on the upper slopes Parnassos can be seen.

The cave is named after the nymph Corycia. Nymphs were minor female deities, daughters of the river and sea gods, and of Ocean and Mother Earth. They were nature spirits, living in the springs, rivers, mountains and caves of the world. They are often depicted in the company of shepherds and their flocks, and with Pan, the god of woods and pastures. His original home was Arcadia (see Chapter 6). His worship was late in coming to the rest of Greece (see Chapter 2, Marathon). Pan and the nymphs were usually worshipped in natural sanctuaries such as the Corycian cave. It is possible to make out the remains of inscriptions to Pan and the Nymphs carved on the cave wall to the right of the entrance. Above the cave, on the higher slopes of Parnassos, Athenian women known as Thyiades performed rites, sometimes called orgies, in honour of Dionysus, every year. They took their name from Thyia, a daughter of Kephisos, a river-god. She was the first to have sacrificed to Dionysus as a god. Parnassos was also later identified as the home of Apollo and the Muses.

Arachova is a seasonal ski resort active for a brief three month period each year. As such it offers broad range of accommodation and provides an alternative to the tourist facilities of Delphi itself.

Delphi (Δελφοί)
The greatest sanctuary of the Greek world. Dedicated first to Mother Earth, Themis and Poseidon, it became the sanctuary of Pythian Apollo after he slew the Python.

In ancient Greece Delphi was regarded as the navel, or centre, of the earth. Zeus is supposed to have released two eagles from opposite ends of the Earth in order to establish the centre. They met at Delphi, and at the exact centre the omphalos, or navel stone, was set up. The original stone in the inner sanctuary of the temple has been lost, but there are replicas visible elsewhere on the site. One can be seen by the Viotian treasury and there is an impressive Hellenistic copy in the museum.

Delphi's mythic origins are as a joint sanctuary and oracle of Gaia, Ge or Mother Earth, together with her daughter, Themis (see Chapter 2 Rhamnous), and Poseidon. Although Poseidon is thought of as the god of the sea, he was also the god of horses and, as here at Delphi, the god of earthquakes. The place was originally known as Pytho, after the serpent Python, who lived in a nearby cave and guarded the oracle. Python was said to be the son of Mother Earth and to have been born from the mud left after the Deucalion flood. The priestess of the oracle was called the Pythia.

At some point Apollo took over the oracle. A simple mythical explanation had Gaia handing on her share to Themis who made a gift of it to Apollo. Poseidon too gave up his share, but only in exchange for the island of Poros. The more common tale is that Apollo killed Python in revenge for his mother's persecution by the serpent on behalf of Hera (see Chapter 2, Braurona). He then established himself at the sanctuary, having persuaded Pan to reveal the art of prophecy to him. Thereafter he was known as Pythian Apollo, that is, as Apollo the slayer of Python. The Pythian Games were set up to commemorate this event. In their original form they were purely a religious event with musical contests.

The cult of Apollo Delphinios, the worship of Apollo in the form of a dolphin, was introduced from Crete. This was responsible for the change of name from Pytho to Delphi. The Homeric Hymn to Apollo tells how Apollo, disguised as a dolphin, brought a Cretan ship bound for Pylos to Kirra, the port on the Gulf of Corinth, so that its sailors could become the first priests of his temple. Delphi (Δελφοι) of course means Dolphins.

Visiting the site

Coming down the hill from Arachova, the ancient site is hidden from view by a shoulder of the mountain. The first part of the complex, the Marmaria or Sanctuary of Athena, lies below the road on the left. Here is the circular Tholos, with its re-erected columns, probably the most photographed edifice in Delphi. A little further on, again below on the left, lay the extensive facilities of the gymnasium, rebuilt in Roman times, and laid out on artificial terraces. Then, at a sharp bend, the cleft in the rocks with the Castalian spring can be seen on the right. Here the Pythia would purify herself before taking her place to deliver the oracle. After another 400M, the main entrance to the Sacred Precinct is also on the right. Although there is little space for car parking, the vast majority of visitors come by tour coach, and cars simply park by the side of the road wherever it wide enough. The museum is to be found a little beyond the main entrance to the site. Do not be put off by the vast array of coaches that line up to disgorge their passengers. People come in great numbers simply because this *is* the most beautiful ancient site in Greece. It is also large and quickly absorbs crowds.

The Sacred Precinct rises steeply up the hillside to the temple of Apollo, and then beyond to the theatre and the stadium. Only as you begin to climb do you become aware of the full glory of the location, the setting resembling a great natural theatre beneath the dramatic grey-red rocks. It is astonishing to realise that everything now visible was unknown before the work of the French excavators, which began at the end of the 19C. Until 1891, the village of Delphi occupied the ancient site, and there was little to be seen. The complete, forcible, removal of the village to its present position, about a kilometre distant, made it

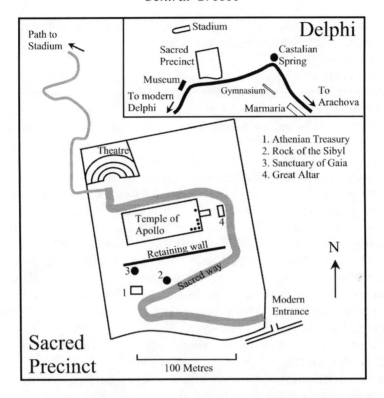

possible for the archaeologists to reveal all that had been buried beneath the landslips and human accretions of millennia. The modern entrance is placed so that the visitor follows the route of the original Sacred Way, which takes a zigzag course up the hill. The path climbs through the remains of monuments, war memorials, statue bases, and treasuries that held the offerings of individual cities. The best known is the re-erected Treasury of the Athenians, another famous image of the site. Above the Athenian Treasury, and half-destroyed by the massive retaining wall of the temple, is thought to be the site of the original Sanctuary of Mother Earth. To the right of it lies the rock of the Sibyl, the place from which the prophecies of the oracle of Gaia were pronounced. The path finally reaches the temple of Apollo on its huge artificial terrace, with the reconstructed Great Altar to the east. This 4C BC temple stands on the site of two previous structures, the earliest supposedly that built by Trophonios and Agamedes. The inner sanctuary was the seat of the oracle and the site of the original Omphalos. The remains indicate that the sanctuary was sunk below the main level of the temple floor. The priestess, the Pythia, sat on a tripod in an underground chamber over a "chasm". Vapours from this chasm induced a trance, and in this state she uttered her prophecies. These were "translated" by a priest into verse.

Archaeologists have looked in vain for such a chasm, casting doubt on the historical accounts. However, recent work by an American team, including geologists, a chemist and a toxologist, has found evidence of a natural explanation. Two geological faults intersect beneath the temple sanctuary. They cut through a structure of bituminous limestone. Heat generated from fault movements vapourised petrochemicals within this layer of rock and the gases rose through fissures below the temple. Spring water around the site has been analysed and found to contain traces of methane, ethane and ethylene. It is known that ethylene, in low concentrations with air, can produce a trance like state. The possibility that there was a fissure in the ground that has subsequently closed or filled up, rather than a gaping chasm, provides a plausible interpretation of the Classical texts. However, the discovery of a natural explanation does not deny the involvement of the gods. Apollo spoke his prophecies through the priestess, a mortal, and simply employed mechanisms from the natural world to accomplish this.

Above the temple is the extremely well preserved theatre, 4C BC with later restorations, including work from the Roman period. Here were held the musical contests of the Pythian Games. About 400M above the theatre is the stadium, equally well preserved, and built on an artificial terrace. It is now seen in its final, Roman, form. From the 6C BC onwards, the Games were greatly expanded to become a major Pan-Hellenic festival. They were held every four years with the full range of athletic events in the stadium, and horse or chariot races in a Hippodrome, located in some unknown spot on the Krisaean plain below.

A complete description of the entire site is outside the scope and purpose of this book. More detailed descriptions and site plans of Delphi are included in every guidebook to Greece ever published, and are available at the site. Note that even a hurried visit is likely to take more than half a day if you wish to include the Marmaria, the Castalian spring, and the Museum as well as the main site. In good weather, the steepness of the site can make a visit a hot and sticky experience if taken at too rapid a pace.

Figure 5 Delphi: The Temple of Apollo

Figure 6 Delphi: The Theatre

4

West from Delphi: Aitolia and Akarnania

The greater part of this chapter describes a circular route around Aitolia and Akarnania, an area little visited by foreign tourists. Here are some of the best-preserved ancient cities of mainland Greece. Kalydon is the site of a sanctuary of Artemis. It was the scene of the myth of the famous boar hunt in which all the great heroes took part. Pleuron, nearby, has excellent remains of a city re-built in the 3C BC. The tragic events leading up to the death of Hercules began here. Thermon, with its 7C BC temple of Apollo was the spiritual centre of Aitolia. Stratos was the ancient capital of Akarnania, whilst at Oiniadai the remains include docks and shipyards preserved from the Classical era. On the northern edge of the region, near Preveza, are the extensive ruins of Roman Nikopolis, the city founded by Augustus after he had defeated Anthony and Cleopatra. Further north again in Epirus lie two of the oldest oracles in Greece, the Necromanteion or Oracle of the Dead on the coast and the Oracle of Zeus at Dodona, inland near Ioannina. Alternatively it is possible to drive directly from Delphi to the Peloponnese via the bridge across the Gulf of Corinth from Antirio on the north bank to Rio.

A. Via Nafpaktos and Mesolonghi

From Delphi, the road quickly leaves the mountains and descends to the sacred Krisaean plain, now densely covered by olive groves. The coast is reached at Itea. Just to the east of the modern town lies the ancient port of Kirra where Apollo brought the Cretan ship so that its sailors could be his first priests at Delphi (see Chapter 3).

Nafpaktos is the largest settlement on this coast and a popular overnight stop. It is still visibly a mediaeval walled town, despite the

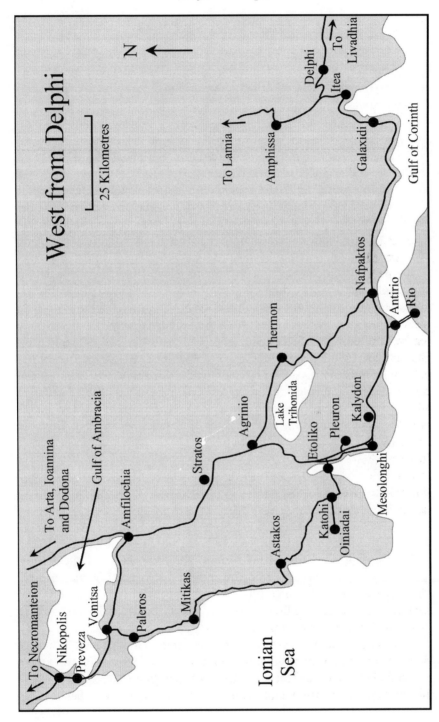

West from Delphi

25 Kilometres

N

modern buildings that attempt to conceal the fact. Although virtually nothing remains of its pre-mediaeval history, apart from some Classical foundations beneath the castle walls, Nafpaktos has a history as old as any in Greece. It was here that the Dorians (the Heraclidae, the descendants of Hercules) were believed to have built their ships in preparation for their invasion of the Peloponnese (see chapter 9). In the middle of the 5C BC it was taken from the Locrians by Athens, who allowed a group of Messenians, expelled by Sparta after an unsuccessful revolt, to settle there. After the battle of Chaironia in 338 BC, Philip II occupied the town and gave it to the Aitolians. However, the town is better known as Lepanto, its Venetian name, and the name given to the famous naval battle fought in October 1571 when the Ottoman Turks were defeated by the combined fleets of Spain, Venice and the Papacy.

The town's main square is by the harbour. From the castle above, walls descend to enclose the original mediaeval town and the picturesque port. The mediaeval history of Nafpaktos is outside the scope of this book, but a worthwhile visit can be made to the castle, either on foot, or by car via a good asphalt road. To walk there, look for a brown sign pointing up a cobbled lane from the harbour square. To drive, leave the square along the main road west, and turn immediately right, at a brown sign, up a narrow road. After 300M another right turn leads uphill to the main gate. Antirio is 11km from Nafpaktos. The cable stayed toll bridge is an astonishing sight and has transformed the crossing of the Gulf. Across the bridge, the road leads straight onto the new Patras by-pass. The elimination of the Patras bottleneck means that Olympia can now be reached in less than two hours.

The Evinos River
Hercules, Deianeira and Nessus the Centaur

From Antirio the main road west follows the coast for another 10km, before turning north inland of Mount Varasova to avoid the Evinos delta. The river emerges from the mountains, becoming increasingly braided as it flows between huge gravel beds. This was the setting for Hercules's encounter with the Centaur Nessus, an event that was to lead to the Hero's gruesome death.

In the latter years of his life Hercules came to the palace of Oeneus, king of Kalydon and Pleuron, to win the hand of Deianeira, the king's daughter (see below, Pleuron). After living in Aitolia for three years he accidentally killed Eunomus, a relative of the king, at a banquet. In atonement Hercules and Deianeira went into exile. They journeyed to Trachis where Ceyx, Amphitryon's nephew was king. (Trachis is due north of Parnassos, on the southern edge of the Lamian plain). Their route took them over the river Evinos where the Centaur Nessus was employed carrying travellers across the river. Centaurs were said to be an ancient and savage people who lived on Mount Pelion. In the Classical era they are represented as half man and half horse. Hercules gave Deianeira to Nessus to carry across the river and began to ford it himself. Nessus, however, ran off with Deianeira and attempted to rape her. On hearing her screams, Hercules shot the Centaur with an arrow. As he lay dying, Nessus told Deianeira that if she took some of his blood and mixed it with his spilt seed and olive oil, the mixture would ensure Hercules's love for her. She secretly gathered the ingredients in a jar, unaware that the Centaur's blood was poisoned by Hercules's arrow, for he famously coated the tips of his arrows with the venom from the Lernean Hydra.

The pair settled in Trachis. Hercules then set out to seek his revenge on king Eurytus of Oechalia, who, some years before, had refused to give up his daughter, Iole, in marriage. Hercules raised an army, sacked the city, killed the king and his sons and carried away Iole. In order to give thanks for his victory, Hercules built an altar to Zeus and sent to Deianeira for a white shirt appropriate for a sacrifice. Deianeira was afraid of losing Hercules's affections to Iole. She coated the shirt with the lethal mixture she had kept secretly. When Hercules put on the shirt the poison seeped into every pore of his body. In agony, he tried to tear off the shirt but it clung to him and he succeeded only in pulling away his own flesh. Hercules asked his son, Hyllus, to carry him to a quiet place to die. He was taken to Mount Oeta near Trachis. Hyllus built a funeral pyre on the peak of the mountain. Hercules climbed on top and ordered it to be set on fire. As the flames rose he was carried to Olympus on a cloud and became one of the immortals. He was finally accepted by Hera and married her daughter Hebe. Deianeira hanged herself in shame for what she had done.

Kalydon (Κάλυδον)

The myth of Meleager, Atalanta, and the Kalydonian boar hunt

The road west continues across the Evinos on a long viaduct and, after a few hundred metres a brown sign appears abruptly on the right, indicating ancient Kalydon. This is the site of the Sanctuary of Artemis

61

Laphria and the location of the myths of Meleager, Atalanta and the hunt for the Kalydonian boar. Just off the road is a tourist kiosk, occasionally manned, with a parking area. The site is unenclosed and free.

When King Oeneus made a sacrifice to the gods, he unaccountably forgot to include Artemis in his dedications. In her anger Artemis sent a huge boar to ravage his lands. Oeneus's son, Meleager, brought together a group of hunters from all over Greece to track down the beast. They included most of the mythical heroic figures: Castor and Polydeuces, Theseus, Jason, Nestor, Iphicles, Amphiaraos and notably Atalanta, the Arcadian huntress (see also Chapter 9, Tegea). The boar was eventually trapped. Atalanta wounded it first, but Meleager struck the blow that finally killed it. Meleager, who had fallen in love with Atalanta, awarded her the hide and tusks on the pretext that she had struck the first blow. His uncles violently objected to the trophies being given to a woman. When they attempted to take them from Atalanta, Meleager killed them. His mother, Althaea, in revenge for the murder of her brothers, then brought about Meleager's own strange death. When he was just seven days old, the Fates had decreed that Meleager would only live as long as a certain piece of wood in the hearth remained unburnt. Althaea had immediately plunged the wood in water to extinguish it and hidden it in a chest. Now she retrieved the unburnt log and threw it in the fire. Meleager promptly died and in remorse Althaea killed herself.

The sanctuary is directly above the car park hidden from view. A track leads off around the flank of the hill. After 50 M the path passes the site of a Bouleuterion, or meeting house, with the remains of tiers of seats built against the slope of the hill. At a fork, 200M further on, a brown sign points left. One hundred metres up this path a pair of very battered signs indicate right to the Heröon and left to the temple of Artemis Laphrias. An Heröon is simply a shrine to a semi-divine hero. This rather elaborate example belonged to the local hero, Leon. It dates only to about 100 BC, probably the city's last period of prosperity. The foundations are of a colonnaded court with rooms on three sides. An extremely well preserved underground burial chamber with stone furniture can be seen through a barred gate. The shrine is surrounded by a fence, but it is not locked. This is a fine example of a sanctuary to a local hero known only within his own community.

The path to the temple leads along a spur of the hill passing the foundations of a stoa. The Sanctuary of Artemis and Apollo was known as the Laphrion. It stood on an artificial stone terrace where the spur overlooks the plain and the sea. The massive retaining walls are still impressive. All that remains of the temple, built in the 4C BC, are foundations. Archaeological finds have shown that this replaced earlier temples of the 6C and 7C BC.

When Augustus forcibly re-settled the inhabitants of the old Aitolian towns in his new city of Nikopolis (see below), the treasures of the Aitolian sanctuaries were given either to Nikopolis or to the other great Roman foundation of the period, Patrai, now modern Patras on the other side of the Gulf. The great gold and ivory statue of Artemis Laphria found its way to the acropolis at Patrai. Pausanias saw it in the 2C AD when it was still being worshipped there. He explains that the goddess was called Laphrian Artemis after Laphrios who was responsible for installing the statue at Kalydon. It is known from Pausanias's description that Artemis was represented as a huntress. It is possible this has some connection with Atalanta. The myth of Atalanta's birth has Artemis sending a she-bear to suckle the infant, when her father, who had wanted a male child, exposed her on a hillside. The cult of Artemis apparently involved an annual festival called the Laphria at which a huge pyre of logs was built in a circle around the altar. Birds and animals were thrown or herded into the circle that was then set alight.

The temple at Kalydon lies outside the 3C BC city walls. They are now reduced to foundations, but can be traced for much of their length. The church, visible a little uphill from the Heröon, stands just in front of the southern walls that climb to the summits of the two hills to the north and enclose the valley in between. Although the most important part of this site is within sight and sound of the main road, it retains a sense of remoteness and you should have it completely to yourself.

Pleuron (Plevron, Πλευρον)
The city where Hercules won the hand of Deianeira. Achelous and the Cornucopia.

Ten kilometres west of Kalydon the main road bypasses Mesolonghi, best known as the place where Byron's heart is buried, and swings north keeping to the coastal plain. After 5km, where the road begins to run close under the hillside, a sign points right to the "Archaeological site of Ancient Pleuron". The site stands on a considerable plateau about 250M above sea level. A reasonable track leads steeply uphill to the southwest gate of the city wall. The climb transforms the view. At sea level the road from Mesolonghi passes through a drab, flat landscape but from the hill above there are magnificent views south across the lagoons and west to the mouth of the Achelöos, 10km away. Offshore, the islands of Kephalonia and Zante may be visible.

After Pleuron was destroyed in 234 BC by Demetrios II in the conflict between the Aitolian League and Macedonia, the city was rebuilt in a higher, more secure position. The relatively late construction date followed by the subsequent removal of most of the population of Aitolia to Nikopolis after 31 BC, means that this 3C BC city is particularly well preserved. Its predecessor, which may have been the city of King Oeneus, is located on the two low hills visible to the south, where some fragments of cyclopean walls can be found. New Pleuron is marked on some maps as Kira Irini.

When Hercules came to Pleuron he no longer had a wife or sons (see Tiryns, Chapter 8, for the events that led up to the Twelve Labours). He sought the hand of Deianeira but found himself in competition with Achelöus, the river god. Achelöus was the father of all the river gods and could assume three different bodily forms, a horned man, a bull and a serpent. The two suitors settled their rivalry with a wrestling match. Achelöus was forced to use each of his three forms in his struggle to defeat Hercules. His final attempt was as a bull but he retired humiliated when Hercules snapped off one of his horns. The nymphs transformed the horn into the Cornucopia, or horn of plenty, from which an abundance of autumn fruits flows. Hercules married Deianeira and settled in Pleuron.

The very well preserved walls that encircle the plateau are over 2km in length and are punctuated by numerous towers and gates. Traces remain of all of the important features of a Greek city. From the gate, a path leads north inside the wall for 100M to the small theatre. This was built in a very unconventional position, with the proscenium hard against the wall and incorporating a tower. Evidence of the city's water supply is found a little to the east of the theatre where there is a huge multi-chambered cistern. Further east again, on the top of the plateau, are the considerable remains of the agora. To the north, the walls climb up to the acropolis where a chapel stood on the remains of a temple of Athena.

B. Via Thermo and Agrinio from Nafpaktos

The inland route from Nafpaktos to Agrinio via Thermo and Lake Trihonida offers an alternative to the busy coastal road. Although the route
is shorter by distance, it will take considerably longer to negotiate. With
stops, Thermo can be reached in about an hour and a half.

The gorge of the Evinos river is reached after 18 km. It is still
spanned by a single-track, second world war, bailey bridge, with a road
surface of rattling and disconcertingly worn wooden beams. This 'tem-
porary' structure must now be well over sixty years old, although the
central pier supporting the two spans is a modern concrete replacement.
The Evinos is named after a mythical king of Aitolia called Evinus who
wanted to keep his daughter Marpessa a virgin. He challenged each of
her suitors to a chariot race where victory would be rewarded by her
hand in marriage. Defeat would mean the loss of the suitor's head. Idas,
the Messenian (see Chapter 9), determined that he would win both the
race and Marpessa. He persuaded Poseidon to give him a winged chariot. In this he was able to carry off Marpessa and elude Evinus, who
gave chase. In despair at his failure, Evinus killed his horses and
drowned himself in the river, which was henceforth named after him.

Thermon is a pleasant, well-watered inland town with a large central
square lined with cafés and tavernas. Originally called Kefalovrisi, it
has adopted the name of the ancient spiritual centre of Aitolia, which is
about 1km south of the town. Approaching from this direction, a sign
indicates the ancient site 1km sharp right down a minor road.

Ancient Thermon
The spiritual centre of Aitolia

There is evidence of settlement on this site from the Late Bronze Age.
Its importance from the Classical period onwards was as the spiritual
centre for the whole of Aitolia. This was focused on the temple of
Apollo Thermios, which also functioned as the meeting place of the Aitolian League. Although the sanctuary is of considerable size and was
surrounded by walls and towers, like Delphi, it was never a city.

The site is completely fenced and open from 8.30 to 15.00, but
closed on Mondays. It is situated on an area of level ground below
Mount Mega Lakkos, at a point where springs emerge from the base of
the hill. On approach, the site lies a little below the road on the right.
There is room to park by the entrance. It is worth walking along the

road a little to gain an overview of the site layout. In particular, it is possible to make out the complete circuit of the precinct walls, built sometime after the invasion by the Macedonian generals, Antipater and Krateros in 323 BC. Alexander the Great had died earlier that year. Athens and Aitolia had taken advantage of the succession crisis to revolt against Macedonian rule. The circuit forms a rough rectangle. The walls consist of a stone base, about 2M in height and still visible, which carried a superstructure of mud brick. Square towers reinforced the walls at regular intervals. The main gate was at the southwest corner of the enclosure, protected by two round towers. The modern entrance is at the northeast corner, close to a second smaller gate in the walls. Just inside the site fence is the temple of Apollo Thermios, the religious focus of the place, now protected by a modern roof. The visible foundations are of a Doric temple with an external colonnade of 5 by 15 columns. It was rebuilt at the end of the 3C BC after its predecessor was destroyed by Philip V of Macedon. He sacked the sanctuary twice in 218 and 206 BC in his war on behalf of the Achaian league against the Aitolians. The original temple was erected c. 630 BC. It is one of the earliest Doric temples known. Both it, and its replacement, only used stone for the foundations and columns. The cella walls were of mud brick and the entablature was wooden. An earlier temple of the Geometric period lies beneath the Doric temple. Below that are the remains of late Mycenaean houses. To the south is a fountain, and beyond are the foundations of two immense colonnaded stoas built on a north-south axis facing each other. The monument bases in front of the stoas would have supported the statues reputedly destroyed by Philip. At the extreme south of the site is a third stoa, built parallel to the southern wall. In the southeast corner are the remains of a Bouleuterion. There are Geometric, Archaic and Mycenaean finds in the museum.

Although the myths of Aitolia are based around Kalydon and Pleuron, it is here that physical evidence of Bronze Age occupation is to be found.

Stratos (Στράτος)
The capital of ancient Akarnania

Agrinio is a further 30 minutes from Thermo. The road follows the northern shore of Lake Trihonida, and after 16km approaches the modern village of Paravola (Παραβόλα). On a conical hill to the left are some remains of Boukation, another ancient Aitolian town. Beyond

Paravola the road quickly reaches the outskirts of Agrinio. Take the early left turn, signposted National Road (Εθνική Οδός). This refers to the main Mesolonghi – Arta road that bypasses Agrinio to the west. This turn-off leads through the outskirts of the large sprawling town, via a maze of roads with intermittent signs. By heading vaguely west and downhill when in doubt, the main road north is eventually reached. Ten kilometres from Agrinio this road crosses the Achelöos barrage, the boundary between Aitolia and Akarnania. Almost immediately, the walls of Stratos are visible, descending the hill to the right of the road. Drive through the line of the walls. In the middle of the modern village of Stratos, which straggles along the busy road, is a brown sign indicating right to "Archaeological Site and Ancient Theatre".

The founding of Akarnania is part of the great series of myths that began with the war of the Seven against Thebes (see Chapter 2). The sons of the Seven, the Epigoni, had avenged their fathers and sacked Thebes. Alcmaeon, the son of Amphiaraos, had slain his mother Eriphyle for her role in his father's death. However, as she lay dying, she cursed him, calling to all the lands of the world to refuse him shelter and bringing down on him the wrath of the Furies also known as the Erinyes or Avenging Deities. Alcmaeon first fled to Psophis in northwest Arcadia. There King Phegeus attempted to purify him and gave him his daughter, Arsinoe, in marriage. Alcmaeon gave her the necklace and robe of Harmonia. The Furies, however, continued their persecution and made the land of Psophis barren. Alcmaeon fled to the mouth of the river Achelöos leaving Arsinoe behind. Since his mother had uttered her curse new land had been formed there by the river's silt. He was able to live unmolested. He married Callirrhoe, the daughter of the river god Achelöus, and had two sons by her. She too wanted the necklace and robe of Harmonia, so persuaded Alcmaeon to return to Psophis. There he obtained them by deception, telling Phegeus that the only way he would be free of the Furies' wrath was to dedicate the necklace and robe at Delphi. Phegeus discovered the truth and his sons killed Alcmaeon. When Alcmaeon's two sons, Akarnan and Amphoterus grew up, they avenged their father by killing Phegeus and his sons. As no one would agree to purify them for these murders, they returned to the land to the west of the Achelöos, which they colonized and called Akarnania.

Stratos was the ancient capital and best fortified city of Akarnania. It is laid out over four ridges and their intervening valleys. It first prospered in the 5C BC and was pro-Athenian in the Peloponnesian War. It was later held successively by the Macedonians, the Aitolians and finally the Romans. When Nikopolis was founded in 31 BC, Octavian forcibly depopulated much of Aitolia and Akarnania, and Stratos lost most of its inhabitants (see Nikopolis below).

This is an extensive site, but the chief points of interest are the theatre and, about half a kilometre away, the temple of Zeus. The walls are 7.5km long, well preserved in many sections. At the highest point of the circuit is a fortified acropolis. The site is effectively unenclosed and entry is free. The village of Sorovigle originally stood within the circuit. It was moved to its present position by the main road and renamed Stratos. Some of the old houses still stand, deserted among the ruins. The right turn from the main road leads uphill a short distance through the new village. A broken gate can be seen directly ahead where the road takes a sharp uphill turn to the right. A footpath leads through the gate into the agora. This was laid out on two levels. The area has been excavated, but the remains are not spectacular. The road continues upwards towards a church on the ridge above, where there is a tourist kiosk on the right. A path leads down into the theatre, concealed on the other side of the ridge. An excellent information board with a good site plan stands by the kiosk. The theatre has been recently cleared. It has well-preserved seats with carved backs and arms still visible. The paved orchestra is intact, together with the drainage system, which still functions.

From the road, the site of the temple of Zeus Stratios can be seen about 500M away to the west on a wooded knoll. The route is clearly shown on the site plan. Drive back down the hill to the sharp right turn that leads onto the rough back road of the village. This briefly descends steeply then climbs even more steeply for half a kilometre. Turn right by an enormous irrigation pipe. After 200M, at the point where the dirt road begins to bear left, a few remnants of wall can be seen up a small slope on the right and a vague path ascends between the orange trees to the temple. A fence surrounds the remains. The temple is very oddly placed astride the circuit wall. Although reduced now to the platform and fallen column blocks, the masonry is still in very good condition, with the stones retaining their finely chiselled edges. In addition to the external Doric columns (6 x 11), there was a Corinthian colonnade inside the cella. The work, carried out at the end of the 4C BC, was never finished. At some later date, it was pulled down again to recover the materials, particularly the metal clamps used to fasten the blocks.

The view extends in all directions, and to the north numerous deserted houses are visible. This gives the site a curiously desolate air, perhaps because the modern resettlement of the village reflects the other resettlement two thousand years earlier.

North to Nikopolis via Vonitsa (Βόνιτσα)

North of Stratos there are two seaside towns at either end of the Gulf of Ambracia. Amfilochia is 30km from Stratos, and Vonitsa is a further 37km along a good road through pleasantly wooded countryside. Despite its proximity to Preveza airport and the package tour destinations on Lefkas, Vonitsa is hardly touched by tourism and is good base for visiting Nikopolis, the Roman city 25km to the north. A new road tunnel beneath the narrow entrance to the Gulf now links the two shores.

Nikopolis

Nikopolis, or Victory City, was founded by Octavian/Augustus after his victory over Mark Antony and Cleopatra at the naval battle of Actium in 31 BC. The city was built on such a massive scale that most of the inhabitants of Aitolia and Akarnania were forcibly moved to populate it. Such social engineering was possible because by that date Greece had been a Roman province for over one hundred years. Today the visible remains are scattered over a wide area and much new archaeological work is in progress.

History

The events that followed the assassination of Julius Caesar in 44 BC left the Roman empire in the joint control of Octavian in the west, and Mark Antony in the east. The alliance between the two men was strengthened by Antony's marriage to Octavian's sister, and destroyed when Antony discarded his wife in favour of Cleopatra of Egypt. The immediate result was a declaration of war by the Senate on Cleopatra and implicitly on Antony. The final outcome was the defeat of Antony and Cleopatra at Actium.

Antony's camp was on Cape Actium to the south of the entrance to the Ambracian Gulf where both his and Cleopatra's fleets were sheltering. Octavian's camp was on the opposite side of the narrows, north of the site of modern-day Preveza. On the morning of the battle, Antony's ships came out to meet Octavian's fleet, which had been blockading the exit from the Gulf. At the height of the battle, Cleopatra inexplicably ordered her ships, anchored behind the main fleet as rearguard, to hoist sail and escape to the open sea. Antony followed shortly after, but the bulk of his fleet was destroyed and burnt. Although it would be another

69

year before both Antony and Cleopatra were dead, the events at Actium effectively marked the end of the struggle for mastery of the Roman Empire. The immense importance of the victory is reflected in the size of the city that Octavian, now Augustus, founded on the site of his camp. Although an artificial creation, the city prospered due to its position on the trading route between east and west. Fifty years after its creation, Strabo was able to comment on a rapidly increasing population. Thereafter Nikopolis's history follows that of the Western Roman Empire as a whole, declining with successive barbarian incursions in the 4C and 5C AD. There was a second period of prosperity in the 6C AD when Justinian rebuilt the walls and many of the basilican churches were founded. The final decline and abandonment was in the late 9C or early 10C AD.

Visiting the site

From Vonitsa take the Preveza road through the new tunnel (toll). Beyond the tunnel follow the signs for Preveza centre and drive through the town. One kilometre north of Preveza's sprawling commercial suburbs, the road runs through the south gate of Octavian's city. On either side of the road are the half-round brick towers that flanked the gate. They stand about 2M high and are currently being refaced to protect the core. Just before the gate, a sign points right to 'Early Christian Basilica'. This church, the Asomatos, lies 100M down a lane, just inside the line of the walls. Dating from the 5C or 6C AD, the ground plan is preserved by a few courses of the walls and the remains of pavements.

Next, the road enters the smaller circuit of Justinian's walls, and passes the museum on the left. Behind are the remains of the 6C Basilica of Doumetios and the bishops' palace. A little further on the road runs parallel for ½km with the best-preserved section of the Byzantine circuit. Here a dirt track leads left to a monumental arched gate. Turn onto the track and park in front of the gate. Justinian's walls still stand to a height of 10M. Stairways gave access at regular intervals to the wall top. Walk through the gate to view the towers protecting the entrance. The fortifications are built of alternating bands of stone and brick in imitation of the walls of Constantinople. You are now outside the Byzantine city, but still within its original, much larger, Roman predecessor. Justinian's walls enclosed only the northeastern quadrant of the original city. Beyond the gate, the track leads through intensively farmed fields for 400M to the Roman odeion. This dates from the founding of the city, is built of brick and concrete and the seating has

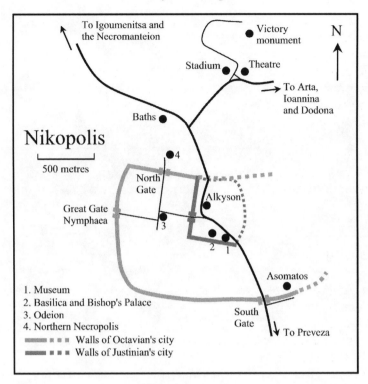

To Igoumenitsa and
the Necromanteion

Victory
monument

N

Stadium

Theatre

To Arta,
Ioannina
and Dodona

Baths

Nikopolis

500 metres

4

North
Gate

Alkyson

Great Gate
Nymphaea

3

2 1

Asomatos

1. Museum
2. Basilica and Bishop's Palace
3. Odeion
4. Northern Necropolis

South
Gate

To Preveza

▪ ▪ ▪ Walls of Octavian's city
▪ ▪ ▪ Walls of Justinian's city

been restored. Originally the structure was roofed. The forum, which
has not been excavated, lay due south. The track reaches a T-junction at
the odeion. To visit the Great Gate 500M to the west, turn left, then
right after 100M. The massive ruined structure standing in the fields is
part of the Nymphaea, the fountains of the nymphs. These stood on either side of the street, in front of the gate. They delivered water from
the river Louros via the city's main aqueduct. Remains of the aqueduct
still exist at Ayios Georgios over 40km to the north in the Louros valley. Each Nymphaeum consisted of a water filled open basin in front of
marble tiled walls with niches, which probably contained statues of the
nymphs. Behind this façade was a massive structure that supported the
high storage cistern fed by the aqueduct. Through the gate ran the De-
cumanus Maximus, the main east-west street. It led through the gate to
the western harbour at Komaros.

The northern gate and recently excavated necropolis are 500M from
the odeion to the right. The foundations of two D-shaped towers flank
the gate. The cemetery, which was in use from the 1C to the 4C AD,
lies on either side of the road beyond the gate, the normal location in

Figure 7 Nikopolis: City gate in Justinian's walls

any Roman city. Extensive excavations have revealed graves of every type. The larger structures have been protected with metal roofing. Beyond the necropolis, the road continued through the northern suburbs to the sacred precinct with its theatre, stadium and gymnasium. These were used for the Actian Games, which had been transferred from their original site at Cape Actium by Augustus.

   To reach the theatre, return to the main road and continue north. Almost immediately on the right of the road is the early 6C AD Basilica of Alkyson, still with the frame of its west door standing. Beyond the northern walls, the road forks, left to Parga and Igoumenitsa, right to Arta. Another public building essential to any Roman city, the baths, can be seen to the left. The great ruin of the theatre lies directly ahead, 500M down the Arta road. The theatre is one of the few monuments in Greece as yet unexcavated. Both it, and the stadium nearby, were two of the first public buildings to be built in Nikopolis. It appears as though the tiers of seating, now completely missing, were built on a natural hillside. Only from behind can the massive buttresses supporting the artificial structure be seen. The construction is once again of brick faced concrete. The stadium lies immediately to the west of the theatre on the opposite side of the by-road to Smyrtoula. Recently cleared, the approach is through the remains of the eastern entrance tunnel. Unusually both ends were rounded. The theatre and stadium stand at the foot of the hill where Augustus built his victory monument, a massive podium faced with bronze rams from the bows of the captured ships with a stoa above. The remains can still be seen a little way above the village of Smyrtoula. The monument was dedicated to Mars (Ares) and Neptune (Poseidon).

Although the remains of Nikopolis can hardly be described as picturesque, a visit does leave a strong impression of a great city lost in the landscape. The isolation of the individual ruins and, in the case of the theatre, the unrestored state, gives a rare glimpse of how all Greek antiquities must have appeared to the first Western travellers of the 18C and 19C.

The Oracle of the Dead and the Acheron gorge
Orpheus and Eurydice. Charon the ferryman to the souls of the dead.

To the northwest of Nikopolis, 35 kilometres along the coast road to Igoumenitsa, is the Oracle of the Dead, the Necromanteion or Nekyomanteion. Here, where an entrance to the underworld was thought to exist, the ancient Greeks would come to consult the souls of the dead, whom they believed had the power to see into the future. Here too, Orpheus descended in search of his wife Eurydice.

The great age of this sanctuary to Persephone and Hades is known from both archaeological finds and ancient written sources. Homer gives a detailed description of Odysseus's visit to the "dwelling of Hades and Persephone" to consult the spirit of Teiresias, the renowned blind soothsayer of Thebes. The sanctuary stands at the end of a low, rocky ridge overlooking the river Acheron, where it flowed out of the now drained Acherousian Lake. Both the river and the lake were believed to form part of the journey to the underworld undertaken by the souls or shades of the dead. Charon the ferryman conveyed the shades across the water to the underworld. His payment was the coin placed in the mouth of every corpse before burial.

Orpheus was a celebrated poet, singer and lyre player who took part in the voyage of the Argonauts. He was the son of Oeagrus, a Thracian king and the Muse Kalliope. His lyre was given to him by Apollo and the Muses taught him to play. After the voyage in search of the Golden Fleece, when he had saved the Argonauts from the entreaties of the Sirens by the greater beauty of his playing, he returned to Thrace and

Figure 8 The Acheron Gorge

married the nymph Eurydice. She however had the misfortune to be bitten by a snake and died from its venom. Orpheus followed her soul into the underworld and used the power of his singing to persuade Hades to allow her to return to the upper world. His desire was granted on the condition that as he led her out of the underworld he did not look back. As he reached the boundary between the two worlds he looked back to see that she was following and consequently lost her forever.

This is the only sanctuary in Greece where the oracular buildings can still be seen. The sanctuary was rebuilt in the 3C BC and destroyed by the Romans in 167 BC, but in consequence, it is particularly well preserved. The layout of the buildings seems to have been deliberately contrived to disorientate the supplicant. At the core of the sanctuary is a windowless hall with extremely thick walls, divided into a central chamber with rooms to each side. Beneath this central room is an underground chamber, partly carved in the rock and with an arched roof. The only method of access was via a series of labyrinthine corridors that ran around three sides of the building. It is thought that a combination of fasting, isolation in the dark interior and possibly foods with a narcotic effect, all contributed to the appearance of the "shades of the dead". However, the find of the corroded remnants of a bronze winch mechanism, suggests that mechanical aids may have assisted spirit manifestations. The remains of the sanctuary are incongruously surmounted by the 18C church of St. John, but the layout of the complex is remarkably complete. The underground chamber, representing the hall of Hades and Persephone, is still accessible by a modern stairway. A visit out of season can easily invoke images of Odysseus's world.

Today the site is much visited in the summer but relatively deserted out of season. Follow the main road to the right turn for Mesopotamos (Μεσοπόταμος). The sanctuary is well sign-posted from here. Opening hours are 08.00 to 15.00 daily.

The Acheron
The entrance to the underworld

Some 12km inland from the Necromanteion beyond the cultivated plain formed by the bed of the drained Acherousian lake, the river Acheron emerges from a dramatic gorge by the village of Gliki (Γλυκή). This is a convincing setting for an entrance to the underworld and the likely location of Aornos, the place where according to Pausanias, Orpheus descended in search of Eurydice.

The gorge is sheer walled and the river has cut down through the limestone mountains to the spring line. As a result water bubbles up through the gravel of the riverbed and out of fissures and openings in the cliffs on both sides. The place is easy to find as it is a popular weekend excursion for local Greeks and there are several tavernas by the gorge mouth (signs for Πηγές Αχέροντα). There is a well-known local path on the south side of the river, the Skala Tzavelanas (Σκάλα Τζαβέλαινας) that provides a high level route into the gorge and leads into the mountains of the Souliot villages, but the simplest and most dramatic approach is to wade upstream through the knee-deep waters of the river. It is possible to penetrate almost a kilometre into the canyon before swimming is required. The gorge can also be explored on horse-back from the riding centre nearby. Rafting on the river is also available in the summer season.

Dodona
The Oracle of Zeus

Further afield, 100km northeast near Ioannina, is the Oracle of Zeus at Dodona, the oldest in Greece. The remains are extensive and the setting spectacular. They include a large well preserved theatre, a stadium and a walled acropolis. Just as at the Necromanteion however, the remains are almost all Hellenistic, dating to the 4C and 3C BC. Nevertheless such is the importance of the site that the new Egnatia motorway has been diverted through a 3km tunnel beneath the area.

To Homer it was "wintry Dodoni". This is an image easy to under-stand for the site stands in a wide but high valley with snow on the mountains until May. The sanctuary was already old by Homer's time. Its origins lie in the third millennium BC when the first deity wor-shipped was an Earth goddess. Votive offerings have been found from the early Bronze Age.

The cult of Zeus was introduced at some time in the first half of the second millennium BC. The centre of the sanctuary was a sacred oak tree. Prophecies were thought to be delivered by the tree itself, for the god spoke through the rustling of the leaves in the wind. According to Homer, the priests who interpreted the divine messages were the Selloi who slept on the ground and had unwashed feet. At this time the site lay outside the Greek world. The introduction of Zeus's worship brought new myths. The original earth goddess became known as Dione and was regarded as one of Zeus's wives. Homer refers to her as the mother of Aphrodite by Zeus. (The better-known version of Aphrodite's birth from the foam of the sea is told in Chapter 5).

The prophetic abilities of Dodonian oak were built into Jason's ship the Argo. Athena had instructed that a beam of this timber be fitted to the prow of the vessel. Called a "speaking timber" it gave the ship itself the gift of prophecy.

Votive offerings from southern Greece first appear at Dodona in the 8C BC. For many centuries religious activity at the site was conducted in the open air. The first buildings did not appear until the 4C BC. By then priests had been replaced by women. According to Herodotus, the priestesses believed that the sanctuary had been founded when a black dove had flown from Egyptian Thebes to Dodona. It had perched on the branch of an oak and with a human voice announced that the spot was to become an oracle of Zeus. This was received as a divine pronouncement. The site flourished in the 3C BC. Pyrrhus built the theatre between 297 and 272 BC. The foundations of the religious buildings that remain are of the Sacred House or temple of Zeus, a temple of Dione and another belonging to Aphrodite. The sanctuary's use as an oracle came to an end when the Romans sacked it in 167 BC.

South from Vonitsa via the coast

A pleasant alternative return route south is via the coast road. This reaches the sea 18km south of Vonitsa at Paleros (Πάλαιρος) and then follows the bare and deserted coastline closely for 45km. The views offshore to the numerous islands are superb. At Astakos the road turns inland, reaching the small town of Katohi (Κατοχή) after another 27km. This is the starting point for a visit to ancient Oiniadai.

Oiniadai (Οινιάδαι)
Here Alcmaeon took refuge from the Furies

Oiniadai is one of the most fascinating Classical sites in Greece yet is seldom visited. The city stands on a low hill surrounded by rich agricultural land formed from the silt of the river Acheloös. In classical times it must have been much closer to the mouth of the river and the sea. Thucydides, writing in the last quarter of the 5C BC, describes it as being surrounded by water in winter. This is the area where Alcmaeon settled to escape his mother's curse (see Stratos). The formation of new land at the mouth of the river was a phenomenon well understood in classical times. Directly offshore lie the Echinades islands. Thucydides explains how the constant silting was slowly joining these islands to the mainland and it is very likely that Oiniadai itself was originally an island. He explains in detail how Alcmaeon was told by the Delphic oracle that in order to escape the curse he must seek out a place that did not exist as land at the time he killed his mother. As he had been wandering Greece for some years he came to the conclusion that enough time had elapsed since his mother's death to form new land from the

77

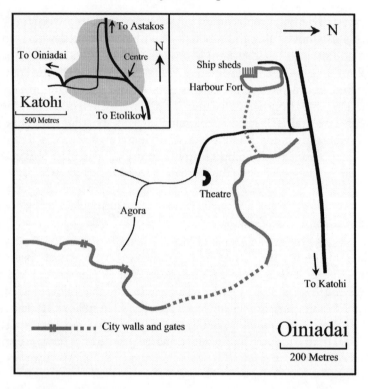

river's silt and the prophecy would be fulfilled. Alcmaeon came to live near Oiniadai and his son Akarnan was eventually to give his name to the entire region.

The site has been recently cleared. The theatre, the agora area, and the well-preserved walls are now all easily accessible. The unique feature of the place is the harbour area, with the impressive remains of 3C BC ship sheds cut into the hillside, protected by a fort above.

Access to the site

In the centre of Katohi (Κατοχή) take a sharp right turn. A battered sign points to "Ancient Oiniadai". A minor road leads through the back of the village. Keep straight on at a crossroads where another sign indicates "Ancient Theatre". At a four-way junction where there are confused signs, turn sharp right. A brown sign after the turn confirms the direction. The road passes through unattractive flat scenery on reclaimed marshland with a rocky hillside to the right. The view is of drainage ditches and bulrushes, until, after 5km, a rocky hill about 50M high appears ahead and to the left. Almost immediately well-preserved walls can be seen descending the hillside. The site entrance is on the left through open gates, with a sign to the Ancient Theatre. A tarmac road ascends towards the theatre. A track on the right leads beneath the harbour fort around to the ship sheds. Just past the gates are recently installed information boards with a good site plan. Drive up to the end of the tarmac road and park. A dirt track leads 200M up to the theatre,

The Theatre, Agora and City walls

The circuit of the city walls is over 6km long. The irregular trace follows steep slopes and cliffs wherever possible. The walls are of impressive polygonal masonry probably dating from the second half of the 5C BC. Certainly there were walls of some form in 455 BC when the city was besieged and taken by the Messenians of Nafpaktos.

The theatre is fenced with a gate that appears to be wired shut. This is a trick. Although the two halves of the gate are wired together, the whole thing slides sideways on runners and is not locked. The theatre, which has been cleared, is a very pleasant spot for a picnic. Almost the whole hill is covered in oak trees. About twenty rows of seats are still in position. The construction has been dated to the 3C BC from inscriptions still visible on the lower rows of seating.

An obvious path continues from the theatre gate up through the trees. At the top of the slope the path forks. To the left stretches the agora terrace. The area has been cleared of vegetation and the foundations of the agora buildings are visible. The clearance of the undergrowth has given the area the air of English parkland. Follow the line of the terrace and bear slightly to the right to reach a section of the fortified circuit that has been cleared to expose a gate and well-preserved sections of wall. Returning to the fork in the path, the other branch leads to a knoll in the centre of the site surrounded by wall foundations. From this point it is possible to see almost the entire hill and gain a good appreciation of the size and extent of the wall circuit.

The Harbour area

Return to the main gate and drive about 200M along the track to the site of the harbour. This area is also fenced and gated. Park in front of the gate, which again is unlocked and simply slides open.

Walk up to the harbour, past walls on the left, until, a hundred metres beyond the gate, the site of the ship sheds opens up, with five slipways cut back into the hillside. They originally faced onto a lagoon that gave access to the sea to the west. The pools at the edge of the slipways give some idea of the original water level. Today they contain terrapins and water snakes. The bases of the columns that supported the roof are in place, and although some modern consolidation of the rear wall in concrete has been necessary, the form of the slipways would be recognisable as such to a modern day shipwright. There is a good pictorial reconstruction of the likely form of the sheds on the information board. It shows the slipways covered by pitched roofs supported on colonnades, looking remarkably like a Venetian Arsenal. Climb up behind the sheds to explore the harbour fort, with its well-preserved tower. The most remarkable feature is the gateway, set at an angle to the wall. It contains a true arch, a rare feature in Greek architecture.

It is worth a considerable detour to see this truly remarkable place.

Figure 9 Oiniadai: Slipways viewed from the harbour fort

5

Athens to Corinth

The Isthmus of Corinth is crowded with archaeological sites. The substantial remains of ancient Corinth, although mainly Roman, are still dominated by the 6C BC temple of Apollo. The Corinthian acropolis, Acrocorinth, is a major site in its own right, and best known as the location of a temple of Aphrodite. The Sanctuary of Poseidon at Isthmia is little visited despite being the location of one of the four great Pan-Hellenic Games. Hera has a beautifully sited sanctuary at the tip of the Perachora peninsula.

Corinth Canal

It is 62km or 45 minutes from Elefsis to the canal by the motorway. Accommodation in the area is available in Loutraki, Ancient Corinth village and around the canal itself. To see the canal it is essential to turn off the motorway. Although the new road obviously has to cross the canal, there is virtually no view. At speed, you may not even be aware of the crossing. There are motorway junctions both east and west of the canal. The exit to the east is signposted Loutraki (Λουτράκι) and is reached almost immediately after passing a toll station. The exit road passes the right turn for Loutraki itself, and then crosses the canal by a steel trestle bridge. Until the building of the motorway, this was the main road and it was a considerable bottleneck. The Geo-Center map is seriously inaccurate in its depiction of the new road arrangements around the canal area. The Road Editions map is better, showing the old and new roads correctly.

The old bridge remains the best, and, apart from the railway crossing a little to the north, the only place to see the deep cutting of the channel. Consequently, it remains a popular tourist stop despite the by-pass formed by the new road. The canal was opened in July 1893 after

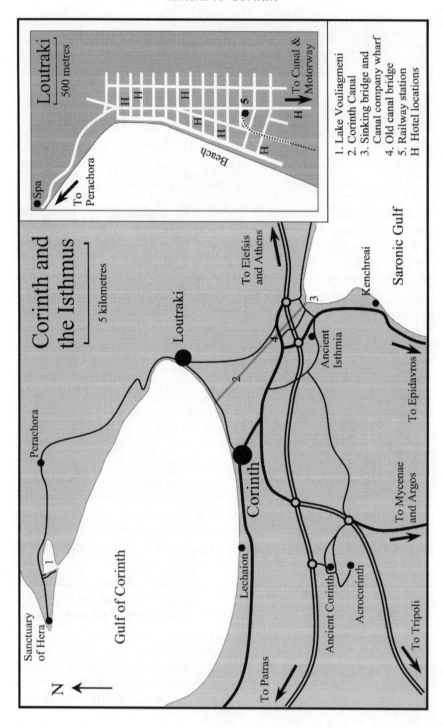

eleven years of work. Plans and attempts to cut a channel have a history starting at the end of the 7C BC. Periander, the Tyrant of Corinth, was the first to consider such a monumental task, but was dissuaded by the oracle at Delphi. The plan was revived by Demetrius Poliorcetes, Julius Caesar, Caligula and Nero, but only Nero actually started work. In fact substantial progress was made in 67 AD. Nero used thousands of war prisoners and slaves. They succeeded in digging a 2km section at the western end of the Isthmus and a 1.5 km section at the eastern end, up to 30M deep and 50M wide. The work was abandoned when Nero returned to Rome to quell revolts and subsequently committed suicide. Traces of these trenches could still be seen in the 19C until obliterated by the modern canal on the same alignment. However a remarkable monument, believed to commemorate Nero's attempt to make the Peloponnese an island, still exists carved into the south face of the cliff above the channel. Unfortunately, this is only visible by sailing through the canal but day cruises are possible from the canal company's wharf at Isthmia. The impetus for the project that finally succeeded in cutting through the Isthmus was the opening of the Suez Canal in 1869. That same year the Greek government passed enabling legislation, but it was another thirteen years before work began. Eleven years of effort and the usual financial crises that accompany all major infrastructure projects finally eliminated the long passage south around Cape Malea. Patras and Piraeus were brought 350km closer by sea.

Perachora (Περαχώρα)
The Sanctuary of Hera, wife and sister of Zeus

The Sanctuary of Hera, the Heraion, at the tip of the Perachora peninsula, is one of the most delightful sites in the area. It is also one of the most important archaeologically, as it is the only Archaic Corinthian site not subsequently built over by the Romans. The sanctuary was first founded early in the 8C BC and may have been connected with the great Argive Heraion (see Chapter 8). Argos was still the dominant political power in the northern Peloponnese at this time. However, the area was firmly under Corinthian control by the Archaic period. It ceased to have any importance after the Roman sack of Corinth in 146 BC.

Hera was the goddess of the plain of Argos. The myths tell of her growing up either near Mycenae or at Stymphalos. Her parents, of course, were Kronos and Rhea. Her birth myth is that of Kronos and the stone related in Chapter 2. She was both the sister and the wife of Zeus.

Figure 10 Perachora: Aerial view of the harbour precinct from the lighthouse at the tip of the peninsula. The 6C BC temple is in the foreground.

Although she at first ignored Zeus's courtship, he tricked her into marriage by appearing before her as a cuckoo in a thunderstorm on Mount Thornax, near Ermioni to the south of the Argolic peninsula. She sheltered the wet bird in her bosom. He promptly resumed his divine shape and raped her, shaming her into marriage. As the wife of Zeus, she was the goddess of marriage.

The sanctuary is 23km, 30 minutes, from Loutraki. The modern village of Perachora is about half way. The village centre can be by-passed

by taking a left fork on the outskirts. Follow signs either for Vouliagmeni (Βουλιαγμένης) or the Heraion (Ηραίον). About 3km from the
sanctuary the road passes Lake Vouliagmeni. This was originally a
fresh water lake, but is now salt, after a narrow cut was made in the 19C
through the spit separating it from the sea. At the far end of the lake a
dirt road branches left to some tavernas. Immediately opposite, on the
right hand side of the road, is an ancient cistern with steps descending.

The main road now crosses a small, level plateau. Half a kilometre
from the lake a very battered, and almost unrecognisable sign, marks
the location of a Hellenistic fountain house. This lies a few metres to
the right of the road. The foundations of an impressive facade of Ionic
columns can be seen with storage cisterns disappearing into the rock
behind. The cisterns were fed by an elaborate collection system of deep
shafts and connecting channels. The fountain stood in the centre of the
town of ancient Perachora, whose fragmentary remains are hidden in
the undergrowth on either side of the road. The road ends in a parking
area with the lighthouse on the promontory beyond. The sanctuary is
hidden below, built around the tiny harbour. An overall view of the site,
and excellent photographs, can be obtained by following the path up to
the lighthouse, now automated and unmanned. The site is unenclosed.

A path leads down to the harbour past the small white chapel of Ayios Ioannis, moved to its present position in 1933. Photographs from the
museum in Perachora village, closed for many years due to earthquake
damage, are sometimes displayed by the church. Arranged around the
tiny harbour are the foundations of the various buildings of the Sanctuary of Hera Akraia, Hera of the heights, probably a reference to the end
of the peninsula. At the foot of the steps from the chapel, there is first
an L-shaped stoa of the 4C BC. Close by is a large altar of the 6C BC,
partly built on top of the original small, apsidal temple dating from the
sanctuary's foundation early in the 8C BC. Beyond this, are the large
square foundations blocks of the 6C BC temple that replaced it. This
long, narrow structure measures 32M by 10M. A semi-circle of burnt
stone, cutting into the foundations, marks the location of a mediaeval
limekiln, and provides graphic evidence of the fate of many ancient remains. Finally, an area identified as a 5C BC agora, occupies the
western corner of the harbour behind the modern jetty.

Above the church, in a small valley, is a second precinct, originally
believed to be a completely separate sanctuary dedicated to Hera Lime-
nia, Hera of the harbour. It is now thought to be an extension to the
original Sanctuary of Hera Akraia, built in the second half of the 8C BC
with a treasury to house the large number of offerings to the goddess.

Walking up the valley from the chapel, further elaborate arrangements for water storage from the Hellenistic period can be seen. A large oval cistern is now open to the sky, but the structure of stone beams that carried the roof, and the steps that gave access to the water, are still in position. The pool at the bottom has a large frog population. Traces of the water channels that fed the cistern are still visible. To the south, on the seaward side of the cistern, are remains of a hestiatorion, a ritual dining room, with some of the stone couches still in place. Further up the valley are the more confused remains of the walled enclosure and treasury itself.

This is a beautiful spot that, on weekdays at least, is usually deserted.

Ancient Corinth
Temple of Apollo. The myths of Sisyphus, Zeus and Asopos. The tragedy of Jason and Medea

From the end of the 8C BC onwards, Corinth was one of the great cities of the ancient world. The city covered a huge area of the low plateau that lies between the coastal plain and the slopes of Acrocorinth. On the summit of Acrocorinth stood the extensive acropolis or citadel. The city had major ports at Lechaion on the Gulf of Corinth and at Kenchreai on the Saronic Gulf. After the end of the Peloponnesian War, a complete circuit wall was built that encircled both the city and the acropolis. Long walls were also constructed from the main circuit down to Lechaion.

The city's main temple was dedicated to Apollo, but the worship of Aphrodite was also important. There was a famous sanctuary dedicated to the goddess on the summit of Acrocorinth. The great Sanctuary of Poseidon at Isthmia nearby, was also controlled by the Corinthians. The Pan-Hellenic festival of the Isthmian Games was held there every two years.

History and Myth

Ancient Corinth, as seen today, is principally the Roman foundation of 44 BC. However, the city's first period of greatness began in the second half of the 8C BC, when it developed as a major trading centre and became the most advanced city in Greece. It was a sea power, founding its first colonies on Kerkyra (Corfu) and Syracuse (Sicily). Its unique position on the Isthmus, with a port on each Gulf, gave it a natural advantage in controlling the flow of east-west trade. From the latter part of the 7C BC onwards, under Periander the Tyrant and his successors, the city reached a level of prosperity sufficient for the undertaking of major projects. The Diolkos, the paved trackway across the Isthmus used for hauling boats from sea to sea, was constructed at this time. New colonies were created on the island of Lefkas and the adjacent mainland. Although Athens and Sparta became the dominant cities in Greece in the 6C and 5C BC, Corinth still remained a major power.

It was at Corinth in 337 BC that Philip II formed the Corinthian league of Greek states after the Macedonian victory in Chaironia the year before (see Chapter 3). Although a Macedonian garrison was installed, the city continued to prosper. Aratos of Sikyon took the city in 242 BC. It became part of a revived Achaian League that was subsequently the major force in the Peloponnese. The League was defeated by the Roman general Mummius in 146 BC and Corinth was comprehensively destroyed. Only the temple of Apollo was left standing.

Julius Caesar re-founded the city in 44 BC. It became the capital of Roman Greece and another period of prosperity, majestic building and population growth began. It remained the finest city in Roman Greece until the second half of the 4C AD when decline began from the ravages of earthquakes and barbarian raids. In the first quarter of the 5C AD, a new city wall was built to enclose a much smaller, and hence more defensible area, just as Nikopolis was to do a century later. A new wave of building activity in the 5C and 6C AD produced large basilican churches outside the wall, and the massive basilica on the shore at Lechaion. From the middle of the 6C AD, the combined effects of plague, earthquakes and Slav invasions caused serious de-population.

The city was reputed to have been founded by Sisyphus, and was first known as Ephyra. Sisyphus was the son of Aeolus and grandson of Hellen, the mythical ancestor of all the Greeks (see Chapter 3). Sisyphus is known chiefly for the torment he was condemned to suffer at the hands of Zeus for revealing divine secrets. Zeus had abducted Aegina, the daughter of the river god Asopos. A river of that name flows into the Gulf of Corinth near Sikyon (see Chapter 6). When Asopos came in search of her, Sisyphus offered to reveal her whereabouts if Asopos would provide a perpetual spring on Corinth's acropolis. Asopos duly created the Upper Peirene spring (see below). Sisyphus then revealed the truth about Zeus and Aegina. Asopos went in search of Zeus, who had laid his thunderbolts aside whilst engaged with Aegina. Caught unawares, he escaped from Asopos by changing himself into a huge rock.

Zeus punished Sisyphus by condemning him to push a similar rock up-hill forever in Tartarus. He would manage to push the rock almost to the top when its weight would overcome him. It would roll back to the bottom of the hill, and his labour would begin again.

Jason, the mythical leader of the Argonauts, came to Corinth after the expedition in search of the Golden Fleece. He lived there for many years with his wife Medea, who had helped him to steal the Fleece. Jason then deserted Medea and divorced her in order to marry Glauke, the daughter of king Kreon of Corinth. Medea took her revenge by sending her children to Glauke with the gift of a poisoned robe. When Glauke put on the robe, it burst into flames and burnt her to death. Glauke's spring or fountain can still be seen within the modern archaeological site. She is reputed to have thrown herself into it in an attempt to escape the effects of the robe. Pausanias describes a memorial near the odeion to the children of Medea, who were stoned to death by the people of Corinth for their part in the murder.

Visiting the Site

The modern city of Corinth on the coast is 5km from the ancient site. It dates from 1858, the year in which Old Corinth was destroyed by an earthquake and largely abandoned. The new town has a utilitarian air and seems to ignore the glories of its predecessors. Old Corinth is now a small village approximately in the centre of the ancient city. For the organised tour industry, Ancient Corinth is a secondary destination. Visitor numbers are lower than at Delphi or Olympia. Consequently, although tourism is important to the village, facilities are on a more modest scale. A significant number of visitors come for the connection with St. Paul, who lived and preached in the city in 51-52 AD.

Access from the motorways that now skirt the area to both the north and the south is straightforward. From the east, stay on the motorway beyond the canal and, at the Tripoli motorway junction, take the right fork signposted to Patra (Πάτρα). After 2km, take the next exit where signs indicate Archaia Korinthos. Follow the road into the village. The short main street, lined with tavernas and tourist shops, leads to a car parking area by the main entrance to the archaeological site. Opening hours are 08.00 to 17.00 or 19.00 in summer.

From Loutraki, follow the old road from the canal, which initially is dual carriageway. Pass through the line of Justinian's walls, built to re-fortify the Isthmus from Slav invaders and still visible. Keep left at the fork for modern Corinth, following signs for Argos and Tripoli. Acrocorinth now looms large, ahead and to the left. The road reverts to a single carriageway and skirts modern Corinth, to the right, before reaching a junction signposted Tripoli straight on and Patra right. Take the right fork that leads onto the motorway west. After two kilometres take the first exit as above. If approaching from the south on the Tripoli motorway, take the exit immediately before the intersection with the Patra highway, and follow the signs for Archaia Korinthos.

Unlike the site of Nikopolis, the major Roman city founded just a few years later (see Chapter 4), there is little impression of a great city on approaching the village from the main road. No massive walls march across the fields into the distance. Although there are traces of the circuit to be found they are not obvious. Not until the village centre is the main archaeological site visible, but again its scale is not immediately apparent, as it lies largely hidden from the road. The successive phases of occupation over two millennia meant that by the end of the 19C, the area of the forum/agora was buried. The view was merely of the few remaining columns of the temple of Apollo emerging from the debris of the Turkish village, destroyed in the War of Independence. The remains seen today are the result of large-scale excavation that began in the late 19C and early 20C. This revealed the entire Roman forum and a section of the Lechaion road leading into it. All the other standard elements of a Roman town plan, theatre, odeion, baths, and amphitheatre exist, scattered about the area. The odeion and theatre are directly opposite the site car park in separate fenced, but accessible, enclosures. They are initially hidden from view as they are cut from the rock of the plateau where it begins to slope away to the north. Of the two, the odeion is the best preserved.

The path from the main entrance approaches the agora from the west, via the museum. Just to the north of the museum stands a massive and mutilated block of rock that was Glauke's fountain. Although now difficult to distinguish, the rock had reservoirs, drawbasins and an elaborate façade. The site is still dominated by the great temple of Apollo dating from the 6C BC. Of the 38 Doric columns that surrounded the building, 7 remain standing. They were each carved from a single block of stone. The temple platform gives the best overall view of the excavations. To the south lies the vast rectangle of the Roman forum, surrounded by the foundations of temples, shops and stoas. Although the majority of the visible structures are Roman, the colonnade of the south stoa is Greek, from the 4C BC. To the east of the temple is the excavated section of the Lechaion road with its typical, careful Roman paved construction. It reached the forum at a set of steps in front of a gateway, or Propylaea. Immediately to the east of the Propylaea is the principal water source of the city, the lower Peirene spring, constantly remodelled over the centuries into an ever more elaborate fountain house.

Peirene was the daughter of the river-god Achelöus (see Chapter 4). Corinth's two ports, Lechaion and Kenchreai, are supposedly named after her two sons Leches and Kenchrias. Kenchrias was accidentally killed by Artemis while hunting and, in weeping for her son, Peirene became a water spring.

Acrocorinth
The myth of Bellerophon and Pegasus. Temple of Aphrodite

The fortress of Acrocorinth consists of a circuit of walls 2.5km in length enclosing the entire mountain top, the entrance complex with its triple line of defences, and a Frankish castle with keep and outer bailey on the highest part of the circuit. Within the walls are the remains of the upper town with its ruined mosques, minarets and cisterns from the period of Turkish occupation. Here too, is the site of the famous temple of Aphrodite and the Upper Peirene Spring with its mysterious water source. Although Acrocorinth was probably first fortified in the 7C or 6C BC, and the circuit was rebuilt in the 4C BC, the ancient walls were destroyed by Mummius in 146 BC when Roman power finally subdued Greece. Local fortification was forbidden within the Roman Empire. Despite the flourishing city that grew from Julius Caesar's new foundation in 44 BC, walls did not rise again on the mountain until the early Byzantine period. Then, the pressure of invaders from the north prompted re-fortification on what remained of the ancient foundations. Following centuries of Slav invasions, the walls were repaired again some time after the re-establishment of Byzantine authority in the Peloponnese in 805 AD. The Franks, the Byzantines, the Turks and the Venetians all added to the fortifications, as each in turn conquered the land and were then themselves displaced.

From the car park at Ancient Corinth, the road continues beyond the village, all the way up to Acrocorinth, passing on the way a Turkish fountain, still in use. It leads directly to a rough parking area a little way below the outer gate. There is a taverna by the car park. The site has no fence as such, but the fortifications, which enclose the entire mountain, still form an effective barrier. Access is by the original gates, which are open 8.00 to 19.00. There is a ticket office just inside the outer gate that dispenses site plans, but at the time of writing entrance is free. The occasional tour bus makes the climb up from Roman Corinth below, but the size of the site will make it feel largely deserted.

The entrance complex defends the only practicable approach to the mountain. Enter by passing through the outer gate (Frankish with Turkish additions), the second gate (Byzantine with Frankish rebuilding and Venetian lower façade) and finally the third gate between a pair of massive towers. Once through the last gate, a path leads up through the shallow valley that occupies the centre of the hill above. To the left of the path is the church of Ayios Dimitrios, still in use, and immediately ahead is a ruined mosque. Above, and to the right, is the shaft of a minaret. On the skyline, the square tower of the Frankish keep is silhouetted.

The path climbs an obvious street between the foundations of Turkish houses. In many places the streets and side alleys are still paved. There are underground cisterns everywhere, often protected only by a loose grating. The isolated minaret stands at the rear of a large terrace that conceals cisterns beneath. A path leads past the terrace and minaret up to the ridge to the left of the keep, where it meets the south walls of the circuit. Turn right along the wall to reach the keep. For the upper Peirene spring turn left. Walk along the line of the ramparts until the square shape of a ruined Turkish barrack block can be seen. The spring, or more accurately a well-house, is below ground. A concrete roof now protects the original Hellenistic vaulted construction. Modern metal steps lead down to the well chamber, where, behind an entrance screen, the source of water has never been known to dry up. Springs usually occur at the bottom of limestone mountains, not at the top. This spring, created by Asopos in his bargain with Sisyphus, remains a geological conundrum.

The spring was the also the place where Bellerophon captured the winged horse Pegasus. Bellerophon learned his skill with horses from his father Glaucus, who was taught by his father Sisyphus. Glaucus's desire to win chariot races at all costs brought him to a gruesome end. He had refused to let his mares breed in the belief that this would make them more spirited. Aphrodite, as the goddess of love and procreation, was offended by this. She caused the mares to bolt, overturning his chariot and dragging him to his death. His ghost was reputed to haunt the area of the Corinth Isthmus. Horses that took fright at the Isthmian Games were thought to have been startled by the ghost known as the Horse-scarer.

Zeus's hatred for Sisyphus was extended to the next generation, for he had placed a curse on Glaucus that he would never be the father of his own children. Accordingly, Bellerophon's real father was Poseidon, who had slept with Eurynome disguised as her husband Glaucus. At birth Bellerophon was called Hipponous. His name was changed when he killed the Corinthian Bellerus and was forced to leave the city. He fled to the court of king Proetus of Tiryns. When he spurned the advances of the king's wife, she accused him of trying to seduce her. Proetus, rather than killing Bellerophon himself, sent him to his father-in-law Iobates, king of Lycia, with a secret letter asking Iobates to kill Bellerophon.

Iobates sent Bellerophon to kill the Chimaera, a fire breathing beast, part goat, part lion and part dragon, in the belief that he was sure to perish. Bellerophon had the foresight to consult the seer Polyeidus, another descendant of Melampous, who advised him to catch Pegasus. He found the horse drinking from the upper Peirene spring and he was able to capture it using a golden bridle given to him by Athena. He then killed the Chimaera by flying over it on Pegasus and shooting it with arrows.

The temple of Aphrodite stood on the summit of the hill behind the spring and is the highest point of the entire site. The foundations have been excavated, but there is now little to see apart from the view.

Aphrodite had a remarkable birth. When Kronos castrated his father Ouranos, he cast his genitals into the sea. Aphrodite was said to born from the foam that spread around them. She was the goddess of love and beauty possessing a magic girdle that made the wearer irresistible in love. She was notoriously promiscuous and had numerous lovers, both gods and mortals. In Corinth sacred prostitution accompanied the worship of Aphrodite. Most guidebooks imply that this activity somehow took place on Acrocorinth, but there is nothing in the ancient sources to indicate this. Prostitution would have been an activity of the city and the ports, where, in any case, there were many other shrines to Aphrodite.

Ancient Isthmia
Sanctuary of Poseidon and the home of the Isthmian games.

The Sanctuary of Poseidon at Isthmia stands on the edge of a line of low cliffs that now overlooks the southern end of the canal. Religious activity in the area may have begun as early as the 11C BC and there was a large Doric temple to Poseidon on the site by the 7C BC. The Isthmian Games appear to have begun in the 6C BC, the date is usually given as 582 or 584 BC. They were held every two years. A new larger temple was built around 465 BC to replace the original that was burnt down. With the destruction of Corinth in 146 BC, the Games on the Isthmus came to an end. For the next 200 years they were in the hands of Sikyon (see Chapter 6). Even though Corinth was refounded in 44 BC by Julius Caesar, the Games probably did not return to Isthmia until 50 AD. They ceased sometime in the 4C AD. In the first half of the 5C AD the Hexamilion (six mile) wall was built across the Isthmus by Theodosius II in response to barbarian attacks from the north. Justinian repaired the wall in the 6C AD and also constructed a fortress against it to the east of the sanctuary. These walls can still be seen.

Today the site sees few tourists as the major monuments were systematically dismantled in the 5C AD to provide stone for the Hexamilion wall. However, the excellent museum, the unique starting gate from the first stadium, and the Roman bath complex with the remains of an enormous Greek pool from the 4C BC beneath, make this a highly worthwhile visit.

In common with the other Panhellenic Games, those at Isthmia were founded as funeral games and have a complex foundation myth. It begins when the infant Dionysus, after being born from Zeus's thigh (see Chapter 2), was given by Hermes to Ino, Semele's sister, to be brought up. Hera, having brought about Semele's death, was still determined to wreak vengeance on Dionysus and anyone helping him. She asked the Furies to drive Ino and her husband, Athamas, insane. In his madness, Athamas killed his son Learchus. Ino took her younger boy Melikertes and jumped into the sea with him, shouting the name of Bacchus (Iacchos/Dionysus). Aphrodite, the mother of Harmonia and therefore grandmother of Semele and Ino, in pity for her grandchild, pleaded with Poseidon to make Ino and Melikertes gods. Poseidon stripped away their mortal remains. Ino became the goddess Leukothea and Melikertes became the god Palaimon. The body of the drowned boy was carried ashore at Isthmia by a dolphin. Sisyphus, king of Corinth, buried Palaimon's mortal remains after they had been washed ashore and founded

93

the Games in his honour. Athenian tradition, however, has Theseus founding the Games in celebration of his victory over Sinus. This was one of the labours he performed on his journey from Troizen to Athens (see Chapter 8).

Although Poseidon was less powerful than Zeus, his role as the god of the sea cannot be understated in a world where sea travel between coastal settlements was so important. He received the sea as his domain when the world was divided between Zeus, Hades and Poseidon, after the fall of Kronos. He was also the god of horses. The Greeks depicted him travelling across the surface of the sea on a chariot pulled by a golden-maned team of horses whose brazen hooves calmed the waves. He was the father of Pegasus. He seduced Medusa in the form of a horse in one of Athena's temples. Outraged at this sacrilege, Athena gave Medusa a head of serpents in place of hair. When Perseus subsequently cut off Medusa's head (see Chapter 8), Pegasus sprang from her blood.

In yet another role, Poseidon was known as the earth-shaker, the god of earthquakes. The location of his sanctuary on the Isthmus between two seas, in an area notorious for its seismic activity, seems very appropriate.

Visiting the Site

The easiest route to the site from the canal area is to take the Epidavros road south from the motorway junction ½km west of the canal bridge (see above). The road runs downhill towards modern Isthmia. The remains of the Hexamilion wall are visible to the right. After 1km, a sharp right turn, with a brown sign, at the small village of Kiras Vrisi (Κυράς Βρύση), leads back up the slope of the plateau to the museum and site entrance. The walls of a Byzantine fortress built by Justinian in the 6C AD appear to the right ½km further on. The south gate, flanked by two round towers, is visible from the road. On the opposite side of the road is the 'new' stadium built sometime around 300 BC. It occupies the floor of a small valley that runs off to the south. It is unexcavated but clearly visible. The museum is a few hundred metres further up the road on the right. Entrance to the site is through the museum. Opening hours are 8.30 to 15.00, normally closed on Mondays. The site is now well provided with plans and information boards.

The museum has excellent displays of finds from the sanctuary and some remarkable glass mosaics found at Kenchreai. The foundations of the temple of Poseidon lie directly behind the museum building. As is usual, it was aligned east-west. The original stadium ran from one corner of the temple towards the southeast. Built in the first half of the 6C BC, it was removed about 300 BC. A stoa that formed part of the temple enclosure was subsequently built over it. However, the starting system has been uncovered. Gates were operated by cords pulled by a starter, who stood in a pit in the centre of the line. This system is clearly illustrated in the museum. Close by are the remains of a Roman temple to Palaimon. Curiously, no evidence of an earlier temple has been found.

The theatre lies in a hollow to the northeast. It is now little more than a large hole in the ground. A little way beyond is the extensive complex of the Roman baths dating from the 2C AD. This is built on top of a much earlier Greek pool of the 4C BC. The baths have now been completely excavated. The showpiece, a huge monochrome mosaic, has been painstakingly restored. It is currently protected by a gravel covering, but there are plans for a permanent protective roof to allow visitor access. The archaeologists have been able to expose a considerable proportion of the original Greek pool.

6

Corinth to Olympia

From Corinth there are numerous routes that can be used to reach Olympia. Three are described below. The first is the most utilitarian, taking the fast coast road directly to the site. The other two routes lead through the mountains of Arcadia, visiting important sanctuaries and the scenes of Arcadian myth. While they can easily be covered in a day, they offer the opportunity for a more extended exploration of the heartland of the Peloponnese.

A. From Corinth via the coast road

This is still the quickest way to reach Olympia and the west coast of the Peloponnese, the more so now that the bottleneck of Patras has been bypassed. The 'new' National road along the coast varies in standard from true motorway at one extreme, to fast, two-lane highway with no central barrier at the other. In this chapter for convenience it is referred to as 'the motorway' to distinguish it from the old road that passes through every coastal town along the way.

Sikyon (Σικυώνα)
The myths of Prometheus and Pandora

Ancient Sikyon lies some 20km from Corinth, about 4km inland from the modern town of Kiato. It was a typical city-state with a small agricultural plain on the coast that formed the basis of the economy. The area was known as Sikyonia in antiquity. The original city was on the plain with its acropolis on an extensive triangular plateau to the south. However, in 303 BC, the city was destroyed by the Macedonian, Demetrius Poliorketes. He refounded it immediately, but chose to build

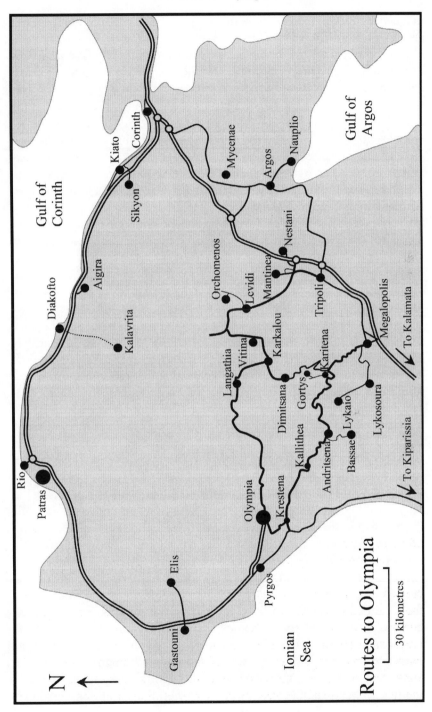

Routes to Olympia

in a better defensive position on the plateau, creating a new acropolis on an upper terrace. This is the city we see today.

Sikyon claims a history as old as any Greek city and has numerous connections with important myths. Apollo and Artemis are said to have come here for purification after killing Python at Delphi. Meleager dedicated the spear he used to kill the Kalydonian boar to Apollo in his temple by the agora. The city numbers one of the Seven against Thebes amongst its kings. Prior to the war between the sons of Oedipus (see Chapter 2), Adrastus, ultimately the only survivor of the Seven, was expelled from Argos by Amphiaraos. He fled to king Polybus at Sikyon, assuming the throne when Polybus died. He was later reconciled to Amphiaraos and returned to Argos.

Sikyon's oldest myth concerns the very beginning of man's relationship with the gods. Prometheus, said to be the creator of mankind, was called upon to arbitrate in a dispute at Sikyon, or Mekone as it was then called, between the gods and mortals over the division of the sacrifice. His sympathies lay with mankind. He butchered and divided a bull in a clever way. He placed the meat of the animal on its hide, concealed by placing the stomach on top, so that it resembled a heap of offal. He then made a great pile of the bones and covered them with fat, so that they looked like the flesh of the animal. Prometheus asked Zeus to choose between them. Zeus was fooled into choosing the bones and fat. Thereafter, this unequal division was to remain the basis of mankind's sacrifice to the gods.

Zeus realised he had been tricked. He punished Prometheus and mankind by withholding the gift of fire. Prometheus's response was to gain entry secretly to Olympus, steal fire and bring it back to the land of men concealed in the hollow of a fennel stalk. Zeus exacted a terrible vengeance on Prometheus. He commanded Hermes (or Hephaistos) to fasten Prometheus to Mount Caucasus with iron spikes. He set an eagle (or vulture) to tear out his liver (or heart) each day. Each night his liver grew back, so that the torture could be repeated the following day. Prometheus's torment would thus last forever.

Zeus's revenge on mankind was more subtle. As Prometheus had created only men, Zeus ordered Hephaistos to fashion the first woman from earth and water, and to give her human attributes including great beauty. Then he sent her to Prometheus's brother, Epimetheus, as a gift. Epimetheus ignored his brother's advice never to accept a gift from Zeus and took Pandora as his wife. Pandora had brought with her a jar containing every human ill; pain, disease, anguish, vice and passion. Although Epimetheus had been warned to keep the jar closed, Pandora's

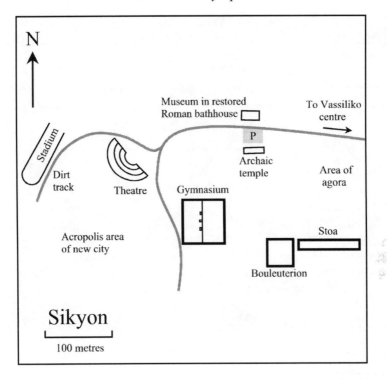

N

Museum in restored
Roman bathhouse

To Vassiliko
centre

P

Archaic
temple

Area of
agora

Stadium

Dirt
track

Theatre

Gymnasium

Acropolis area
of new city

Stoa

Bouleuterion

Sikyon

100 metres

curiosity led her to open it and all the ills that now plague mankind were released. Only Hope remained behind, so that men would be able to bear the ills they were now condemned to suffer.

Tourists do not usually visit Sikyon, possibly because it is surprisingly difficult to find, despite being clearly marked on most maps. Approaching from the motorway, take the Kiato (Κιάτο) exit and follow the road downhill to the centre of the town that stretches along the old coast road. Turn right, back in the direction of Corinth. On the outskirts of the town, immediately after a Lidl supermarket, take a right turn with a small blue sign indicating Archaia Sikyona. At the next junction there is another blue sign. Go left at the fork signposted to Moulki (Μούλκι). At the next junction, with a Stop sign, turn left. The road passes under the motorway. Take the left turn signposted Archaia Sikyona. The road reaches the outskirts of Vasiliko (Βασιλικό), renamed Sikyona on some maps, and winds up the edge of the plateau into the centre of the village. This appears to be the only signposted route to the site. There are shorter alternatives, but local knowledge is required to navigate the maze of roads. If lost, follow any signs to Moulki or Vassiliko.

Figure 11 Sikyon: carved stone seating in the theatre

Drive right through the village where a sign to the Archaeological Museum, by the church, confirms the direction. On the far side of the village the first brown sign appears. The Hellenistic city occupied much of this flat plateau. The museum buildings are on the right, housed in a well restored brick-built Roman bathhouse of the 2C or 3C AD. Despite the signs and the well-kept appearance, the museum is permanently closed. However the site, which is essentially unenclosed and free, now has information boards with good site plans.

The public buildings that remain visible are almost a textbook list of the elements the Greeks considered essential in a city; temples, a theatre, stadium and gymnasium, fountains with a good water supply, and the all-important agora. On the opposite side of the road, beyond the parking area, is a fenced compound with an unlocked gate. This contains the buildings that surrounded the agora. Visible immediately to the left of the gate are the foundations of an Archaic temple dating originally from the 6C BC. This is the only building known from the original city when this area formed the acropolis. The temple was remodelled in the Hellenistic period and incorporated into the design of the agora of the new city. Carved crosses are visible indicating its later use as a

Christian church. It may be the temple of Apollo 'in the marketplace' described by Pausanias. Beyond the temple, to the left, are the foundations of a colonnaded stoa over 100M long and a Bouleuterion, or council-house. These formed the south side of the agora. To the right, on the west side, is a well preserved gymnasium, elegantly laid out on two levels and originally surrounded by colonnades. The two levels are linked by three stairways, still intact. Two elaborate fountains flank the central stairway. The one on the left still retains its colonnaded draw basin.

The large 3C BC theatre lies 200M from the museum and is built into the slope that divides the plateau into two terraces. The upper terrace was the acropolis of the new city. Of the original 50 tiers of seats, eight rows are preserved. In addition to the normal system of steps, two vaulted corridors gave access to the diazoma, the corridor that divided the seating of the auditorium into two sections. A Roman fountain is built against the stage buildings. About 200M up the track that forks right in front of the theatre, is the stadium, partly built in a natural cleft in the hillside, and partly on an artificial terrace with massive retaining walls of polygonal masonry. This, presumably, was the location of the Isthmian Games during the period when they were lost to Corinth.

Aigira (Egira, Αιγείρα)
Theatre and sanctuary of Tykhe

Ancient Aegira lies 5km inland from the coastal village of the same name, 40 km west of Kiato. Although it has no great myths to tell, its well preserved and well-excavated Hellenistic civic centre offers a pleasant detour from the coast road. The site is easy to find and has tremendous views out over the Gulf. There are exits from the motorway onto the old coast road both east and west of Aigira. At the eastern end of the village a signposted turn towards the sea loops under the main road and motorway, before beginning to climb. Passing the school, it swings around to the right, then continues uphill for a total of 5km. Where it begins to level off, there are signs for the scant remains of the Mycenaean Citadel to the right, and for the Ancient Theatre to the left, initially hidden below the road. A short walk leads to the gate of the well-fenced site. Entrance is free and the site should normally be open 8.30 – 15.00. If closed there are still excellent views of the excavations and the theatre, even from the wrong side of the fence. The theatre is built into the lower slopes of the acropolis hill. A large part of the seating is preserved, carved from the rock of the hillside. In front, on a flat terrace overlooking the Gulf, is a complex of buildings dating from around 280 BC. This includes temples, shrines and a sanctuary to Tykhe. The theatre and sanctuaries show evidence of rebuilding into the Roman period. Tykhe, or Fortune, was a goddess widely worshipped as the guardian of a city's luck. Pausanias's description of the city bears out the identification of the various shrines. He mentions a sanctuary of Zeus, a shrine to Apollo, another to Artemis with a statue of Iphigenia, as well as a statue of Tykhe in its own building. Both the head of a statue of Zeus and a figure of Tykhe have been found.

Kalavrita railway
The Vouraikos gorge

Diakofto (Διακοφτό) is another seaside resort 18 km west of Aigira. It is the terminus for the narrow-gauge railway line that climbs up the gorge of the Vouraikos (Βουραϊκός) river. The trip gives access to the most spectacular, and otherwise inaccessible, part of the gorge between the coast and the mountain village of Zachlorou (Ζαχλωρού). The walk down the gorge, part of the E4 long distance footpath, also offers a unique opportunity to experience the mountains on a route that is entirely downhill. Take the motorway exit 4km to the east of Diakofto onto the old coast road. Signs appear for the 'track train', a reference to the fact that the narrow gauge line also operates on a rack and pinion system for much of its length. The coast road crosses the narrow gauge track and a right turn is signposted to the railway station. The road winds down through the village to the station.

The journey from Diakofto to Kalavrita takes just over an hour. Train times can be checked in advance at **www.ose.gr**. Zachlorou is thirty minutes and halfway up the line. The walk back down from this point takes about 3 hours and a head for heights is needed when crossing the bridges. A note of the train times is also useful when walking through the short tunnels. Note that Zachlorou is also known as Mega Spileo, and this is the name prominently displayed on the end of the station building.

Rio, and the southern end of the new bridge across the Gulf of Corinth, is 48km west of Diakofto. Here the Gulf of Corinth is just 2km wide. Beyond Rio, the road reaches true motorway standards, bypassing Patras, Greece's third largest city, an important port and previously a major bottleneck. Once past Patras, the mountains recede to the south and the road traverses the wide coastal plain of northern Ilia. From Patras it is 110km to Olympia. After 68km the road reaches the Gastouni crossroads. A left turn here leads to the archaeological site of ancient Elis, (see Chapter 7). The road bypasses the large town of Pyrgos then leads directly to the centre of the modern village of Olympia.

B. From Corinth inland via Langathia

The road around the coast can give the unfortunate impression that Olympia lies at the end of a motorway. A more appealing route, and one that more readily fulfils expectations of Arcadian landscapes, is the road from Tripoli through the mountains, via Vitina and Langathia. This road approaches Olympia down the beautiful, largely deserted Alpheios valley and leads directly to the sacred precinct before reaching the town, where the pastoral spell is broken.

The starting point for the main mountain section of this route is Nestani, an attractive village on the eastern border of Arcadia. It now gives its name to an intersection on the Tripoli motorway about 60km from Corinth, and about 8km after the motorway bores its way through the mountains via the Artemission tunnel. From the motorway intersection, a short spur leads west for 4km to the main Tripoli – Vitina - Langathia road. Nearby are the little visited ancient cities of Mantinea and Orchomenos. To start this route from Nauplio and the Argolid, see Chapter 8.

Nestani (Νεστάνη)
The Arcadian myth of Poseidon's birth. The Golden Hinds of Artemis.

The picturesque village of Tsipiana, now renamed Nestani after its ancient predecessor, lies in a bowl-shaped valley beneath the slopes of Mount Artemisio, on one of the ancient routes from the Argolid. The mountain formed the border between Arcadia and Argolida.

Above the village towers the distinctively shaped massif of Goula. The low hill of the ancient acropolis is immediately behind the village and overlooks the small plain through which the motorway now runs. A ruined tower and a well-preserved gate represent the visible remains of the 4C BC fortifications. At the foot of the acropolis hill is Phillip's spring, no doubt rebuilt numerous times over the centuries, but reputedly first erected by Phillip II in 338 BC. After his victory that year at the battle of Chaironia (see Chapter 3), he journeyed south to make diplomatic preparations for the creation of the Corinthian League the following year.

To visit the village and its modest archaeological remains, turn right almost immediately at a crossroads after leaving the motorway. Follow the signposted road back under the dual carriageway for 4km. On entering the village, the one-way system first leads right, up the hill, and then left after 200M. A T-junction a little further on leads left to the square. From here, another left completes the circle returning to the starting point. To reach the acropolis and Philip's spring, turn right at the T-junction above, then immediately left, indicated by a brown sign reading 'Ancient Acropolis'. A narrow lane leads up a slope for a few hundred metres to the low wooded hill that formed the original defended area. Park by the church and cemetery on the left where there are more brown signs. The spring, or more accurately fountain, is just below the church by the schoolyard. A short walk up a green lane leads to the gate of the acropolis circuit. From the hill there are superb views of the village with the truncated cone of Mount Goula in the background. This is the view that often appears in Greek pictorial guidebooks of the region. In the other direction, the hill overlooks the plain and the motorway. Pausanias refers to this plain as the Waste, and comments on its propensity to flood. Despite modern drainage, flooding still occurs. After a wet winter the plain can become a shallow lake split in two by the motorway embankment.

The area is steeped in legend. Pausanias tells us that somewhere on the plain, by the road to Mantinea, was a fountain known as the Lamb Spring. The Arcadians had a different version of the birth of Poseidon from that described in Chapter 2 where Kronos swallowed each of his children by Rhea. They believed that Rhea left the newborn Poseidon in a sheep pen with the lambs. She tricked Kronos, telling him that the child she had borne was a horse, and she presented him with a foal, which he then swallowed. The name of the spring commemorates the place of Poseidon's birth in the sheep pen.

The worship of Artemis in Arcadia was very old. A shrine and statue to Artemis once stood on the summit of Mount Artemisio. She was often represented hunting in the mountains on a chariot drawn by four golden antlered deer. There were, in fact, five of these 'Golden Hinds' sacred to Artemis. The fifth roamed free in Arcadia's mountains. Hercules's third labour was to capture this creature and bring it alive to Eurystheus at Mycenae (see Chapter 8). Known as the Keryneian Hind,

Hercules tracked it across the mountains until it took refuge on Mount Artemisio. Various versions of the story have him catching it with nets, pinning its front legs together with an arrow, or simply wearing it down by the chase. As he was carrying it to Mycenae on his shoulders, he was accosted by Artemis and Apollo. Artemis accused him of trying to kill her sacred animal. Hercules defended himself, blaming Eurystheus for the burden of the Labours, so Artemis allowed him to complete his task.

Mantinea (Μαντινεία)
A famous battle site. Sanctuary of Horse Poseidon.
Church of Ayia Photeini.

The name Mantinea appears in ancient Greek history as the site of recurring battles between Sparta and various alliances of cities. The first Battle of Mantinea was just one episode of the twenty-seven years of conflict now called the Peloponnesian War in which a quadruple alliance of Mantinea, Argos, Elis and Athens was comprehensively defeated by Sparta in 418 BC. Thirty three years later, in 385 BC, the city itself was besieged by the Spartans, under Agesipolis, and razed to the ground. Agesipolis used a novel method of breaching the walls. The city lay in the centre of its level plain, presumably originally a lake-bed, surrounded by mud-brick walls. Unusually, the river Ophis flowed right through the centre of the city. Mud brick walls were usually built on a socle, or foundation layer, of stone. Agesipolis's ruse was to damn the river at its exit from the city. The resulting flood rose above the level of the stone foundations causing the saturated mud brick to collapse. The defeated Mantineans were forced to demolish what was left of their walls, abandon their city, and return to live in the villages that had been their homes before the city was founded.

Just 14 years later, in 371 BC, Sparta was decisively defeated by Thebes led by Epaminondas, at the battle of Leuktra (see Chapter 2). The Mantineans then rebuilt their city, possibly with the help of Theban architects. The walls they raised were again of mud-brick on stone foundations, but the river was channelled into a moat that ran right around the elliptical circuit. Where the river had previously been a weakness in the defences, it was now an additional barrier. The foundations of these walls, surrounded by the now dry moat, are still visible today. In less than 10 years, however, there was general disenchantment in Arcadia with the new Theban dominance. Mantinea joined an unlikely alliance of Achaia, Elis, Athens and Sparta against Thebes. In

Figure 12 Mantinea: The church of Ayia Photeini

362 BC, Epaminondas marched into the Peloponnese and at the second battle of Mantinea Thebes again won a decisive victory. However, Epaminondas himself was killed in the battle and with the loss of his leadership, the brief period of Theban hegemony in Greece came to an abrupt end.

Visiting the Sites

A right turn onto a minor road where the spur from the motorway reaches the Tripoli - Vitina highway, leads in 3km to the remains of ancient Mantinea. Alternatively, an earlier right turn on the spur road, signposted to the village of Milia (Μηλιά), leads past the scanty remains of the Sanctuary of Horse Poseidon, perhaps also related to the myth of Poseidon's birth. Drive through the village. On the northern outskirts a brown sign on the right indicates the site, 100M across a meadow. Within a small, locked compound are the modest foundations of a temple from the Archaic period. The earliest temple on the site was supposed to have been built of oak logs by the famous architects Trophonios and Agamedes (see Chapter 3). The road continues north for a kilometre until a left turn leads back to the Mantinea road.

Mantinea was built in the centre of the plain. Although its mud brick walls have completely disappeared, the foundations still exist, almost intact. The road passes straight through the western half of the oval 4km circuit. With over 100 towers and 9 or 10 gates, it must have been a magnificent sight. Now it is easy to miss the point where the road crosses the line of walls.

However, it is impossible to miss the amazing modern church of Ayia Photeini built in 1972 by the side of the road, inside the ancient city. The building, often described as resembling a folly in the English country estate sense, is a consecrated church and should be treated as such. Built in a confused mixture of brick and stone, its style has been variously referred to as a combination of Minoan, Byzantine, Egyptian and Classical. It is probably best described as the work of an aspiring Greek Gaudi. Within the well-tended grounds of the church are other structures that might genuinely be called follies. The church will probably be open, but the entrance is concealed at the rear. The interior is as idiosyncratic as the exterior, although the ground plan still follows the normal conventions of an Orthodox church.

The church stands directly opposite the gates to the archaeological site. A fenced avenue leads to the excavated area. Although enclosed, access is possible at all times. The path first reaches the small theatre, one of the few in Greece constructed completely on flat land. The normal raised auditorium was built of banked earth behind semi-circular retaining walls. Two or three rows of its seating remain in situ. Beyond the theatre is the agora, surrounded by the foundations of temples and stoas with various dates from the 4C BC to the 2C AD. Brown signs give the names of the principal monuments, but the general impression is of scanty remains in an overgrown meadow.

To the north is the conspicuous conical hill of Gortsouli, the site of the original acropolis, inhabited since the Neolithic period. A good view of the whole plain can be obtained from this vantage point. To reach it, continue along the road from Ayia Photeini. After crossing the line of the walls again on the northern side of the circuit, the right turn for the church of Panayia Gortsouli is indicated by a very battered sign. A dirt road climbs the hill to the church, built almost entirely from re-used ancient materials. A brown sign announces 'Prehistoric Acropolis'. The oval circuit of the city walls can be traced in the fields below.

Arcadian Orchomenos   (Ορχομενός)
Ancient theatre. Temples of Apollo, Aphrodite and Artemis

From the Mantinea junction, the main road climbs gently uphill in fast sweeping curves, reaching Levidi (Λεβίδι) after 15km. From here it is a short detour of 8km to the beautifully isolated remains of ancient Arcadian Orchomenos, not to be confused with its namesake near Thebes. An archetypal Arcadian city, it is named after its mythical founder Orchomenos, a son of Lykaon (see Lykosoura below). Though the

Figure 13 Arcadian Orchomenos: The view north from the Orchestra of the Theatre. Carved stone throne in the foreground.

monuments themselves are modest, the site is worth visiting for the glorious views alone.

Fork right in the centre of Levidi, where the turning is signposted for Ancient Orchomenos. At the next junction carry straight on, following the sign for Nemea. After a further 2km, another sign points left to Ancient Orchomenos. The road climbs through the tiny modern village built on the site of the ancient lower town. Keep right at an obvious fork, with an easy-to-miss sign to "Ancient Theatre and Agora". The road becomes a rough, but quite driveable track that winds for 1km above the village. It begins to level out and passes the overgrown remains of a wall-tower on the left. Just beyond, there is room to park and turn round. The road continues for only another 50M beyond this point. Suddenly there is a proliferation of brown signs. Follow an obvious footpath for about 300M to the theatre, superbly situated looking out over the plain.

The theatre area is fenced but the gate is not locked. A few rows of the seats remain and two stone thrones still stand at the rear of the orchestra. Above, on the grassy summit of the acropolis hill, are the foundations of the agora, the bouleuterion and temples to Apollo, Aphrodite and Artemis Mesopolitis. The hillside is carpeted with flowers in the spring. Snow lies on the distant peaks even in May. There is every chance of having this splendidly isolated place completely to yourself.

To Langathia (Langadhia, Λαγκάδια)
The myths of Atalanta, the Arcadian huntress.

From Levidi a good, usually deserted road continues to climb into the empty mountains. It passes a right turn north for Patras and Kalavrita after 10 km and in another 10km reaches the mountain village of Vitina (Βυτίνα). Three kilometres beyond Vitina a minor road runs south for 1km to the village of Methydrion (Μεθύδριο) where there are fragmentary remains of the ancient city of the same name. This is the territory of Atalanta, the famous huntress and companion of Artemis and the place where, according to Pausanias, she had the racetrack used for the contests for her hand in marriage.

Atalanta was the daughter of Iasus and Clymene. Although she was rejected at birth by her father and exposed in the open countryside, she was nursed by a she-bear sent by Artemis and survived to be rescued and brought up by hunters. When she reached adulthood she determined to remain a virgin and continued to live the life of a huntress in the wilderness where she is depicted as a companion of Artemis. She was famous for her fleetness of foot. The centaurs Rhoikos and Hylaios attempted to rape her but were killed by her arrows. After the adventure of the Kalydonian boar hunt she was recognised by her father. When he decided that she should marry she agreed to accept whichever suitor could defeat her in a deadly footrace. Each prospective bridegroom would sprint down the racecourse pursued by Atalanta, fully armed. If he was able to stay ahead of her his reward would be her hand in marriage. If he was caught the outcome would be instant death. Many young men met their end in this way. When Melanion came to try his hand, he brought with him three golden apples given to him by Aphrodite. As he raced in front of Atalanta he dropped each of the apples in turn. Atalanta was unable to resist them and stopped to pick them up. By this ruse Melanion was able to stay ahead of her. The pair were married and had a son, Parthenopaios, one of the Seven against Thebes. Their marriage was shortlived however, for having offended Zeus by making love in one of his sanctuaries, they were transformed into lions.

Twelve kilometres further on, at Karkalou (Καρκαλού), is the left turn for Dimitsana. This attractive mountain village lies at the very head of the Lousios gorge some 8km to the south and is the ideal centre for exploring the area. The village is built on the site of ancient Teuthis and fragments of its walls are incorporated in the buildings that form the centre on the hill. The gorge is famous for the numerous monasteries built against its cliffs and offers excellent walking opportunities (see also Ancient Gortys below).

Ten kilometres north of the Dimitsana junction, after crossing the watershed, Langathia comes into sight, spilling down the hillside above the gorge formed by a tributary of the Ladon (Λάδωνας). The character of the road changes abruptly, narrowing and winding its way through the picturesque village. Beyond the village, the road winds on its ledge high up above the well-wooded gorge. There are stunning views in all directions with the purple of the Judas trees visible in April and May. The contrast with the bare slopes of the mountains to the east could not be greater.

The Ladon and Erymanthos valleys to Olympia
Poseidon and Demeter. Pan and Syrinx. Hercules and the Centaurs.

After Stavrodromi (Σταυροδρόμι), just 12km from Langathia, the road improves, climbs over a watershed into the broad valley of the Ladon, and keeps to the valley for the next 8km. This is the heartland of Arcadian myth. Here on the banks of the Ladon, Poseidon caught Demeter when she hid from him disguised as a mare. He found her grazing among the mares of Onkios of Thelpousa. (Onkios was a son of Apollo. Thelpousa was an ancient city in the hills above the Ladon). Transforming himself into a stallion, he coupled with her. The outcome was the birth of Despoina (see Lykosoura, below) and the horse Arion. Pausanias mentions a Sanctuary of Demeter somewhere by the river. The myth has her bathing and purifying herself here after her liaison with Poseidon. He describes a statue called Washing Demeter in the sanctuary commemorating this event. He also tells us that the birth of

110

Arion led to the name 'Horse Poseidon' being used for the first time. Here, too, is another spot where Hercules is said to have captured the Keryneian Hind. The Ladon valley was where Pan pursued the nymph Syrinx. She rejected his advances, but being unable to escape, she asked the nymphs of the river to change her form. She became a reed among the marshes. All that was left of her was the sound of the wind in the reeds. Pan immortalised her name by cutting reeds of different sizes, creating the instrument called the Syrinx or Pan pipes.

Beyond the hamlet of Daphni, the road climbs the ridge of hills that separates the Ladon and Erymanthos valleys. After passing a left turn for Tripotamia, meaning literally three rivers, the great bowl in the hills, where the Alpheios, the Ladon and the Erymanthos all meet within a kilometre, can be seen to the south. All around is the epitome of an Arcadian landscape; deciduous trees and cypresses clothing the hillsides, with grazing sheep beneath. The road begins to drop down towards the Erymanthos. Below, on the left, can be seen the broad strand of the braided riverbed. Here was the setting of Hercules's fourth Labour.

The story of the fourth Labour is straightforward. Hercules was commanded to bring back alive the Erymanthian Boar, which had been ravaging the countryside to west and north of the river, the area of Mount Lambia and Mount Erymanthos. Having tracked it down, he drove it into a deep snowdrift, trapped and bound it, and carried it back to Mycenae. However, it was during this hunt that he came to fight the Centaurs, a savage race that originally lived on Mount Pelion, the peninsula south of modern Volos. They came to be represented in mythology as half man and half horse. They were expelled from Pelion in their fight with the Lapiths, another ancient race.

Hercules had to pass through the area known as Pholoe, west of the Erymanthos. Mount Foloi (Φολόη) lies just to the north. He was entertained there by Pholus, the Centaur. Pholus prepared roast meat for Hercules who persuaded him to open a jar of wine to accompany the meal, despite Pholus's protestations that it belonged to all of the Centaurs in common. The smell of the wine attracted the other Centaurs, who came to Pholus's cave armed with rocks and up-rooted fir trees. Hercules drove them away with his arrows. They fled in every direction, some to Malea, some to Elefsis. Nessus, who was later to be responsible for the death of Hercules, fled to the river Evinos (see Chapter 4). Pholus, wondering at the power of the arrows to kill the giant Centaurs, pulled one from a corpse. It slipped from his hand and pierced him in the foot. He died instantly, for the arrows' tips were coated with poison from the Lernean Hydra. Hercules gave him a magnificent funeral burying him at the foot of the mountain that henceforth bore his name.

The road crosses the Erymanthos bridge. This marks the border between Arcadia and Ilia. In many respects the lightly wooded landscape of Ilia is more arcadian than Arcadia. Finally the broad valley of the Alpheios is reached after another 10km. A new road is being constructed through the valley, but is not yet open. On the approach to Olympia, the Coubertin monument and Mount Kronos are passed on the right; the ancient stadium and entrance to the sanctuary are on the left. The modern village lies beyond the bridge over the river Kladeos.

C. Via Megalopolis

This route again uses the motorway to reach central Arcadia quickly via Megalopolis, 25km beyond Tripoli. From Megalopolis it crosses the mountains to the south of the Alpheios valley, via Karitena, Andritsena, and Kallithea. Hidden away in the hills to the west of Megalopolis are two of the most important sacred sites of Arcadia, the Sanctuary of Despoina at Lykosoura and, high above on the summit of Mount Lykaion, the Sanctuary of Zeus.

Megalopolis
The largest theatre in mainland Greece.

Ancient Megalopolis, Great City, was an artificial creation, born of the desire to create a capital for Arcadia after the defeat of Sparta at Leuktra in 371 BC. With Mantinea, Messene and Argos, it formed part of Epaminondas's ring of cities designed to contain any resurgence of Spartan power. Sparta had always had a policy of opposing urban development among its neighbours (see Mantinea above). Before the foundation of Megalopolis, the Arcadians had lived in small villages or townships. Pausanias gives a list of forty communities that abandoned their homes to create the new capital.

Sparta made repeated, but unsuccessful, attempts to destroy the new city. In 353 BC they were defeated with Theban help. In 331 BC it was Macedon that assisted the Arcadians. In 234 BC the Spartans were defeated when a hurricane blew down their siege engine. Finally Sparta successfully sacked the city in 223 BC, but it was a partial and short-lived victory. Two thirds of the population escaped into Messenia. Two

112

years later, after the Spartans' decisive defeat by Macedon, they returned. However, once Greece had been absorbed into the Roman Empire, Megalopolis ceased to have any political logic. Its great walls crumbled away and its population dispersed. Pausanias, in the 2C AD, could still describe the city's major temple and monuments. The twelve-foot tall bronze statue of Apollo that had been brought from the temple at Bassae (see below) could still be seen in the agora. However his description is of a ruin.

Megalopolis now lies 1km to the west of the Tripoli – Kalamata road. The motorway beyond Tripoli is still under construction and ends about 15km short of Megalopolis. Guidebooks tend to be unkind to the town, somewhat unfairly, because the area immediately to the west is dominated by two power stations burning the locally mined brown coal. Centred on a large pleasant square, it is an unpretentious working town. The ancient city lies 1km to the north of the town on the Kariteña road. It was built on either side of the Hellison River, a tributary of the Alpheios, and laid out on a massive scale, with a wall circuit over 8km long. Today the only monument that retains a sense of this scale is the theatre. Immediately beyond the edge of town a sign points left along a track towards a small, steep hill, 200M from the road and 100M from the river. The theatre, built into the north slope of this hill was the largest in mainland Greece. Unfortunately, with the exception of the lower rows of seats, it is not well preserved. The Thersileion, the great square hall that stood directly in front of the theatre, was built as the assembly hall of the Pan-Arcadian League. It was fronted by an open portico that formed the original skene for the theatre. The two structures were thus linked and perhaps were both used for League meetings. The Thersileion was destroyed about 222 BC and not rebuilt. Eventually the theatre acquired a Roman stone stage. All that can be seen today are the foundations stones of the rows of pillars that supported the Thersileion roof. The extensive agora lay on the other side of the river. Virtually nothing remains.

Lykosoura (Λυκόσουρα)
The sanctuary of Despoina.

In the hills above Megalopolis lay some of Arcadia's most sacred areas. At Lykosoura there were sanctuaries of Pan and Despoina. The famous Sanctuary of Zeus stood on the summit of Mount Lykaion. Both these remote sites are easily accessible by car.

The Arcadians believed themselves to be descendants of the Pelasgians, the people of Pelasgos, a mythical first man who sprang from the earth. His family provided a foundation myth for all the ancient cities of Arcadia. His son, Lykaon, is said to have founded the city of Lykosoura and this is the basis for its claim to be the oldest city in the world. Lykaon's sons in turn founded the other ancient cities of Arcadia, from Alifera and Phigalea in the west (see Chapter 7) to Orchomenos and Mantinea to the east. Lykosoura was one of the few Arcadian cities unaffected by the founding of Megalopolis. Its inhabitants refused to abandon their own homes and the Arcadian League was reluctant to force the move because of the sanctity of the city.

Lykaon's only daughter was Callisto. Her son Arkas by Zeus (see the myth of Callisto and the bear, Chapter 2) became king after the death of Lykaon's eldest son, Nyltimos. Arkas was taught agriculture by Triptolemos, who himself had been taught the secret by Demeter (see Elefsis, Chapter 2). Thereafter the people were called Arkadians.

Open cast mining of the local brown coal has changed, and continues to change, both the landscape and the road layout to the west of Megalopolis. Modern maps do not reflect this accurately. To reach Lykosoura from Megalopolis, take the Karitena (Καρίταινα) road from the town centre. About 300M from the main square a blue sign, in Greek only, points left to 'Αρχαιολογικός Χώρος', heading towards the power stations. Turn left at a junction where confused signs (Προς Κιπαρίσσια and Προς Μαυριά) indicate the villages of Kiparissia and Mavria straight on, and a faded blue sign for Lykaio (Λύκαιο) points left. Pass a large works and continue towards the second power station. Go through a small village and follow signs for Kalivia Karion (Καλύβια Καρυών) and Lykaio (Λύκαιο). Then cross the Alpheios over a modern concrete bridge, to reach Kalivia Karion in the shadow of the power station. At a fork, with a host of confusing signs and a large descriptive board showing the mountain and its sights, turn left. Two kilometres later, at another fork, a badly drawn sign points right to Lykosoura and Lykaion.

After reaching the wooded hills, a brown sign indicates an ancient cistern by the left hand side of the road. At a fork another brown sign points left to Ancient Lykosoura just before the village of the same name. The road climbs the hillside and ends after ½km at the site gate. The sanctuary is open daily 8.30 - 14.00, closed on Mondays. The museum, just inside the gate, is unfortunately permanently closed. The sanctuary lies out of sight below the museum on a lower terrace. The city lay to the west. Fragments of its walls are hidden on the hillside.

Despoina, which simply means Mistress in Greek, was the daughter of Demeter and Poseidon (see above). She bears a close resemblance to Demeter's daughter by Zeus, Kore or the Maid. However while Kore's true name, Persephone, is well known, that of Despoina has never been revealed. Pausanias tells us that she was the most worshipped god in Arcadia, and that her name could not be disclosed to the uninitiated. Her worship involved mystery rites, perhaps related to those at Elefsis.

The sanctuary consists of a 2C BC temple on earlier foundations, a long colonnaded stoa and a monumental altar on several levels where offerings were made and the mystery performed. The temple is a plain rectangle with a porch fronted by six Doric columns. In the main body of the building, the cella, are the remains of a mosaic floor, currently protected by gravel and plastic sheeting, and the pedestal that supported the cult statues. This group of marble figures by Damophon of Messene, consisted of a central statue of Demeter and Despoina sitting on a double throne, with a figure of Artemis to the left and Anytos to the right. Anytos was a Titan, supposed to have been responsible for Despoina's upbringing. Pausanias claimed that the two central figures were carved from a single block of stone. Reconstructed fragments of the group are displayed in the National Museum in Athens.

The path down to the terrace from the museum gives a panoramic view of the site and the layout of the buildings can clearly be seen. The temple is directly below. Its portico faces east. The stone frame of an unusual side door to the south is still in place. It faces a long series of steps, or possibly seats, built against the slope of the hill. These may have been connected with the mysteries or may simply be a retaining wall. The footing slabs of the stoa mark its position along the terrace to the east of the temple. Above, at the level of the museum, a brown sign in front of a great oak tree marks the site of the Megaron, or Hall, where the cult altar stood.

Somewhere on the hill above was a Sanctuary of Pan with a colonnade and a statue. Pausanias writes of climbing steps to reach it. In front of the statue a perpetual flame burnt. There was also an altar to Ares and idols of Aphrodite, Apollo and Athena. It remains unexcavated. Pan was very much an Arcadian god whose worship did not spread to the rest of Greece until after 490 BC. Little is known of his mythology before this date and there are many versions of his birth myth. Generally, he is regarded as the son of Hermes and variously Dryope, Thymbris, Callisto, Orneios or Penelope. Images of Pan usually show him with horns, pointed ears and the legs and tail of a goat. His ugliness was said to have caused his mother to run away from him in fear. Originally he

Figure 14 Lykosoura: The Temple viewed from the south with the side door facing the rows of seats built into the hillside.

was an oracular god and gave oracles through the nymph Erato, wife of Arkas. Pausanias records that the prophecies Erato delivered in verse were written down and that he had himself read them. As the god of shepherds and their flocks, Pan is depicted wandering in the mountains of Arcadia playing his reed pipes. Travellers who came upon him in the hills were often filled with terror or *panic*. Despite the lack of visible remains, it is not difficult to imagine his presence in this lonely spot.

In a smaller fenced area, on the opposite side of the road from the museum, are some further remains, including a large square bath, or fountain, on another small terrace formed by retaining walls. The site guard will unlock the gate on request.

Mount Lykaion
The Sanctuary of Zeus

The whole of Mount Lykaion was considered sacred by the ancient Arcadians. In the earliest myth, Lykaon, son of Pelasgos, founded not just the city of Lykosoura, but also the Lykaian Games on the mountain. He created the title of Lykaian Zeus, that is, Zeus of the Wolves. Arcadia claimed Mounta Lykaion as the birthplace of Zeus. The accepted myth was that he had been born on Crete. However, the Arcadians believed that the name referred to an area on the eastern slopes of the mountain called Kretea and that Rhea bathed the infant Zeus in the river Neda to the west (see Phigalea, Chapter 7). The river is named after one of the nymphs charged with his upbringing.

The altar to Zeus on the peak of the mountain was famous in antiquity for human sacrifice. Pausanias, in recounting the achievements of Lykaon, adds that he slaughtered a child, poured its blood on Zeus's altar, and at that moment was turned into a wolf. Thereafter, Pausanias refers to the practices at the altar only as 'secret sacrifices' and refuses to explain their nature further. He clearly believed that human sacrifice here was a reality. Yet, when the Greek Archaeological Service excavated the area of the altar at the beginning of the 20C, they found nothing but animal bones along with pottery fragments, clay figures and iron implements. Their finds indicated that the altar was first used in the late 7C BC. However recent excavations have now shown that there was activity here from 3000 BC although again only animal bones have been found.

The site divides into two main areas. The facilities for the Games were located on a small plateau below the final peak of the mountain. Here are the remains of the Hippodrome, with a stadium laid out in its centre. This is the only example of a racetrack for horses still visible anywhere in Greece. By the 2C AD the site was no longer being used. Nearby are the ruined foundations of a hostel, a stoa and a bathhouse. Somewhere nearby was another Sanctuary of Pan. On the peak stood the sacred precinct, or temenos, of Lykaian Zeus with the great ash altar above. The sanctity of the precinct was such that entry was totally forbidden. More remarkably, it was said that no living thing cast a shadow inside the precinct. Those who disregarded the prohibition on entry would die within a year.

It is 16km from Lykosoura to the peak of Lykaion. From the fork for the museum continue uphill, first through the village of Lykosoura, then through modern Lykaio, ignoring turns to left and right. After another 5km follow a sign left for Ano Karies (Ανω Καρυές). At the next junction, by a small church, Ano Karies is to the right, and Mount Lykaion to the left. A little further is a well-restored fountain with picnic tables. Beyond this, the raised circular stone platform of a threshing floor is visible below the road. At a final fork, keep left uphill. The asphalt road ends in the Hippodrome itself. To the left are the scattered remains of the hostel and stoa spread across the hillside. The bathhouse is beyond the far side of the Hippodrome slightly to the right. The unsigned dirt road that forks left uphill 200M before the Hippodrome, leads to the summit and the altar of Zeus. Half way up keep sharp left where another track goes straight on. Continue, making a complete circuit around the hill. Unless the winter weather has left the dirt road in a poor state, it is passable to vehicles, with care, all the way to the summit, where it ends in a flat area of about an acre, immediately below a conical mound.

After a short walk to the top of the mound, the visitor is rewarded with a brown sign for the altar and temenos of Zeus Lykaios and a view of half of the Peloponnese. As at Olympia, the altar itself was simply a huge mound of ash. Just below is a modern church, no doubt on an earlier foundation. To the left of the church, facing the Hippodrome below, are the two column bases on which stood the famous golden eagles mentioned by Pausanias. To the east are the twin power stations in the plain of Megalopolis. To the west the temple of Apollo at Bassae in its huge white tent is visible on the horizon 8km away.

Karitena (Καρίταινα) and Ancient Gortys
The Sanctuary of Asklepios

The route to Karitena from Megalopolis follows the broad valley of the Alpheios northwest. The distinctive outline of Karitena, on its hill crowned by a mediaeval castle, is visible from a considerable distance. Below this hill, the Alpheios forces its way through the mountains in a narrow gorge. After 16km the road reaches the Dimitsana junction. From here a minor road winds up the hill for 3km to the main square of Karitena. From the centre of this attractive village, signs point left to a footpath up to the castle on its rock hanging over the gorge. Founded by Hugh de Bruyéres in 1254, it is worth a visit for the view alone.

Beyond the square, the road continues downhill towards Atsicholos (Ατσίχολος) and the Lousios gorge. This is the easiest route to ancient Gortys. The Classical city stood on a small plateau above the gorge, but the most interesting of the remains are those of the Asklepion, or Sanctuary of Asklepios, beautifully situated by the river near a small chapel and an old pack-horse bridge.

Asklepios was the god of healing, although born a mortal. He was revered as the founder of medicine. The myth of his birth and life is a complicated story of divine jealousy and retribution. He was the son of Apollo and Koronis, daughter of Phlegyas, a Thessalian king. Apollo had fallen in love with Koronis and slept with her. Filled with rage at

118

his daughter's liaison with Apollo, Phlegyas set fire to the god's temple in Delphi. In retribution, Apollo killed him with his arrows and sent him to be punished in the underworld. Despite being pregnant with Apollo's child, Koronis had fallen in love with Ischys and now slept with him. A raven, that Apollo had left to watch over Koronis, told him of her infidelity so he killed both her and her lover. However he snatched Asklepios, her unborn child, from her funeral pyre unharmed. Later, Epidavros was to become known as the supposed birthplace of Asklepios, and a different version of his birth myth was told there (see Chapter 8).

Apollo entrusted the Centaur Kheiron (Chiron) with the upbringing of the infant Asklepios. Kheiron was a son of Kronos. He was said to be the wisest of the Centaurs, having learnt the skills of hunting, medicine, music, gymnastics and prophecy from Apollo and Artemis. Many of the great heroes are described as his pupils. While Asklepios was growing up, Kheiron taught him hunting and the art of healing. Asklepios became so skilled in this art that he was able to cure even those thought to be beyond hope. For this reason perhaps, he was said to be able to raise the dead. Another aspect of his myth however, explains that Athena had given him some of the blood of Medusa (see Chapter 8). Blood drawn from her left side would raise the dead, while that from the right would kill instantly. Eventually, after Asklepios had raised either Glaucus or Hippolytus from the dead, Zeus determined to stop men cheating death, and killed Asklepios with a thunderbolt. Later, at Apollo's request, he was resurrected as a god and Zeus placed him amongst the stars.

From Karitena the road towards Atsicholos runs north down to the river. By the modern bridge is the extremely picturesque single arched structure of its older Turkish predecessor. The road climbs the hill on the west bank for 3km. Half a kilometre before Atsicholos itself, a dirt road on the right with a sign for Αρχαία Γόρτυς, leads to the ancient sites. After 1.2km the dirt road forks. The right fork passes the acropolis of Gortys whose 4C BC walls and towers are visible across a field to the left. Beyond are the Kalamiou monasteries (Μονή Καλαμίου), which can be visited. The left fork continues to the riverside, 3km further on, by the small white chapel of Ayios Andrea (St. Andrew) possibly dating from the 11C AD. Another old arched bridge connects with both Elliniko and Stemnitsa on the Dimitsana road, via dirt tracks in the process of being upgraded

The Asklepion is just opposite the bridge and not immediately obvious as it is now below ground level. The best preserved feature of the

119

site is the elaborate bathing complex first built in the 4C BC. This structure had a pool with benches and individual niches, a furnace and a hypocaust system for heated rooms suggesting that health spas are not a modern idea. The large Doric temple of Asklepios, just to the north, originally held a statue of the god as a beardless youth. There are other remains scattered to the south including the foundations of houses, perhaps designed to accommodate visitors or patients.

The location alone makes Gortys worth a visit. From this spot it is possible to walk the length of the gorge as far as Dimitsana (see above). The inaccessibility of the area was a positive attraction for those seeking a monastic life, and monasteries were first established here in the 10C and 11C AD. A shorter walk can be made to the Prodromou monastery by following an obvious path up the west bank of the river. After about 1km the path crosses the river by the Prodromou bridge, then climbs to the monastery built into the cliff. On weekdays the gorge will be almost deserted.

Andritsena (Ανδρίτσαινα) to Olympia

From the Dimitsana junction below Karitena, the road west follows a serpentine route climbing for 35km up to the mountain village of Andritsena. It first crosses the Alpheios on a modern concrete bridge high over the gorge. Below is its unique mediaeval predecessor, a Frankish bridge incorporating a chapel against one of the piers. Beyond the bridge, the first section of the road describes an almost complete circle around Karitena providing a seemingly endless succession of views of the village and its castle.

Andritsena is possibly the most attractive of all the mountain villages, retaining an air of isolation and dignity. The wooden balconies of its houses overhang the road and a network of alleys climbs the hill above. Near the school, the Nikolopoulios library, founded in 1840, has over 20,000 volumes including rare English works about Greece. The village's main tourist attraction, the temple of Apollo at Bassae about 15km away, is described in Chapter 7.

Beyond Andritsena the road winds down the southern fringes of the Alpheios valley, the bare hillsides gradually giving way to a more verdant landscape. At Krestena (Κρέστενα), 45km from Andritsena, a right turn, signposted for Olympia, leads via Makrisa (Μακρίσια) and the Alpheios barrage to the modern village of Olympia.

7

Olympia and Ilia

Olympia
The greatest sanctuary of the Greek world.

Modern Olympia, like modern Delphi, exists purely to service the tourist trade. All routes into the village lead to the one main street. Hotels are visible everywhere on the small network of side streets. Although huge numbers of people visit the site, most come in organised groups and, when the tour buses leave for the day, the village can be surprisingly quiet. The archaeological site is ½km to the east of the village. The entrance to the site is to the right of the road immediately after crossing the Kladeos bridge. The archaeological museum is hidden at the far end of the large car park opposite. The site is open daily from 8.00 until 19.00. To see it without the vast number of people that arrive during the day, it is essential to start at 8.00. Weekends in particular are busy, as large numbers of Greeks now join the foreign visitors.

Olympia lies in the nome or county of Ilia (Ηλεία). The ancient name of Elis (Ηλις) was used both for the region as a whole and for the principal urban centre about 35km northwest, whose remains are still visible (see below). According to the records kept by the Elean officials who administered the Olympic Games in the Classical period, the first Olympiad was held in 776 BC. However, this was regarded as simply a restoration of earlier Games founded or restored by the great heroes and the gods themselves. This early mythology is extremely complicated, and the order in which the elements were added is not clear. Both Pelops and Hercules have important roles, but as Olympia is first and foremost the Sanctuary of Zeus, the foundation myths go back to his birth.

In the conventional, rather than the Arcadian, myth of Zeus's birth, Rhea entrusted the upbringing of the newborn Zeus to the Kouretes of Mount Ida on Crete. The Kouretes were five brothers. The eldest brother was called Herakles. (Not the Herakles, stepson of Amphitryon,

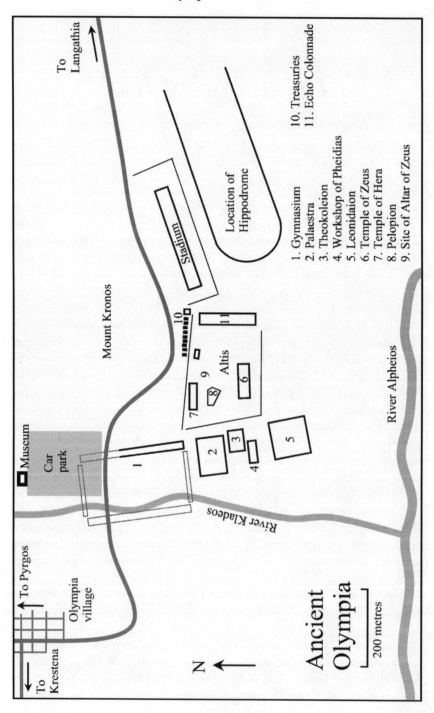

Ancient Olympia

200 metres

1. Gymnasium
2. Palaestra
3. Theokoleion
4. Workshop of Pheidias
5. Leonidaion
6. Temple of Zeus
7. Temple of Hera
8. Pelopion
9. Site of Altar of Zeus
10. Treasuries
11. Echo Colonnade

To Langathia

Location of Hippodrome

Stadium

Mount Kronos

Altis

River Alpheios

Museum

Car park

To Pyrgos

Olympia village

To Krestena

River Kladeos

N

who we know as Hercules). This Herakles organised the very first Games in celebration of Zeus's triumph over Kronos. His brothers raced among themselves. Apollo raced with Hermes and beat Ares at boxing. A later version of this myth has Klymenos, a descendant of Herakles of Crete, founding games at Olympia and setting up an altar to Herakles and the other Kouretes. Yet another legend has Endymion, son of Aethlios, and grandson of Zeus, driving Klymenos from the throne of Elis and creating a race at Olympia for his sons, with the throne as prize. However, the most important myth in the creation of the sanctuary at Olympia, is that of Pelops, who not only gained control of Olympia and celebrated the Games in great style, but also gave his name to the entire Peloponnese. His role was commemorated on the east pediment of the temple of Zeus, the centrepiece of the sanctuary, where a series of monumental sculptures depicted his famous chariot race (see below). The Pelopion, his sacred enclosure, was one of the earliest structures at Olympia.

Pelops's story begins with the myth of his birth. His father was Tantalos, king of Lydia and a son of Zeus by the nymph Pluto. At first, Tantalos was a favourite of the gods and often attended their banquets. He in turn invited the gods to a banquet where he secretly served up his son, whom he had cut to pieces and boiled. All the gods realised the true nature of the meat they were offered and refused to touch it. Demeter, however, was distracted with grief for her missing daughter Persephone and, without realising, ate part of Pelops's shoulder. This was not the first of Tantalos's crimes. He was said to have betrayed Zeus's secrets and also to have stolen the food of the gods. Zeus sentenced Tantalos to eternal torment in the underworld. He was forced to stand in the waters of a lake beneath the boughs of an overhanging fruit tree. Whenever he stooped to drink, the waters receded. Whenever he reached out for the abundant fruit hanging within reach, the wind would blow it away from his outstretched hand. Above the tree a huge stone was balanced, constantly threatening to fall and crush him. Thus he was condemned to perpetual thirst and hunger with the means of relief tantalisingly close but unreachable.

Zeus resolved to restore Pelops to life. He ordered Hermes to collect his limbs and boil them afresh in the cauldron. To replace his missing shoulder, Demeter gave him a new one of ivory. The reconstituted Pelops was of such beauty that Poseidon fell in love with him and gave him a winged chariot pulled by a team of immortal winged horses, capable of travelling over the sea. Although Pelops inherited his father's kingdom, he was forced to emigrate by barbarian invasions. He came to

Elis bringing his great wealth with him. Here he sought the hand of Hippodameia, daughter of Oinamaos, king of Pisa, a town very close to Olympia. Unfortunately, Oinamaos was determined to prevent his daughter marrying, either because he was in love with her himself, or because an oracle had foretold he would die at the hands of his son-in-law. He had already disposed of many of Hippodameia's suitors by challenging them to a chariot race with his daughter's hand as the reward for victory. The penalty for defeat was death. Although Oinamaos gave each contestant a considerable start in the race, he had been given his horses by Ares and there were none swifter. He was always able to overtake the unfortunate suitor and kill him with his spear. Pelops, of course, also had horses that he had received by divine gift. But to ensure that there was no possibility of defeat, he bribed Myrtilos, Oinamaos's charioteer, with the promise of half the kingdom if he would help him to defeat his master. Myrtilos replaced the lynch pins on the axles of Oinamaos's chariot with wax substitutes. At the critical moment in the race, when Oinamaos was poised to transfix Pelops with his spear, the wheels of his chariot came off and he was dragged to his death. Pelops took possession of the throne and married Hippodameia, but refused to keep his bargain with Myrtilos. He murdered him by casting him into the sea. As he died, Myrtilos cursed Pelops and all his descendants. Pelops's new kingdom flourished. He took possession of Olympia, and the Games he held in honour of Zeus surpassed any held before. Partly because of his wealth and partly because of judicious marriages by his many children, he eventually became the most powerful king in what became known as the Peloponnese. His son, Atreus, was to become king of Mycenae (see Chapter 8).

A further myth has Hercules, stepson of Amphitryon, founding or re-founding the Games. He was himself a great-grandson of Pelops and was said to have created the sanctuary known as the Pelopion and to have been the first to sacrifice to Pelops there. His Twelve Labours were the subject of a sculptured frieze inside the temple of Zeus. Hercules's connection with Olympia began with the fifth Labour imposed on him by Eurystheus. He was instructed to clean the cattle yard of Augius, better known as the Augian stables. Augius was the great grandson of Endymion and king of Elis. He owned 3000 oxen, and his cattle yard had not been cleaned for 30 years. Their dung filled the yard and was spread across the pastures making them unusable. Hercules was given only one day in which to perform his task. Seeking to profit from his Labour, Hercules went to Augius and, without mentioning his obligation to Eurystheus, offered to clean the yard in one day, in exchange for a tenth part of his cattle. Augius agreed, despite his belief that the task was impossible in so short a time. Hercules diverted the river Phenios, so that it flowed first through the cattle yard and then across the pastures, clearing everything in its path. Augius, on hearing that Hercules had been commanded by Eurystheus in his task, refused to pay the agreed price, arguing, that in any case, it was the river gods who had done the work. When Augius's son, Phyleas, testified that both parties had made their bargain under oath, Augius banished him from Elis. Later, after the completion of his Labours, and various other adventures, Hercules took his revenge on Augius. He captured and looted Elis with an army raised from Argos, Thebes and Arcadia. Pylos and Pisa fought alongside Elis. Hercules sacked Pylos, but left Pisa untouched. The Delphic oracle had warned him that Pisa and its territory, including Olympia, belonged to Zeus. Having taken his revenge, he handed Elis back to Phyleas, because of his honourable conduct. Tradition then has Hercules holding the Games, pacing out the distance for the footrace himself by placing one foot in front of another 600 times. Iolaos, his companion and nephew, won the chariot race, Castor won the foot race and Polydeuces won the boxing.

Pausanias records that the Games died out after Hercules held them. They were not revived until the reign of Iphitos. Tradition has the Delphic oracle instructing Iphitos to renew the Games and institute the Olympic Truce. This established that the land of Elis was sacred to Zeus. No one could enter armed with weapons. During the period of the Games, warfare between Greek states had to cease wherever it took place. A list of victors, produced in the 5C BC but starting with the very first foot race, gives this date as 776 BC. The winner of this simple race of one stadion, 600 ancient feet, was Koroibos of Elis. He can be considered the first non-mythical Olympic victor.

Over the centuries, the Games became ever more elaborate. The Pentathlon, which consisted of the long jump, discus, javelin, running and wrestling, began in 708 BC. The first horse races were held in 648 BC and the first chariot races in 408 BC. The Games grew from a simple one-day event to a major spectacle lasting 5 days. They were to last for over a thousand years.

Although, for most of this period, control of the Games was in the hands of the Eleans, it was disputed by the town of Pisa, to which the sanctuary had originally belonged. This seems to be reflected in the various foundation myths, where one version has a king of Elis holding the Games, and another, a king of Pisa. In the Elean records, the Games held in the brief periods of Pisan control, were not recognised as Olympiads. The dispute frequently led to conflict which was finally resolved in 472 BC by the complete defeat and destruction of Pisa. The temple of Zeus was said to have been built from the spoils of this war.

The Games continued well into the Roman period, ending only in 393 AD when Theodosius I suppressed every pagan festival in the empire. His namesake, Theodosius II, had the sacred precinct burnt. In the centuries that followed, earthquakes and landslips caused much destruction. The collapsed buildings were subsequently buried by silt and mud as the river Alpheios changed its course, sweeping away the Hippodrome in the process. By the 19C there was little to see. Excavation by German archaeologists began as early as 1875. Not until after the Second World War were the resources available to clear the completely buried stadium. Today the site is pleasantly wooded again, as it was in antiquity, and the Alpheios flows unseen ½km to the south. In the 2004 Olympics, the shot-put events were held here.

Visiting the Site

Although it was the size of many Greek cities, there was no permanent settlement at Olympia. At the centre of the site was the Sanctuary of Zeus, a walled precinct filled with temples, altars and statues. Around this precinct were administrative buildings, training facilities, bathhouses, and, of course, the structures necessary for the Games themselves, the stadium and the hippodrome.

Even after over 100 years of effort Olympia is not fully excavated. This becomes apparent immediately on entering the site where the remains of the gymnasium emerge from the ground to the right of the path. Only the south east corner of this huge colonnaded court (210M x 100M) has been excavated. The northern part extends under the road and beneath the car park. The western side has been swept away by the river Kladeos. The gymnasium was designed to allow the runners to practice in all weathers. Its long eastern colonnade was the same length as the stadium.

The gymnasium is the first of a line of buildings that supported the religious and athletic life of the sanctuary. Beyond the gymnasium is the palaestra, also used for athletic practice. Continuing south the next building is the Theokoleion, or priests house. Behind that is the workshop of Pheidias, later converted into a Christian church, and further again is the Leonidaion, an elaborate colonnaded building that formed an hotel for distinguished visitors. These structures occupy the western

126

part of the site. To the east is the trapezoid enclosure of the Altis, or Sacred Grove, the Sanctuary of Zeus itself. The sanctuary was dominated by the Doric temple of Zeus erected in the mid 5C BC. It stands on a 3M high platform and must have towered over the other buildings. It contained Pheidias's famous ivory and gold statue of Zeus seated on a throne, one of the Seven Wonders of the World. His workshop, nearby, was constructed to the same dimensions as the interior of the temple, so that the statue, which was built in sections, could be fully assembled and then re-erected in its final resting place when complete. After the closure of the sanctuary at the end of the 4C AD, the statue may have been carried off to Constantinople. The destruction of the temple by earthquakes in the 6C AD completed the work of Theodosius. The columns on the south side still lie as they fell. A single column has recently been re-erected.

The temple of Zeus was a relative latecomer to the Altis. The temple of Hera in the northeast corner of the enclosure is much older and was completed in about 600 BC. It was probably a joint temple of Zeus and Hera before the temple of Zeus was built. Later it seems to have functioned as a Treasury for the sanctuary. The oldest sacred area that can still be identified is the Pelopion, a grove that contained a low mound and an altar to Pelops, surrounded by a wall. This dates from 1100 BC. There was apparently a similar enclosure to Pelops's wife, Hippodameia. Olympia may, like Delphi, originally have been a sanctuary and oracle to Gaia. Pausanias mentions an altar to Mother Earth, but this has not been found. It may have been outside the Altis itself, on Mount Kronos, the conical tree covered hill immediately to the north. This was said to have an altar to Kronos on its peak, although no trace remains. In total, Pausanias lists 69 altars in the Altis.

The altar of Zeus stood, not in the usual position in front of its own temple, but to the east of the temple of Hera and the Pelopion. Like the great altar on Mount Lykaion, it was built from the ash of the sacrifices. It stood 7M tall. Not surprisingly, not a trace of such fragile material remains. To the north of the Altis, a line of Treasuries stands on a terrace at the foot of Mount Kronos. These small, temple-shaped buildings were used to house offerings from individual cities, principally Greek colonies. The eastern side of the precinct is bordered by the remains of the Echo Colonnade, named after its seven-fold echo and dating from the reign of Philip II of Macedon. Behind the colonnade is the Stadium, reached by a vaulted tunnel at the northeast corner of the Altis. The stadium was rebuilt three times, the last being in the 4C BC. The earlier versions ran into the Altis. Each successive rebuilding moved the track east and enlarged the spectator terraces. Sometime in the Middle Ages the river Alpheios changed its course and washed away a large part of the eastern and southern terraces. The stadium was filled with silt and mud to a depth of 5M. When this vast mass of material was removed, it revealed the original track level with the starting and finishing lines in position and the water supply around the edge of the track in place. The excavated sediment was used to reconstruct the spectator terraces to their 4C form. The re-created stadium was inaugurated in June 1961.

Although women were prohibited from attending the Games and, in fact, from the whole area north of the Alpheios, there was a separate festival of Hera with its own foot races, held every four years. Pausanias tells us that the races took place in the stadium over a slightly shorter course. They were for virgin girls, who ran in short tunics, with their hair let down and their right breast and shoulder bared. These games also had a mythical beginning and were said to have been founded by Hippodameia in thanks for her marriage to Pelops.

Horse racing took place in the Hippodrome, which lay further south and east of the stadium. Its circuit was over 1km long. Although there is a good description of it from Pausanias, who gives a detailed explanation of the elaborate system of starting gates, the physical remains have been completely swept away by the river. As at Isthmia, the racecourse was reputed to be haunted by a Horse-scarer. The horses panicked as they galloped past a small tumulus by the side of the course. The horse-scarer was said to be variously Myrtilos, Oinamaos or Horse-Poseidon himself.

New archaeological work is in progress at the site. Information boards are being erected with good site plans. Because much of the site was buried for centuries, the finds displayed in the museum are particularly fine. The major sculptural groups from the temple of Zeus are displayed there, and a visit is recommended.

Ancient sites of Ilia

If Olympia represents Greece to the organised tour, then the remainder of Ilia must be considered undiscovered territory. Of course, a few foreign visitors do reach the sites described below, but it is more than likely that they will be deserted. Ancient Elis, to the north, is little visited despite the close connection between the city and Olympia. To the east, Typaneai and Alifera are glorious, isolated locations that provide a marvellous introduction to exploration of the broad Alpheios valley.

Olympia and Ilia

This is the landscape that most closely resembles the 'arcadian' image people carry of Classical Greece. South of Olympia is the more intimate landscape of the Neda valley. Although the remains of ancient Lepreo and Phigalea are not outstanding in their own right, the beauty of their locations completely justifies a visit. It is possible to combine Typaneai, Alifera, Lepreo and Phigalea with a visit to the temple of Apollo at Bassae in a long day's circular tour.

Ancient Elis
The Olympian competitors' training ground.

To reach ancient Elis (Ηλις, also Ilida, Ηλιδα), from Olympia, take the main road to Pyrgos (Πύργος). Keep to the bypass around the town and, after 23km towards Patras, turn right at the Gastouni crossroads. The site is signposted from this point and lies 10km along the road just after the village of Avgio (Αυγείο). The modern road cuts right through the site, which has been recently cleared. New archaeological work is in progress. The museum lies to the left of the road, just after the first excavations become visible.

Elis was not only the administrative centre of the Olympic Games but also the place where the athletes spent their last month of practice prior to the competitions themselves. The city therefore had to provide training facilities and it is known to have had gymnasia and running tracks. The site is generally accessible, even though the new excavation work is fenced off. The museum stands on a slight ridge overlooking the Pinios valley to the north and has a good site plan. It is open every day 08.30 to 15.00, but closed on Mondays. A path leads from the side of the museum to the theatre built against the natural slope. The cavea, or auditorium, was of simple earth construction but with retaining walls to give the necessary curvature. Unusually, there was no stone seating. The buildings of the agora stretched to the north and west and are currently being re-investigated. Good views of the new excavations can be obtained from the road, as the modern surface is several metres above the original ancient street levels.

The archaeological work at the site has shown a history of settlement from the 11C BC onwards. Political leadership of Ilia from a central site may therefore correspond with the role of Elis in the mythical history of Olympia.

Typaneai (Platiana)

Ancient Typaneai, also possibly identified with Homeric Aipy, can be found off the Krestena – Andritsena road on a small hill above the modern village of Platiana (Πλατιάνα). The unenclosed site has no known mythological connections, beyond the single mention of Aipy in the Iliad, and the visible remains are modest, but it is still a superb example of a rural city of the 4C or 3C BC in miniature. Inside the circuit wall that completely encloses the flat-topped hill, is the tiny theatre, an equally small agora, water storage cisterns, and two Christian churches perhaps on the sites of earlier sanctuaries. The setting is spectacular with views in all directions over the archetypal arcadian landscape.

The village of Platiana lies just off the main road to Andritsena, about 18km from Krestena. The turn for the village is well signposted and there is the usual brown sign indicating 'Archaeological Site'. The road leads ½km up into the village. Entering the village, the road narrows. Keep right at a fork, then at a T-junction with a brown sign turn right. This goes through the top of the village on an asphalt road winding between the houses. Keep left at a fork on the edge of the village and follow the road uphill. The new tarmac surface soon turns to gravel. This is a well-used back road that eventually leads to Zacharo on the coast. At a junction, a brown sign indicates left. At a final junction where the right fork leads over the hill and down towards Zacharo, another brown sign points left. After about 200M a final brown sign appears, placed apparently at random, by the side of the road. The site lies on the hilltop above. Ignore this sign and carry on up the dirt road until, a few hundred metres further on, the road ends. There is ample space here to turn around. The total distance from the main road below is 5km. The route to the summit is concealed about 20M past the end of the road, on the right. From here a path, newly improved with steps, climbs the scrub-covered slope. After 200M, a line of walls appears on the crest of the hill. The path emerges onto the flat summit a few metres to the east of the small theatre built directly against the circuit wall.

Although the seats of the theatre are in very poor condition, the curve of the cavea can still be made out. A single stone throne remains. The unusual layout of the theatre mirrors that of the much better preserved example at Pleuron (Chapter 4). The hill forms a long, narrow, steep-sided ridge or plateau over 600M long but in places hardly 30M wide. The hilltop has recently been cleared of the trees and scrub that were beginning to conceal much of the remains. It appears to be divided into several terraces, natural or enhanced by human intervention. For the most part, the buildings of the interior are reduced to foundations. The walls, which are probably 3C BC, closely follow the north edge of the ridge, and are visible for much of their length as two or three courses of regular, squared blocks. To the south, the walls run east to west halfway down the slope, so that a considerable area of steep ground is incorporated into the circuit in addition to the flat area of the ridge. The walls are generally more impressive when seen from below. Immediately to the west of the theatre, the highest terrace forms a small acropolis, and seems to have been fortified separately. The remainder of the terrace to the east of the theatre may have been the agora. A large cistern is cut into the rock and traces of the lining, of plaster reinforced with tiny stone fragments, remain. It is not obvious how cisterns on such an isolated height would be kept supplied with water. Further east again, it is possible to make out the trace of two mediaeval churches of simple basilican form with apsidal east ends. At the very eastern end of the plateau, a little way down the slope to the south, a gate can still be identified.

Ultimately though, you do not come here for the fragmentary remains, but to wonder at such a magnificent location for a town. The stunning views include the coast to the south, the mountains east towards Andritsena, and the great bowl of the Alpheios valley to the north. Olympia and mass tourism are ten miles away, as the crow flies. It could be a thousand.

Alifera (Aliphera, Αλίφειρα)
Temple of Athena and sanctuary of Asklepios.

Ancient Alifera lies on top of a high, wooded hill above the modern village of the same name about 12km up the valley from Platiana. It was an Arcadian border town named after Alipheros, a son of Lykaon (see Chapter 6, Lykosoura). It was known for its sanctuaries of Asklepios and Athena. The city had its own version of Athena's birth myth.

Alifera seems to have existed from at least the 6C BC, but lost much of its population when Megalopolis was founded. It was conquered by Philip V of Macedon and later became one of the cities of the Achaian League. By Pausanias's time it was reduced to a small town.

Athena was the daughter of Zeus by his first wife Metis, a daughter of Oceanus and Tethys, and the personification of wisdom and prudence. The story of Athena's birth is a strange one. Zeus had lusted after Metis, but she had resisted his advances and used her ability to

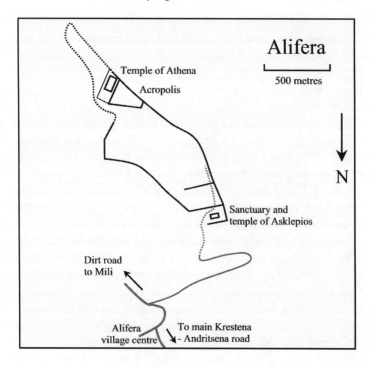

change her form to escape him. However, such was Zeus's determination that eventually she relented and became pregnant. Zeus then learned from Gaia and Ouranos that it had been foretold that Metis would first bear a daughter, Athena, and afterwards a son who would overthrow Zeus, as he had overthrown his own father Kronos. To avoid this, Zeus copied his father by swallowing Metis. Some time later, Zeus developed a terrible headache that made him howl with pain. His cries brought Hermes who realised the cause. He called for Hephaistos to bring a wedge and cut a hole in Zeus's skull. Out sprang Athena, fully grown and dressed in armour.

Athena combined the qualities of her parents, acquiring her power from her father and her wisdom from her mother. Her appearance fully armed represents her role as protector of cities. Although she is now identified principally with Athens, many cities claimed her as their patron deity. She was also the goddess of law and order, and hence the protector of social stability. Her birth from Zeus's head was supposed to have happened by the banks of the river Triton. The myths generally place this river in Libya, or in Viotia, but the Aliferans believed that Athena was born and raised in their country. They had a legend that connected the river to a water-fountain called Tritonis. Pausanias tells us that Alifera had an altar of 'Zeus in Bed' commemorating Athena's birth and a fine bronze statue of the goddess. There can be little doubt of her importance to the city, for the foundations of a large temple dedicated to her can still be seen on the hilltop.

Twelve kilometres from Platiana, towards Andritsena, is the tiny roadside village of Kato Amigdalies (Κάτω Αμυγδαλιές). Take a left turn here, where there are various signs for the Archaeological Site. The road follows the edge of a side valley and passes the gate of the monastery of Sepetou hidden below. After 4km the road runs downhill into the modern village of Alifera. At a T-junction, a brown sign indicates right to Archaia Alifera. The road quickly turns to gravel. Turn sharp right by more signs and climb slowly uphill. (The dirt road that carries straight on at this point eventually returns to the main Andritsena road near Mili further up the valley). After about ½km, the road forks right to some farm sheds. Take the left fork that winds uphill. If the track is heavily overgrown, park at this point and walk. After 1km there is a sign and a notice board with a good pictorial representation of the site. An obvious footpath from here winds up through scrub vegetation. If in doubt, continue uphill. The entire site is unenclosed.

The path first reaches the temple of Asklepios, a plain, rectangular building with three courses of its walls in situ. In the centre of the temple, the base of the cult statue is still in position. There are foundations of the altar to the east. Another building opposite was perhaps the healing area of the Asklepion. Above, the hill is divided into a series of large terraces, cleared of undergrowth. The largest of these formed the main area of the city but is now virtually devoid of buildings. Beyond, at the highest point of the hill, a fortified area may have been the acropolis. Here are the best preserved sections of wall. From this point there is a good view of the whole site and the line of the walls can be traced to the north. Behind the acropolis, on a lower terrace, are the massive foundations of the temple of Athena. This Doric temple dates from the late 6C BC. It was built on a north-south axis like many Arcadian temples. It was surrounded by a colonnade of 15 x 6 columns. Here stood the bronze statue of Athena seen by Pausanias. As at Platiana, the views extend in all directions. Here they are even more spectacular.

The city's Necropolis lay on the lower slopes of the hill to the east and south. A well-preserved Hellenistic tomb dug into the hillside, with an elaborate pedimented front, can be seen by taking the dirt road to Mili (Μύλοι) mentioned above. It lies by the roadside 1½km from the fork.

Bassae (Bassai, Vasses, Βάσσαι, Βάσσες)
The temple of Apollo the helper.

The remarkably well-preserved temple of Apollo at Bassae stands on the rocky slopes of Mount Kotilion, 14km above Andritsena. Old post-cards are still available that show views of the temple standing roofless, but otherwise almost complete, in wild and open countryside. However this view has not been seen for two decades. A long term conservation project is in progress, designed to restore and protect the building. A massive tent has been erected over the temple, completely enclosing it. As engineering, this structure is almost as imposing as the monument it now conceals, although the covering is now stained and patched and becomes more so with the passing of each winter. More importantly, the visitor seeking to view the temple is completely restricted to the estab-lished opening times (8.30 – 15.00 daily). Approaching Andritsena from Krestena, the right turn for Bassae is at the entrance to the village. The road climbs steeply up the left hand side of a deep valley. Circular stone threshing floors can be seen in numerous places, evidence of the intensity with which this landscape was once farmed. The tent enclosing the temple can be seen from some distance as a brilliant white mass on the hillside. The eye has difficulty resolving its size and form. The site lies a short distance above a car park by the side of the road.

Commentators from the 19C onwards would describe the temple as standing in isolation on a remote mountain. This is certainly how it ap-pears today. In the 5C BC however, this was far from the case. It was the centre of a sacred precinct, or precincts, that stretched over ½km up the mountain to its peak. In addition to the temple of Apollo, there were further temples to Artemis and Aphrodite and numerous other buildings to the north, of which only traces now survive. The sanctuary's parent city was Phigalea, 6km to the southwest. The temple to Apollo was the fourth built on the site, which seems to have been in use since the 7C BC. The citizens of Phigalea rebuilt the temple in about 420 BC in gratitude to Apollo for saving them from a plague. The dedication is therefore to Apollo Epikourios, that is, Apollo the Helper. The work was entrusted to Iktinos, the architect of the Parthenon. The temple was unknown to Western Europe until 1765. At the beginning of the 19C it became one of the first sites in mainland Greece to be investigated. Cockerell and others found the interior of the temple full of stone blocks, sculpture fragments and frieze slabs. From this debris they were able to recover the sculptured frieze that ran around the interior walls depicting battles between Centaurs and Lapiths and between Greeks and

Amazons. This frieze is now in the British Museum. Today, inside the tent, the temple is difficult to appreciate as a whole, and the interior is no longer accessible to the public. Nevertheless it is still possible to distinguish the building's unusual features. Its orientation, like that at Alifera above, is north to south. It was roofed not with clay tiles, but with slabs of Parian marble. The external colonnade is virtually complete, consisting of 6 Doric columns on the short axis and 15 on the long. Inside the cella, the two rows of internal Ionic columns are not freestanding, but are connected to the side walls by short extensions or buttresses. The southern-most pair of these is set diagonally to the wall, and between them stood a single Corinthian column, the earliest known. Unfortunately only drawings of its acanthus capital survive.

The southern third of the cella, separated from the main part by this curious arrangement of pillars, contained the cult statue. This may have faced the door placed in the eastern side wall, another unusual feature. No base for a statue has been discovered, but the expedition of 1812 discovered statue fragments on this spot. Whether this replaced the bronze statue of Apollo that Pausanias tells us was taken to Megalopolis, or whether that always stood elsewhere, is unknown.

Above the temple there are extensive views over the bare mountains. The dome of the other great sacred site of Arcadia, Mount Lykaion is visible 8km to the east.

Phigalea (Figalia, Phigaleia, Φιγαλεία)
An unexcavated classical city

Ancient Phigalea is an extensive site, almost entirely unexcavated. A village still occupies the centre of the ancient city, and the original water sources are still in use. Although modern signs now point out the obvious sights around the village, there is clearly still much to be found. Here, perhaps, the visitor can recapture a little of the atmosphere of 19C exploration, when antiquities remained to be discovered.

From Bassae the road leads downhill towards the Neda gorge. The road first skirts the village of Dragogi (Δραγώγι) and then reaches the larger settlement of Perivolia (Περιβόλια) after a total of 8km. Here, a sharp left turn is signposted to ancient Phigalea. After 2km the road cuts through the line of the ancient city walls and 1km further reaches the modern village, beautifully situated on a plateau high above the deep gorge of the Neda. Ancient Phigalea was yet another Arcadian town named after a son of Lykaon, in this case Phigalos. The site seems to

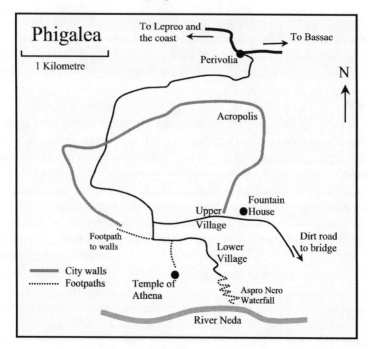

have been continuously occupied since the Late Bronze Age. It had a history of antagonism with Sparta, was a member of the Aitolian and Achaian Leagues, and was still occupied in the Roman era. The city has never been excavated or even accurately surveyed. The visible remains are widely scattered. The circuit of the walls is almost 5km in length. Long sections with towers, dating probably from the 4C BC can be explored. At the edge of the village, the road suddenly acquires a marble paved surface, recently laid. At a junction this swings left and leads through the upper village passing a fountain built into the wall, a new café-bar and the church. On the far side of the village it reaches the remains of the Hellenistic fountain house beneath a massive plane tree. The water still flows into the ancient draw-basin, in front of which are the foundations of the elaborate columned façade. A dirt road, in the process of being improved, continues on down to the river Neda and a new concrete bridge to the south.

Straight on at the junction above, a dirt road leads in 100M to an information board describing the area and several direction signs. A footpath leads off to the right to the best preserved stretch of walls. Nearby, hidden in the undergrowth, are traces of a colonnaded stoa that formed one side of the agora. The dirt road swings left and leads to the lower village, invisible at this point, and surprisingly large. After 50m another track, with a brown sign, 'Archaeological Site', leads right, onto a low hill to the remains of a small temple of Athena. The excavations are fenced but not locked. By keeping straight on into the lower village, it is possible to walk down into the gorge and the waterfall of Aspro Nero (Ασπρο Νερό, White Water). The road zigzags down through the houses to a well maintained but steep path. There are numerous signs. Here, in the Neda, Rhea bathed the infant Zeus (see Chapter 6, Lykaion). In antiquity, as it does today, the river formed the boundary between Ilia and Messenia.

Behind the village, the walls climb towards the acropolis hill. A church now occupies the site of a sanctuary of Artemis Sotiros, the saviour, on the summit. Recent work on improving the road through the upper village has revealed ancient stones just below the surface. Somewhere, there is a temple of Dionysus. There is much more of ancient Phigalea waiting to be found.

Lepreo (Λέπρεο)
Temple of Demeter

Lepreo is a small site, beautifully situated above a wooded valley within sight of the sea. Inside the ruins of the circuit wall of the acropolis stand the remains of a 4C BC Doric temple of Demeter. The site can be visited by making a small detour on the road from Phigalea to the coast. It is unenclosed and easily accessible.

Lepreo had no shortage of foundation myths. From Herodotus there is a myth linking the city with the descendants of the Argonauts. The crew of the Argo accompanying Jason on the great expedition for the Golden Fleece were often known as the Minyae, or Minyans, because so many of them were descendants of King Minyas (see Chapter 3, Orchomenos). Early in their journey, the Argonauts called in at the island of Lemnos. The women of Lemnos had previously killed all the men of the island in revenge for the ill treatment they had received. They proceeded to take the Argonauts as lovers, and as a result the island was repopulated. The descendants of the generation that the Argonauts fathered also called themselves Minyae. Three generations later, the Minyae were driven out of Lemnos by Pelasgian invaders. They made their way to the Peloponnese and were welcomed by the Spartans because their great heroes Castor and Polydeuces had been among the Argo's crew. Although the Minyae were given allotments of land and

137

Figure 15 Lepreo: The Temple of Demeter

took Spartan wives, they soon began to demand power within Sparta and were condemned to death. They were freed by a subterfuge of their wives who, being Spartans themselves, were able to visit them in prison. They exchanged clothes with their husbands, who made their escape in disguise. The majority of the Minyae made their way to Triphylia, the southern part of Elis, and founded six new towns for themselves, one of which was Lepreo.

Pausanias offers three separate explanations of Lepreo's origin. In the first, Lepreo is named after its unfortunate first settlers who contracted leprosy. In the second, the town was founded by Leprea, daughter of Pyrgeus. In the third, and most elaborate tale, its founder is Pyrgeus's son, Lepreos, famous for taking part in an eating contest with Hercules, in which each of them slaughtered, cooked and ate an ox. Having proved that he was as great an eater, Lepreos foolishly challenged Hercules to a fight. He was killed and buried at Phigalea.

From Phigalea, return to the Bassae road. West from Perivolia, the road is forced north by the deep ravines formed by tributaries of the Neda. The road passes through the villages of Petralona and Nea Phigalea. The countryside gradually acquires a green, wooded aspect again after the austerity of the mountains. Approaching the modern village of Lepreo, a brown sign indicates the slight remains of prehistoric Lepreo on the left. Drive through the village. On its western edge, a brown sign

138

points right to, 'Archaeological Site – Acropolis of Lepreo'. A rough and steep concrete road that requires first gear for the first 200 metres quickly leads to a good asphalt surface. After 1.7km, at the point where the tarmac becomes dirt, another sign points to the right up a footpath. The road is shaded by pine trees and there is room to park.

The path almost immediately reaches the walls of the acropolis. A simple outline map of the site has been painted on a board beside the first stretch of fallen masonry. It shows the acropolis to be roughly L-shaped. The best preserved section of the circuit is that immediately visible. One of the towers has been converted into a roofed shed. Beyond, the walls enclose the southern section of the citadel that forms the precinct of the temple of Demeter. The whole area is attractively wooded and much of the interior of the acropolis is still olive grove. However, the area round the temple has been cleared and the foundations are well preserved. The well-weathered stone drums from the collapsed columns have been carefully laid out to one side of the temple. The surroundings are superb and the view magnificent.

Beyond Lepreo, it is further 8km to the main coastal highway at Kato Taxiarches (Κάτο Ταξιάχες). Olympia is then 40km to the north.

8

Corinth to the Argolid

The Nome of Argolida, Argolis or the Argolid, has the greatest concentration of archaeological sites in Greece, together with a wealth of myth. The area is relatively compact and can easily be explored from a fixed point. A week would be required to see all that the area has to offer. For many people, Nauplio will be the most convenient base, with the archaeological sites of Mycenae, Epidavros, Tiryns, Midea, Lerna, Asine, Argos and the Argive Heraion all within a radius of fifteen miles. A number of coastal resorts, Palaia Epidavros, Tolo, Drepanon, can be used as cheaper and, out of season, quieter alternatives. All of these places can now be reached from Athens airport in less than three hours.

There are three possible routes south from Corinth. The first follows the old Corinth-Tripoli road, past the junctions for Nemea and Mycenae, and then on to Argos, where a left fork leads to Nauplio on the coast. The second takes the coastal road, turning left for Epidavros shortly after crossing the Corinth canal. At Palaia Epidavros the road turns inland for Nauplio. The third and quickest route follows the Tripoli motorway to the Sterna (Στέρνα) interchange. Leave the motorway here and follow the improved road that runs southeast to join the first route above, just north of Argos.

Palaia Epidavros (Παλαιά Επίδαυρος)
The site of the ancient city that controlled the great Sanctuary of Asklepios 10km inland.

Heading south from the canal for 35km the coastal road reaches first Nea Epidavros (Νέα Επίδαυρος). This 'New' village is new only in the sense that its oldest structures belong to the crumbling mediaeval castle above the village. Seven kilometres further on is the left turn for the seaside village and small holiday resort of Palaia (old) Epidavros, built

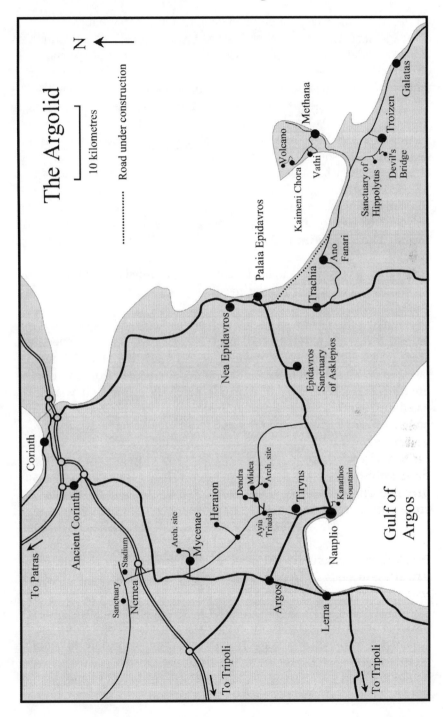

N ←

The Argolid

10 kilometres

·········· Road under construction

Corinth

To Patras →

Ancient Corinth

Sanctuary
Nemea
Stadium

To Tripoli →

Mycenae
Arch. site

Heraion

Ayia
Triada

Dendra
Midea
Arch. site

Argos

To Tripoli →

Lerna

Tiryns

Nauplio

Kanathos
Fountain

Gulf of
Argos

Epidavros
Sanctuary
of Asklepios

Nea Epidavros

Palaia Epidavros

Trachia

Ano
Fanari

Volcano

Kaimeni Chora

Vathi

Methana

Sanctuary of
Hippolytus

Devil's
Bridge

Troizen

Galatas

on the site of the Classical city and now attempting to rename itself Archaia (ancient) Epidavros. Note that the brown sign at this junction that reads "Small Theatre of Epidavros" refers to the theatre of the classical city described below, while the sign that reads "Ancient Theatre of Epidavros" refers to the Sanctuary of Asklepios 10km away.

The village centre is five minutes downhill from the main road. There is a spacious square by the quayside, reached by following the signs to the harbour. The village is built around a pleasant bay, with a headland to the south on which stood the ancient city. This is a typical city site of the Classical period, built on a defensible promontory surrounded by the small agricultural plain that formed the basis of the economy. It was known to Homer and appears several times in the complicated history of the Peloponnesian War, when it was an ally of Sparta. The antiquities that remain visible are modest but include the small theatre and the site of a sanctuary of Aphrodite. The promontory is largely unexcavated and much of it remains cultivated. The fragments of masonry that appear among the orange groves would indicate that there is more to be revealed.

To reach the theatre, walk around the harbour and follow the road along the shore below the headland. Take the path between fenced orange groves indicated by a brown sign. At a junction after 200 metres take the path to the right and, after 300M, it emerges from the orange groves to reveal the theatre. Recently carefully restored, it was dedicated to Dionysus and could seat 2000. It was first built in the 4C BC and modifications were made right up to the Roman period.

Above the theatre, a white church crowns the low hill. This occupies the site of a Sanctuary of Aphrodite. To reach it, follow the broad path that climbs to the left of the theatre. After 200M, a crude wicket gate on the right leads via an obvious path uphill to the church. Behind the church are quite substantial remains of the sanctuary walls. Visible from here are those sections of the city wall that still stand across the southern flank of the headland. The main church of the village is on the much smaller rocky outcrop to the north of the harbour. This is built on the site of a Sanctuary of Hera. Below, in the shallow water of the harbour, traces of ancient walls can still be seen.

It was along this coastline, between Troizen and Athens, that Theseus performed his labours on his journey to claim his birthright. At Epidavros, Periphetes, a son of Hephaistos and lame like his father, would waylay travellers and murder them with his huge club. Theseus was able to parry his blows, wrench the club from his grasp and kill him with it. Thereafter, Theseus used the club himself.

Corinth to the Argolid

Troizen (Troezen, Trizina, Τροιζήν, Τροιζήνα)
Birthplace of Theseus and scene of the death of Hippolytus.

Ancient Troizen lies 25km to the south of Epidavros, a little way inland on the edge of the fertile coastal plain that formed its territory. As the birthplace of Theseus, the city has a rich mythology and both its myths and history are closely linked to Athens. When Xerxes's army marched into Attica and Athens was evacuated, Troizen sheltered much of the population.

Both Athena and Poseidon were worshipped as the city's patron deities. This unusual joint patronage was said to be Zeus's solution to a dispute between the two gods for control of the territory. The city's coins reflected this arrangement, showing both Athena's face and Poseidon's trident. The city is named after Troizen, a son of Pelops. He and his brother, Pittheus, came from Pisa (see Chapter 7), becoming joint kings with Aetios from the previous ruling family. However the sons of Pelops held the real power. When Troizen died, Pittheus consolidated the previous scattered settlements into one city, which he named after his dead brother.

Troizen lies on the coast of the Saronic Gulf and an earlier king of the area, named Saron, is said to have given his name to this sea. He was hunting deer one day when a hind fled into the sea to escape from the hunt. Saron dived in and swam in pursuit. It led him out into open water where he was overwhelmed by the waves and drowned.

The most famous of Troizen's myths are those of Theseus and his family. This story begins with the dynastic struggles of king Aegeus of Athens. His father, Pandion, had been expelled from Athens by his cousins, the sons of Metion. Pandion fled to Megara, between Elefsis and Corinth, and Aegeus was born there. When they became adults, Aegeus and his brothers, Pallas, Nisus and Luycus attacked Athens and Aegeus recovered the kingship. Aegeus's concern was now for the future of his dynasty. As neither his first wife Meta, nor his second, Chalciope, had borne him sons, he feared that his brother Pallas's 50 sons would overthrow him. Suspecting that his childless marriages might be the work of Aphrodite, the goddess of love, he therefore introduced her worship into Athens for the first time. He also decided to consult the oracle at Delphi about the problem but received the usual enigmatic prophecy that he did not understand. The oracle told him that he should not untie his wine-skin until he had reached the heights of Athens or he would one day die of grief. From Delphi, he went to Corinth to meet Medea, celebrated for her skill in magic. She offered to

143

cure him of his childlessness in exchange for his protection should she ever need it. From there he journeyed to Troizen to visit Pittheus. Aegeus, if he had understood the oracle, would have refrained from drinking. However Pittheus managed to make him drunk and then sent him to bed with his daughter Aethra. The next day Aegeus realised what he had done. Fearing that Aethra was pregnant, he told her that if she gave birth to a son, she should rear him without telling him who his father was. By this enforced secrecy Aegus hoped to protect the child from Pallas's sons. He then hid his sword and sandals under a large rock, known as the Altar of Strong Zeus. Before returning to Athens, he told Aethra that if the child could move the rock when he grew up and retrieve these objects, he should be sent to Athens with them. In due course, Aethra gave birth and the boy Theseus was brought up in Troizen by his grandfather Pittheus. However the myths manage to introduce doubt as to his parentage because they have Poseidon sleeping with Aethra on same night as Aegus.

When Theseus came to manhood, Aethra revealed the story of his birth. She took him to the altar stone, which he was able to move with ease to recover the sword and sandals. The altar has been known ever since as the Theseus Stone. Although his mother encouraged him to sail to Athens, Theseus insisted on making the journey by land. He wished to emulate the deeds of Hercules, his second cousin, by ridding the coast of the all the robbers and villains that infested it. These adventures became known as the Labours of Theseus.

Meanwhile, Medea had fled to Athens from Corinth after murdering Glauke (see Chapter 5). Aegeus had married her and she had borne him a son, Medus. When Theseus arrived in Athens, Medea recognized him immediately. Wishing to protect the position of her own son, she pointed out Theseus to Aegeus as an assassin. She arranged for Theseus to be invited to a banquet where Aegeus would offer him a cup of poisoned wine that she had prepared. However, when the moment came, Aegeus saw the carved hilt of the sword that Theseus carried and immediately recognized him as his son. General rejoicing followed. With Medea's plans destroyed, she fled from Athens with Medus. Theseus's next great adventure was to lead to the tragic death of Aegeus foretold in the prophecy.

While Theseus was growing up, Aegeus had been involved in a war with King Minos of Crete. Minos's son, Androgeos, had come to Athens as a guest of Aegeus to compete in the Panathenaic Games. After he had won in every competition, Aegeus had sent him to kill the Marathonian bull that Hercules had originally brought from Crete as his seventh Labour. Unfortunately, Androgeos was killed and Minos, seeking revenge, attacked Athens with his army, eventually extracting a terrible tribute from the Athenians. Every nine years Athens had to send seven maidens and seven youths to Crete as prey for the famous Minotaur, half bull, half man, kept in the labyrinth at Knossos.

When the third of these tributes was due, Theseus volunteered to be one of seven youths. He slew the Minotaur and escaped from the labyrinth with the help of Ariadne, Minos's daughter. Before setting out for Crete he had arranged that, on the return voyage, a white sail would be hoisted in place of the normal black, to signal the success of the expedition. As his ship approached Athens, he forgot his plan, and Aegeus, seeing the black sail, threw himself into the sea in despair, thinking that his son had perished. Henceforth the sea was known as the Aegean.

After his father's death, Theseus became king of Athens. He had a bastard son, Hippolytus, by Antiope, queen of the Amazons. After concluding a treaty with Deucalion of Crete, he married Deucalion's sister Phaedre, by whom he had two further sons. In order to avoid any dispute over the succession, he sent Hippolytus to Pittheus at Troizen, who adopted him as his heir. When, later, Phaedre travelled to Troizen with Theseus, she fell in love with Hippolytus on sight. She built the temple of Peeping Aphrodite next to the gymnasium where he trained each day naked, so that she could watch him unobserved. Eventually, when he had come to Athens for the Panathenaic festival, she sent him a letter confessing her love. Hippolytus was horrified and rejected her. Phaedre, in despair, wrote a note to Theseus accusing Hippolytus of raping her and then hanged herself. Theseus immediately banished Hippolytus from Athens. In his rage he also prayed to Poseidon to slay his son. Hippolytus had set off with his chariot and horses for Troizen. At a point where the road led by the seashore, Poseidon created a gigantic wave that carried a monstrous bull ashore. Hippolytus's horses were terrified. They bolted, overturned the chariot, and Hippolytus, tangled in the reins was dragged to his death.

Pausanias gives a detailed description of the city of Troizen. In his time, all the buildings that claimed a connection with the city's myths were still standing. As well as the temple of Peeping Aphrodite and the Theseus Stone, he describes a shrine or temple to Saviour Artemis, said to be where Dionysus returned from Hades with Semele, and where Hercules brought back Kerberos on his twelfth Labour. Today the visible remains are small-scale and scattered but curiously evocative.

From Palaia Epidavros, the main road swings west towards the Sanctuary of Asklepios and Nauplio. To reach Troizen, take the left fork that heads south towards Kranidi (Κρανίδι) and Portoheli (Πορτοχέλι). After 12km, beyond the village of Trachia (Τραχειά), a left turn signposted to Galatas (Γαλατάς) and Poros (Πόρος) heads back towards the coast via Ano Fanari (Ανω Φανάρι). This twisting route through the hills will eventually be bypassed by a new road being driven south from Palaia Epidavros along the shoreline.

Both the ancient city and the modern village of Trizina lie 2km inland of the main road. A prominent sign for the Poros centre of Psisiculture and a battered green sign for the archaeological site (ΤΡΟΙΖΗΝΑ ΑΡΧΑΙΟΤΗΤΕΣ) mark a right fork onto a narrow country lane. This leads, via a further left turn with a similar set of signs, to a brown sign for the Sanctuary of Hippolytus, pointing right, ½km, up a dirt track. There is room to park at the end of the track.

The site, which is unenclosed, consists of the Sanctuary of Hippolytus itself, the remains of a building complex tentatively identified as an Asklepion, and the more extensive remains of a Byzantine bishop's palace or church. Known as the Palaia Episkopi, this incorporates the remains of a Classical temple possibly that of Peeping Aphrodite.

Hippolytus was worshipped here as a Hero. Annual sacrifices were made and there was a tradition that a girl about to be married would bring a lock of her hair to the shrine to be dedicated. The graves of Hippolytus and Phaedre are said to be somewhere nearby.

For the most part, the ruins are reduced to their foundations, but some arcaded walls of the palace are still standing surrounded by a confusion of ancient blocks and pillars. The Asklepion has a complex arrangement of water channels still visible. In the distance can be seen a solitary tower, the principal fragment of the city walls still standing.

Return to the tarmac road. One kilometre further on, a sharp right turn at another junction leads to the tower and the Devil's Bridge. Here on this corner, directly beneath the road signs, is the rock said to be the Theseus Stone. Behind the Stone, half hidden by undergrowth, are some ruins, possibly Roman brickwork, identified by an old green sign as the site of a Sanctuary of the Muses.

The tower and other fragments of the city walls are ½km along the gravel road to the right. The lower half of the tower is classical, the upper half, mediaeval. After another ½km, the road ends by the edge of a small gorge. A path leads on to a natural rock arch over the narrow ravine known as the Devil's Bridge. The line of an ancient aqueduct and traces of its channel still exist.

Methana (Μέθανα)

Beyond the Theseus Stone, the road continues into the modern village of Trizina and then loops back to the main road. Offshore is the volcanic peninsula of Methana. Almost an island, it is connected to the mainland by a low, narrow isthmus. The main town is known for its warm water spa. The entire mountain is formed from ancient lava domes and lava flows. At its north-western corner is the site of the only volcanic eruption known on mainland Greece in historic times. Recorded by Strabo, the eruption is thought to have occurred in the 3C BC. It produced a new dome with a crater about 100M in diameter and 25M deep. The lava flows were over a kilometre long and extended to the sea on one side and to the village of Kaimeni Chora (Καημένη Χώρα) on the other. This name translates literally as burnt village.

To visit the volcano, take the road east from Methana town towards Vathi (Βαθή) and Megalochori (Μεγαλοχώρι). Vathi is an attractive fishing village built around a picturesque harbour, with tavernas on the quayside. A road runs south along the beach to ancient Methana, whose walls stand prominently on a small headland. Below the walls, a tiny Byzantine church now sits 2M below modern ground level.

The hamlet of Kaimeni Chora sits at the very edge of a lava flow, about 5km beyond Vathi. The houses have been built in positions that make it appear that the lava has flowed quite recently and stopped just short of their walls. To reach the volcano, drive through the village onto the dirt road that climbs the hillside beyond. The road initially climbs away from the volcano before doubling back. After about 1km a signed path leads off to left. The way-marked path briefly descends before rising to the crater. Although steep, it is a short and worthwhile walk offering a unique opportunity to enter a volcanic crater. In early spring the ground is carpeted with wild cyclamen.

Ancient Epidavros
The Sanctuary of Asklepios

Today, Epidavros is known principally for its magnificent theatre and the annual summer festival of Greek drama held there. It is a major tourist destination and much visited. There is no difficulty in finding the site as the main road south from Palaia Epidavros leads straight to it. Its fame throughout antiquity was as the principal Sanctuary of Asklepios, the healing god and the founder of medicine. The theatre was just one element of the various buildings in the sacred precinct. Although the cult of Asklepios appears to have originated in Thessaly, it reached Epidavros in the 6C BC and had spread throughout the Greek world by the 4C BC. The original Thessalian myth of his birth and upbringing was related in Chapter 6. In the later version, however, although Asklepios is still the son of Apollo and Koronis, his birthplace has become Epidavros itself.

Phlegyas, Koronis's father, was renowned for his plundering and cattle thefts from neighbouring states. Koronis accompanied her father on a visit to the territory of Epidavros when he came to gauge the military strength of the inhabitants. She neglected to tell him she was pregnant by Apollo, and gave birth secretly on Mount Titthion, a mountain to the northeast of the sanctuary. There she abandoned the child. A herd of goats was grazing on the mountain guarded by a goatherd and his dog. One of the goats left the herd to give the infant milk, and the dog stood guard over him. The goatherd came in search of his missing animals and found the child. When he attempted to pick him up, a flash of lightning warned him of the child's divinity and he turned away. Human intervention was avoided and the myth of Asklepios's divine upbringing and his tutelage by Apollo and Artemis was maintained.

The sanctuary was always controlled by the city of Epidavros on the coast. The first healing god worshipped here was Apollo himself. The art of healing was closely related to the art of prophecy, as the knowledge of medicine and healing was thought to be divinely revealed. A separate Sanctuary of Apollo Maleatas has been found about 600M to the northeast of the theatre. Excavations have revealed a succession of altars, the earliest dating from the Mycenaean period, and two temples to Apollo, the first dating from the 7C BC. Unfortunately this part of the site is not normally open to visitors.

The worship of Asklepios seems to have been introduced towards the end of the 6C BC alongside that of his father Apollo. From this date the sanctuary grew in size and importance. By the 4C BC, Asklepios was established as the main healing god of the Greeks. New sanctuaries were built everywhere, including Athens itself, the island of Kos and the Greek cities of Asia Minor. Those at Gortys (see Chapter 6) and Alifera (see Chapter 7) were erected in the 4C BC. The magnificent complex at Messene (Chapter 9) was probably built in the 2C BC. The cult had already spread to Rome by the 3C BC.

By the 4C BC, the sanctuary was the equal of Olympia in size and facilities, and had acquired a wide range of functions. The original religious buildings, the temples and altars, were surrounded by a complex

148

of facilities for patients, visitors and, no doubt, tourists. As well as the amenities of a fashionable health resort, there was also the infrastructure necessary for the Asklepieia, a Pan-Hellenic festival of athletic games and drama competitions held every four years. This included a stadium, a gymnasium and the theatre. The sanctuary provided both a spiritual and a practical approach to healing. Treatments could be as simple as rest cures or involve medicines based on herbs. There is evidence that surgical procedures were performed. However, cures were also sought from the god by incubation, that is, by sleeping in the sanctuary over-night, in the hope of receiving advice in dreams or healing directly by divine intervention.

Asklepios was not envisaged as acting alone. His wife, Epione, was the goddess of soothing. His daughters also were responsible for differ-ent aspects of medicine and healing. Panakeia was the goddess of cures, that is, the medicines themselves. Her name of course gives us the word panacea, or cure-all. Akeso was the goddess of the process of healing and curing. Iaso was the goddess of recovery, while Hygeia was the goddess of good-health and was often worshipped in conjunction with her father (see Chapter 9, Messene). Finally, his son, Telesphoros, had a role as the god of convalescence. The importance of this divine family can be gauged by the opening lines of Hippocrates's Oath of Medical Ethics: "I swear by Apollo the Physician and Asklepios and Hygieia and Panakeia and all the gods and goddesses…..".

The site is completely enclosed, but has long opening hours, usually 8.00 to 17.00 daily and until 19.00 in the summer. Driving into the very large car park, the foundations of the sanctuary buildings are visible di-rectly ahead inside the fenced area, but the theatre is hidden in a fold of the hillside ahead and to the right. The stadium lies to the left of the car park. As at other major archaeological sites, detailed site-plans and in-numerable guidebooks are available.

Today the theatre appears to be the most important part of the site and the modern summer festival reinforces that impression. It is cer-tainly the most beautiful of all Greek theatres, although the landscaped pathways and other modern paraphernalia associated with the festival have served to separate it somewhat from the rest of the sanctuary. Built by Polykleitos in the 4C BC, it has been sensitively restored and is fa-mous for its perfect acoustics. The remainder of the site, unlike Delphi or Olympia, is much less visited, although new restoration work is in progress, which may make the rather fragmentary remains more acces-sible. The buildings, on the whole, are reduced to their foundations. They date principally from two periods, the 4C BC, when the sanctuary was at the peak of its fame, and the 2C AD when the Romans renovated the site and erected new facilities.

From the entrance by the museum, paths bear right uphill to the theatre, or left to the main area of the sanctuary. Here the visitor passes first the Katagogeion, or guest house. Further east is another square building, identified as a gymnasium. It can be recognised by the remains of the curved seating of a Roman odeion built later within its internal court. Beyond, is the temple and altar of Asklepios himself. Only the foundations remain. It was originally surrounded by a Doric colonnade of 6 by 11 columns and contained a gold and ivory statue of the god. A dog lay at his feet.

The snake was sacred to Asklepios, possibly as a symbol of regeneration because of its ability to shed its skin. Just to the west of the temple are the remains of a building in the form of a rotunda. Also known as the tholos, its labyrinthine foundations of concentric walls still stand. Its purpose is uncertain. One possibility is that it contained a sacred snake pit. Immediately to the north of the temple and tholos were the buildings of the abaton, or Enkoimeterion. These took the form of two adjacent colonnaded stoas. They were the dormitories where the sick spent the night hoping to dream. These buildings crowd around the eastern end of the stadium. This is built in natural depression and some of the stone seating survives.

Nauplio (Nauplion, Navplio, Ναυπλιο)
The myths of Nauplios and Palamedes.

Nauplio was the capital of the Peloponnese under the Turks, again under the Venetians, and was the first capital of modern Greece. It is rightly regarded as one of the most attractive towns of the mainland. Located at the head of the Gulf of Argos on a prominent peninsula, it is in essence a Venetian town, still dominated by its late mediaeval fortifications. It has retained much of its character, although tourism is now the main occupation. With its almost traffic free centre and pleasant paved squares, it makes an ideal base for exploration of the Argolid.

Approaching from Corinth by either the old road or the motorway, it is first necessary to negotiate the town of Argos and its one-way system. Although this seems to consist almost entirely of back lanes, it is, in fact, reasonably well signposted. The road emerges from the narrow streets south of the town where it crosses the line of the narrow gauge Peloponnesian railway. Shortly after passing on the left the low hill of

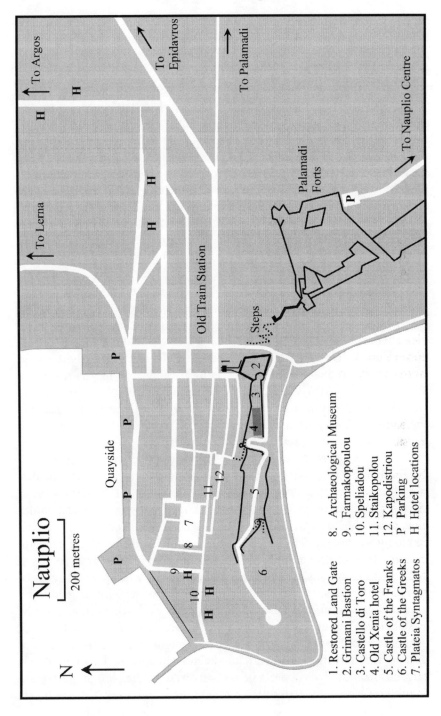

1. Restored Land Gate
2. Grimani Bastion
3. Castello di Toro
4. Old Xenia hotel
5. Castle of the Franks
6. Castle of the Greeks
7. Plateia Syntagmatos
8. Archaeological Museum
9. Farmakopoulou
10. Speliadou
11. Staikopolou
12. Kapodistriou
P Parking
H Hotel locations

Tiryns, whose cyclopean walls are clearly visible, the modern suburbs of Nauplio are reached. One kilometre from the centre, at a T-junction, a sharp right turn leads to the old town. Note that there is no obvious right of way here. Left at this junction is the road to Epidavros. If approaching from this direction, the sign at the junction indicates right to Argos and straight on to the centre (Κέντρο). After 300M, there is a sign to the right for "Seaside Parking". This street leads onto the quayside and the road runs along the harbour front for half a kilometre. The old town is to the left, sandwiched between the sea and the acropolis. Large areas of the quay are fortunately given over to car parking. Approaching Nauplio from the south, from the old road to Tripoli, look out for the right turn at Mili (Μύλοι) signposted Nea Kios (Νέα Κίος) and Nauplio. This road follows the curve of the bay all the way to the Nauplio quayside. An irritating detour to Argos is the consequence of missing it.

Nauplio's foundation myth is a by-product of the tales of Danaus's fifty daughters (see Argos below). Poseidon had been in dispute with Hera over which of them should have the patronage of the territory of Argos. A tribunal of the local river gods ruled in Hera's favour. In revenge Poseidon withdrew the rivers' water, so that they flowed only during heavy rain and were dry in summer. Danaus, when he came to Argos, realised the cause of the drought, and sent his daughters to search for water. Amymone, one of the fifty, came across a sleeping Satyr in her search. When he attempted to rape her, she called to Poseidon for help. He appeared and drove off the Satyr. Poseidon then lay with the girl, and, as a gift, revealed the Lernean springs to her. The result of their union was a son, Nauplios, the supposed founder of the city.

The heights of Palamadi above the town are named after Palamedes, Nauplios's son. Both Palamedes and his father have important roles in the story of the Trojan War, although these legends have caused confusion from the time of Strabo (1C AD). He believed that Nauplio's founding myth must be a much later invention, as the mythical genealogies would require Nauplios to be over 200 years old to have fought at Troy. It is easy to see why the city would wish to appropriate these myths. Palamedes was known as a great inventor who introduced lighthouses, navigation, weights and measures as well as new letters to the alphabet of Cadmus. When preparations were being made for the great expedition to Troy, Odysseus (Ulysses) sought to avoid going to war, despite the oath he had sworn to defend Helen (see Chapter 9). He feigned madness by yoking a horse and an ox to the plough, and began to till the fields. Palamedes placed Odysseus's infant son Telemachus in front of the plough forcing Odysseus to expose his pretence of insanity. Odysseus joined the expedition but took his resentment of Palamedes's trick with him. Once at Troy, he took his revenge by forging a letter from the Trojan king Priam to Palamedes. He arranged that this should be discovered in Palamedes's tent and accused him of treachery. Palamedes's punishment was to be stoned to death by the Greeks. His father eventually avenged his death when the victorious Greeks returned from Troy. Placing false fire beacons on the dangerous coast of Euboia, he lured many ships to their destruction.

Nauplio was probably the naval station of Argos in Mycenaean times, but had become an independent city-state by the 7C BC. When war broke out between Argos and Sparta in about 625 BC, Nauplio sided with Sparta. Sparta was defeated and Argos annexed Nauplio, whose inhabitants fled to Messenia. When Pausanias visited the city sometime in the second half of 2C AD, it was abandoned and he saw only the ruins of a temple of Poseidon and the famous Kanathos spring where Hera annually washed to renew her virginity. Today only the spring can still be seen (see below).

The connection between Nauplio and the Venetians begins as early as 1082 when a treaty was agreed between Venice and the emperor Alexios I, giving Venice not only rights of free trade within the Byzantine Empire but also trading and residential areas in several cities including Nauplio. Following the capture of Constantinople in 1204 and the subsequent division of the Byzantine empire between the Franks and Venice, the Peloponnese was invaded and conquered by Geofrey de Villehardouin and Guillame de Champlitte. By 1206, they had gained control of the greater part of the territory and Nauplio fell to them in 1210. The Franks were to hold the town for 160 years until it was purchased by the Venetians in 1388 from the last of the Frankish line.

Nauplio remained Venetian until 1540 when it was taken by the Turks. There was a further brief period of Venetian rule from 1686 to 1715, during which the magnificent fortifications on Palamadi were erected. The Turks held it until the Greek War of Independence when they were finally expelled in 1822. They were not completely driven from the Peloponnese until 1828 after which Nauplio was temporarily the first capital of Greece. Today there is little to see of Nauplio's ancient past and the principal pleasure is simply walking around the attractive streets of the old quarter. Although the town is dominated by its fortifications, both on the ancient acropolis directly above the harbour and the enormous complex of forts on the heights of Palamadi, the remains are almost entirely mediaeval and, as such, are outside the scope of this book. The acropolis walls are in any case best viewed from below as the interior is partly occupied by modern hotels and partly an overgrown wilderness. The fortifications of Palamadi are, however, well preserved and well worth a visit. The energetic way to reach the site is by the highly visible 900 steps that climb directly up from the town. The easier route is via the main entrance on the opposite side of the rock. This can be reached in ten minutes by car up a modern road (see plan). Opening hours are usually 08.00 to 17.00 or 19.00 from April. There are ticket offices at both entrances.

The town possesses an excellent archaeological museum housed in a fine, secular Venetian building, originally an arsenal or naval depot, which occupies one side of the main square. It houses numerous Mycenaean finds from the surrounding area, including a unique suit of Mycenaean body armour found at Dendra (see below).

Ayia Mona and the Kanathos Fountain
The spring where Hera renewed her virginity.

Hera was the patron goddess of all the cities of the plain of Argos. She was the goddess of women and marriage and her various titles represent the stages of a woman's life in Greek society; girl, bride, wife, and widow. She was able to represent each of these stages by her ability to renew her virginity each year when she washed in the spring of Kanathos. Today a fountain in the garden of the monastery of Ayia Moni (Αγία Μονή) is thought to occupy the site of the spring. The monastery, also known as Zoothohos Pigi (Ζωοδόχου Πηγής), the water of life, lies a little way out of the town, 2km from the main road.

To visit it, take the Epidavros road east, turning right just before reaching the army barracks on the left hand side of the road, before the suburb of Aria. The right turn has a sign for Ayia Moni. After ½km, at a T-junction, another sign points right. A sign by a car-park outside the monastery wall confirms its identity. The garden is accessible at all times and the spring, or fountain, is found just inside the wall by a small gate. The water of the spring is thought to have spiritual power to this day. It is not unusual to see people arriving by car and filling numerous large water containers.

The Mycenaean sites of the Argolid

The most famous Bronze Age site of the Argolid is, of course, Mycenae itself. It is one of the four most visited tourist destinations of mainland Greece along with Olympia, Delphi and Epidavros. The citadel of Tiryns however, whilst no less impressive, receives noticeably fewer visitors and offers a much clearer impression of a Mycenaean palace layout than that at Mycenae. Those who prefer to have a site completely to themselves should visit Midea. This hilltop citadel ranks third in terms of visible remains among the Mycenaean cities of the Argolid. Whilst it lacks evidence of palace structures inside its substantial walls, it is virtually unvisited, and has the added advantage of being unenclosed. Argos too, was an important site, and although little remains from the Bronze Age, there is still much to see there.

The foundation myths of the Argive cities
Danaus and his fifty daughters. The myths of Perseus.

The sheer number of myths describing the history of the cities of Argolis is a testament to the central importance of the area in the late Bronze Age. The earliest mythical chronologies are complex and link to virtually every other major legend of the Greek heroic age.

The histories of Argos, Mycenae and Tiryns are intertwined and, at first, the myths describe a single dynasty controlling the whole area. The story begins with Phoroneus, son of the river god Inachus, who was said to be the first man to gather people together into communities. The town he founded was called Phoronikon, or Phoronea. His successor was his grandson Argos, the son of his daughter Niobe by Zeus. She was said to be the first mortal that the god slept with. With a divine connection established, the city was renamed Argos. This dynasty continued to reign at Argos for several generations until, during the reign of Gelanor, Danaus came to Argolis and deprived him of his kingdom.

The story of Danaus's takeover is, as so often in myth, a tale of rivalry between two brothers. Belus, king of Egypt and brother of Agenor from whom Cadmus and the kings of Thebes were descended (see Chapter 2), had two sons, Danaus and Aegyptus. Belus had given them kingdoms, Arabia to Aegyptus, and Libya to Danaus. Each fathered 50 children; Aegyptus had 50 sons by various wives, and Danaus, 50 daughters. When the brothers quarrelled, Danaus fled with his daughters to Greece, fearing the strength of his brother and his sons. He landed near Lerna and travelled to Argos where he claimed the throne from

Gelanor. His claim was based on his family's decent from Io, daughter of Inachus. Gelanor naturally believed that Danaus's claim was worthless, but the following night a wolf attacked the cattle grazing by the city wall and killed the leading bull. The people of Argos thought that the bull represented Gelanor, the wolf Danaus, so they duly elected Danaus as king. In the belief that the wolf had been sent as an omen by Apollo, Danaus founded a temple of Apollo Lykios, Wolf Apollo, in his honour. Meanwhile, Aegyptus's sons had followed Danaus to Argos, seeking to marry his daughters. He was forced to accede to their demands, but arranged that each daughter should take a concealed dagger with her to her bridal bed. There, they murdered their new husbands on the wedding night. It was said that they finally paid a price for this mass murder, for after they had died natural deaths, they were condemned to fetch water forever in jars like sieves. The only survivor of the 50 brothers was Lynceus whom Hypermnestra refused to kill. Later when Danaus died, or perhaps after he was killed by Lynceus in revenge for the death of his brothers, he succeeded his father-in-law. Lynceus was succeeded in turn by his son Abas.

The next chapter of the story brings to an end the rule of a single king over the whole of the Argolid, and recounts the birth myth of Perseus, the first of the great heroes of Mycenae, and his fantastic adventures. Abas had twin sons, Proetus and Akrisius, whom he instructed to rule alternately when they inherited the kingdom after his death. When the time came, they ignored their father's instruction and attempted to settle the succession by force of arms. Akrisius managed to expel Proetus, who fled to the court of King Iobates of Lycia. There he married the king's daughter Anteia. Returning to Argolis, backed by a Lycian army, he was able persuade his brother to divide the kingdom. Akrisius retained the area around Argos itself, while Proetus took control of Tiryns, Midea and the coast.

An oracle had told Akrisius that his daughter, Danae, would give birth to a son and the boy would eventually kill his own grandfather. In an attempt to prevent this, he shut Danae in an underground dungeon, but despite his precautions Zeus came to her in a shower of gold and she bore a son, Perseus, by him. Akrisius refused to believe that Zeus was the child's father and, still hoping to avoid his fate, he cast Danae and the infant adrift on the sea in a chest. However, they were washed ashore on the island of Seriphos where they were rescued by Dictys, who brought them to his brother, Polydectes, the local king. Here Perseus grew up. Polydectes fell on love with Danae and sought marriage, but the young Perseus stood in his way. Polydectes then contrived a way to remove Perseus from Seriphos. Pretending that he intended to marry Hippodameia (see Chapter 7) he sought wedding gifts from his friends and Perseus foolishly promised him that he would obtain any gift he named, even the head of the Gorgon, Medusa. Polydectes took him at his word.

The Gorgons were three hideous maidens, usually represented with hissing serpents instead of hair. Their gaze was so terrible that those who looked at them were turned to stone. Perseus, as the son of Zeus, was fortunate to have the guidance of Athena and Hermes in his quest. Athena gave him a polished shield as a mirror to avoid looking at Medusa directly. Hermes gave him a sickle with which to cut off Medusa's head. They then guided him to the Graea, sisters of the Gorgons. These strange creatures were old women from birth. They had only one eye and tooth between them, which they passed to one another as needed. Perseus took away the eye and the tooth refusing to return them until the creatures had shown him the way to the Nymphs who guarded the winged sandals, magic wallet and helmet of invisibility that belonged to Hades, god of the Underworld. Having obtained these magic devices, he flew to the home of the Gorgons and, coming upon them asleep, cut off the head of Medusa with the sickle, using the mirror to guide his blow. Putting the head in the wallet, so that it would be safe from human gaze, he was able to escape the other Gorgons because the helmet made him invisible.

Perseus returned to Seriphos by way of Ethiopia. As he approached the coast he came across Andromeda, chained naked to a rock. Her mother Kassiopeia had foolishly boasted that Andromeda was more beautiful than any of the Nereids, the sea-nymph daughters of Nereus, the old man of the sea. When the Nereids complained to Poseidon over the insult, he sent a sea-monster to ravage the land. Kassiopeia's husband Kepheus, the king of Ethiopia, consulted the Oracle of Ammon (this famous oracle was that consulted by Alexander the Great during his campaigns in Egypt) who told him that his land would only be saved if Andromeda was sacrificed to the creature. Perseus had fallen in love with her on sight. He came to an agreement with Kepheus that she should become his wife if he killed the monster. He beheaded it and released Andromeda, but was then confronted by her uncle Phineus to whom she was already betrothed. Perseus was only able to escape from Phineus and his followers by revealing Medusa's head, which turned them all to stone.

Perseus eventually reached Seriphos with Andromeda. There he found his mother Danae and Dictys had taken refuge in the temple to

157

escape the violence of Polydectes. He went immediately to the palace and with his eyes averted, once again uncovered the Gorgon's head. Polydectes and all his court were turned to stone. His final act with Medusa's head was to give it to Athena who set it in the middle of her shield. He finally returned to his birthplace of Argos with Danae and Andromeda. Akrisius had not forgotten the oracle predicting his death at the hands of his grandson and fled to Larissa in Thessaly. By coincidence, athletic games were being held there and Perseus went to take part. He entered the Pentathlon. When he came to throw the discus he accidentally hit Akrisius and killed him; the prophecy could not be avoided.

Although Perseus was now the legitimate heir of Akrisius, he did not want to inherit the land of the man he had killed. He therefore exchanged kingdoms with Megapenthes, who had succeeded his father, Proetus. Megapenthes became king of Argos. Perseus became king of Tiryns and also fortified Medea and Mycenae. Other versions of the myth however, have him as the founder of Mycenae, in Greek Mykenai (Μυκεναι). One tale relates that he built the city at the spot where the cap of his scabbard, in Greek a Mykes, fell to the ground. Another version explains that the city was founded where he pulled up a mushroom, also a Mykes, and water gushed from the spot

Perseus was succeeded by his son Electryon, whose accidental death at the hands of his nephew Amphitryon, stepfather of Hercules, was related in Chapter 3. Electryon's brother, Sthenelos, then became king. Both Electryon and Sthenelos had married daughters of Pelops. Sthenelos invited his brothers-in-law, Atreus and Thyestes, to rule at Midea. When Sthenelos died the kingdom of Tiryns and Mycenae passed to his son, Eurystheus. It was Eurystheus whose birth had been hastened by Hera to deny Hercules the throne of Perseus, and whom Hercules was to serve when performing the Twelve Labours. When Eurystheus in turn died, the male line of Perseus was effectively at an end. His sons and those of Electryon were all dead, and Amphitryon was banished. The Mycenaeans therefore consulted an oracle that advised them to choose a king from the sons of Pelops, Atreus and Thyestes. After a complicated tale of deception and divine intervention, Atreus became king, but the by-product was hatred and rivalry between the brothers. In Greek mythology the sins of the fathers are visited on the sons and even on subsequent generations. The curse that Myrtilos had placed on the house of Pelops (see Chapter 7) was to lead to a tragedy of death and revenge that lasted for three generations, ending only after Orestes had killed his mother and her lover (see Mycenae below).

Tiryns (Τίρυνς)
Hercules and the Twelve Labours

The citadel of Tiryns is unmistakeable on its low hill by the side of the main Argos to Nauplio road. With its massive circuit of cyclopean walls, virtually complete, it was both a palace and a fortress. The sea is now 2km away, but may have once reached almost to its walls when the hill was an island in the marshes. The site is completely enclosed with opening hours 08.00 to 15.00 daily, 19.00 in the summer months.

Hercules has a very strong connection with Tiryns. Although he is usually said to have been born in Thebes, some versions of the myths claim that his parents were only banished from Tiryns after he has been born there. His return was to be another act of Hera's jealousy.

After he had defeated the Minyans and had married Megara (see Chapter 3), his fame spread far and wide. Hera's jealousy was aroused anew, and she inflicted a fit of madness on him. Not knowing what he was doing, he killed his own children by Megara, and two of the sons of Iphicles, his half-brother. Eventually, Hera released him from his madness but in his grief he went into exile, going first to king Thespius to be purified. He then proceeded to Delphi to ask the oracle for guidance on how he could atone for the murders. He was told that he should go to live at Tiryns and serve King Eurystheus for twelve years, performing whatever tasks he commanded. At the end of this period, the oracle prophesied that he would become immortal.

Originally there were ten Labours. Eurystheus, however, refused to count the second because Hercules was helped by Iolaos, his nephew, who accompanied him on many of his adventures. He also refused to count the fifth because of Hercules's bargain with Augius (see Chapter 7). He therefore set two more Labours bringing the total to twelve. The first six Labours took place within the narrow confines of the Mycenaean kingdoms of the northern Peloponnese. The later Labours took Hercules to the limits of the Greek world, with the final two placed in completely mythical locations.

The first Labour that Eurystheus demanded was for Hercules to bring him the pelt of the Nemean Lion. Hercules succeeded, returning with the Lion across his shoulders. Eurystheus was so surprised and intimidated by Hercules's obvious power that he forbade him to enter the city again, demanding that he should leave the results of his labours outside the city gate in future. As an added precaution, Eurystheus had a huge bronze jar made. This was buried in the earth and from then on he hid in it whenever Hercules returned. The second Labour took place close by, at Lerna. Hercules was sent to kill the many-headed Lernean Hydra whose very breath was said to bring death. After he had killed the beast he used its gall as a deadly poison for his arrows. For the third Labour Hercules was sent to bring back the Keryneian hind alive. In the fourth he was set the task of capturing the Erymanthian boar. Both these tales were related in Chapter 6. The fifth required Hercules to clean the stables of king Augius (see Chapter 7, Olympia). The sixth Labour was the last to take place nearby. Hercules had to clear the Stymphalian Marsh of the man-eating birds that flocked there. They were said to have brazen claws, wings and beaks. They used their feathers as arrows to kill men. Athena gave Hercules a set of bronze castanets, made by Hephaistos. The noise he made with them scared the birds into the air where he was able to kill them with his arrows.

The next four Labours took Hercules far from Tiryns. The seventh task was to capture the Cretan bull. This myth is intertwined with that of Theseus and the Minotaur. Poseidon had sent a bull to king Minos for him to sacrifice, but Minos had kept it and sacrificed an inferior animal. Poseidon's revenge for this deceit was to make Minos's wife, Pasiphae, fall in love with the bull. The outcome was the Minotaur, a creature with a bull's head but the body of a man. Afterwards Poseidon's bull roamed the Cretan countryside destroying everything in its path. Hercules succeeded in capturing it and brought it to Eurystheus who then set it free. Its wanderings eventually brought it to Marathon. Here it killed Androgeos, Minos's son. The subsequent events led to Theseus's slaying of the Minotaur (see above). Eventually Theseus himself killed Poseidon's bull at Marathon.

For his eighth Labour Hercules brought the flesh-eating Mares of Diomedes from Thrace to Eurystheus. The ninth involved fetching the Girdle of Hippolyte, queen of the Amazons, a mythical race who lived somewhere near the Black Sea. The tenth Labour was to capture the cattle of Geryon, the three-bodied monster who lived on the island of Erythia, said to lie at the western end of the Mediterranean Sea. On reaching what is now known as the straits of Gibraltar, he erected a pillar on each cape. From then on the straits were known as the Pillars of Hercules.

Eurystheus then demanded two further Labours, which were to prove the most difficult of all. For the first of these, the eleventh Labour, Hercules had to bring Eurystheus the Golden Apples of the Hesperides. The apples, or the tree that bore them, had been presented to Hera on her wedding day by Gaia. Hera had entrusted the gift to the

Hesperides, the daughters of Atlas, for safekeeping. Hercules had no idea where to find them, but he forced Nereus, the old god of the sea, to reveal their whereabouts. Nereus advised him to send Atlas, the Titan, to retrieve the apples.

Atlas had been condemned by Zeus to bear the weight of the heavens on his shoulders because he had led the Titans in the war with the Olympian gods when Zeus had deposed Kronos (see Introduction). When Hercules reached the garden of the Hesperides, he offered Atlas a respite from his burden if would fetch the apples. Hercules rested the weight of the heavens, usually represented as a celestial globe, on his shoulders. Atlas returned with three apples but had no intention of resuming his punishment. Hercules, however, promised him that if he would just take the load for a few seconds while he placed his lion-skin on his shoulders as a pad, he would hold up the heavens while Atlas took the apples to Eurystheus. Atlas was foolish enough to be deceived by this trick and found himself back in his accustomed position. Hercules then completed his task.

In his final Labour Hercules had to capture Kerberos, the three-headed dog that guarded the entrance to the underworld. Hades agreed he could take the animal to the upper world on the condition that he subdued it without the use of his weapons. Hercules held the creature by the throat and brought it out of the underworld through a chasm in the ground at Troizen.

The Archaeological site of Tiryns

The walls visible today date from the 13C BC, but the site seems to have been inhabited from the Neolithic period. It was deserted by the 2C AD. The remains were first excavated in 1886 by Schliemann, fortunately with the help of William Dorpfeld. The massive walls enclose two distinct areas, an upper citadel with its complex of palace buildings, and a lower circuit, possibly used as a refuge for the people and animals of the town that stood outside the walls. The circuit walls stand to over half their original height. The palace, however, was constructed of more fragile materials. The walls were of mud brick on a low limestone base. Where columns were used, they were of wood on a stone base. As a result, only the foundation courses remain but fortunately this is sufficient to reveal the layout.

From the ticket office, the entrance route is up the original approach ramp beneath the outer wall. This is arranged so that an armed man would approach with his unshielded right arm exposed to the wall and its defenders. At the head of the ramp an opening, narrowed in antiquity, pierces the outer wall. This opens into a long, massively walled corridor. To the right is the lower circuit. To the left the corridor leads, via a series of gates and courtyards, to the main entrance of the palace.

First, there are two monolithic gateways 45M apart. Beyond the second, the corridor opens into a courtyard in front of the elaborate double porch that formed the entrance to the palace complex itself. Built into the outer wall of this court are the first of the massive rows of chambers unique to Tiryns. They are often referred to as casemates after their resemblance to the vaulted chambers built into late mediaeval fortifications. Behind a colonnade, a vaulted corridor in the thickness of the wall ran the length of the courtyard. Six doors in the rear of the corridor opened into vaulted chambers. These have now partly fallen down the hillside, and originally would not have been open at the rear. Usually referred to as store-chambers, it is tempting to speculate whether they could in fact have been stables. Although it has been noted before that the approach ramp to the citadel is practicable for chariots, no mention appears to have been made of how horses were accommodated within the palace.

Through the double porch lies the forecourt of the palace. To the south of this court, but at a much lower level, is another set of 'casemates', reached by an L-shaped stairway. Again, a vaulted corridor runs in the thickness of the wall and gives access to five storerooms, this time well preserved. On the opposite, north, side of the forecourt, another entrance porch opens into a colonnaded court. Across this court, triple doors lead, via an ante-room, to the great hall or megaron itself. Off to the left of the antechamber is a bathroom, still recognisable as such. The presence chamber has as its centrepiece a large circular hearth and, to one side, the base of a throne is preserved. This progression from the entrance ramp through a succession of gates and elaborate entrances is the ceremonial logic of the palace layout. Additional apartments, often identified as the women's quarters, or Queen's megaron, lay to the east of the great hall. They were reached by a dogleg corridor from the double porch between the first and second courts.

North of the palace complex another court, possibly a service area, gave access from its west side to an elaborate staircase, set within a sickle-shaped curve of the outer wall. This descends to a small postern gate. Even more complicated were the arrangements for securing the water supply in times of siege. At the northern end of the outer enclosure, two underground passages were constructed under the west wall to connect to cisterns fed by springs.

Work is in evidence all over the hill and outside the walls. As well as new archaeological investigations, remedial work is in progress to stabilise recent earthquake damage. As a result, various areas of the site may be inaccessible. However, the most impressive views of the site can be obtained by walking around the outside of the walls.

Mycenae (Mikines, Μυκήνες, Μυκήναι)
The myths of Atreus, Thyestes, Agamemnon, Aegisthus and Orestes

Mycenae lies some 4km to the east of the old road from Argos to Corinth. It is well signposted from a crossroads 10km north of Argos. The road first reaches the modern village of Mikines. Like its counterparts at Delphi and Olympia, this exists primarily to cater for the large numbers of visiting tourists, most of whom arrive by tour bus. The village is therefore busy during the day but can be surprisingly quiet at night. A stay in one of its many hotels would be a convenient way of reaching the site when it opens at 08.00, unfortunately now the only way of avoiding the crowds. Two kilometres beyond the village the road ends at a large car park by the site entrance. Opening hours are normally 08.00 to 17.00 and until 19.00 in the summer.

The remains of the citadel of Mycenae still seem to possess a presence that lives up to the weight of the myths that envelop the site. The myth that dominates the imagination today of course, is that of the expedition to Troy to bring back Helen. This, however, is merely one chapter in the rich mythology of the Argolid. As we have seen in the introduction above, the dynasty founded by Phoroneus was replaced or usurped by that of Danaus. This came to an end with the sons of Perseus and the kingdom passed to Atreus, of the house of Pelops. The Trojan War was to be just one event in a tragedy that began with the rivalry between Atreus and his brother Thyestes. At the same time as Atreus and his brother were feuding, the sons of Oedipus were engaged in their own dynastic struggle. This involved the nobility of Argos in the war of the Seven against Thebes (see Chapter 2).

After Atreus assumed the kingship, he had banished Thyestes. He then discovered that Thyestes had seduced his wife, Aerope, and become her lover. To exact his revenge, Atreus pretended to forgive Thyestes and recalled him to Mycenae. There he killed Thyestes's twin sons and served their flesh up at a banquet, just as his grandfather Tantalos had done with Pelops. After Thyestes had eaten his fill, Atreus

163

revealed what he had done. Thyestes fled horrified into exile for a second time, vowing to have his revenge. He went to the oracle at Delphi to ask how he might obtain vengeance. He was told that he must have a son by his own daughter Pelopia, for this child was destined to avenge him. He followed the oracle's advice by raping his daughter when she went to wash by a stream one night. In the darkness he was able to keep his identity secret, but as he crept away he realised he had lost his sword.

Meanwhile, famine had come to the lands of Mycenae. Atreus asked the oracle for a solution and was advised that Thyestes must be recalled to the city. Atreus went to search for him and came to the kingdom of King Thesprotus at Sikyon, where Thyestes and Pelopia had taken refuge. Thyestes had left the city before Atreus arrived. When Atreus met Pelopia he assumed she was the daughter of Thesprotus. Falling in love with her, he asked Thesprotus for her hand in marriage. Thesprotus agreed, without revealing her true parentage. The couple returned to Mycenae with Atreus unaware that Pelopia was carrying his brother's child. The child was born and called Aegisthus. Atreus brought him up thinking that he was his own son.

Several years passed without news of Thyestes. Atreus sent Agamemnon and Menelaus, his sons by Aerope, in search of him again. They met him by chance on the way to Delphi. Seizing him, they carried him back to Mycenae and imprisonment. Atreus ordered Aegisthus to kill Thyestes in his sleep. However Thyestes awoke at the crucial moment and found Aegisthus standing over him with his own sword. Disarming the boy, he asked him where he had obtained the sword. The boy replied that he had been given it by his mother Pelopia. Thyestes commanded the boy to fetch his mother. When he put the same question to his daughter, she replied that it had belonged to the man who had raped her. When Pelopia realised that she had been raped by her own father, she killed herself in shame. Aegisthus discovered who his true father was and, in fulfilment of the oracle's prophecy, killed Atreus. Thyestes was restored to the throne. Agamemnon and Menelaus were forced into exile.

After many adventures, Agamemnon and Menelaus settled at the court of Tyndareus of Sparta. Agamemnon married Tyndareus's daughter Clytemnestra and Menelaus married her sister Helen. Menelaus became king of Sparta after Tyndareus. Agamemnon then recovered the throne of Mycenae from Thyestes. He may have done this peaceably, or he may have overthrown him, the stories differ. Aegisthus was forced into exile and denied his inheritance. Agamemnon became the most powerful king in Greece. He had a son, Orestes, by Clytemnestra and three daughters, Electra, Iphigenia and Chrysothemis. When Helen, Menelaus's wife, was carried off by Paris, Agamemnon was chosen as the overall commander of the force raised against Troy. His absence, for the Trojan War lasted 10 years, gave Aegisthus, who did not join the expedition, his opportunity to exact revenge.

Clytemnestra could not forgive Agamemnon for the sacrifice of their daughter Iphigenia at Aulis (see Chapter 2). Aegisthus's seduction of Clytemnestra was therefore made the easier by her resentment of her husband. Once he became her lover, Aegisthus behaved as though he had taken power in Mycenae. He and Clytemnestra plotted to kill Agamemnon on his return from Troy. To ensure they were prepared, they arranged that the coast should be watched so they would know the instant he landed at Nauplio. Agamemnon arrived with his Trojan concubine, Cassandra. The lovers killed Agamemnon, Cassandra, and the two children she had borne him. They would have killed his son Orestes as well, but Electra spirited him away to their uncle, king Stophius, in Phokis.

Aegisthus reigned in Mycenae for 7 years. During this period Orestes grew to manhood and in the eighth year he returned to Mycenae to avenge his father's murder. However, he killed not only Aegisthus but also his mother Clytemnestra. For this matricide he was pursued by the Furies, who sent him mad. The Delphic oracle told him that he could only escape his madness by retrieving the statue of Artemis from Tauris. This story was told in Chapter 2. Finally, he returned to Mycenae to discover that Aletes, son of Aegisthus and Clytemnestra, had seized power in his absence. Orestes killed him and reclaimed the throne. This was the final act of violence in the tragic history of the kings of Mycenae.

The Archaeological site of Mycenae

As at Tiryns, the walls of Mycenae date from the 13C BC, replacing and extending an earlier circuit of the 14C BC. Again, the site has been inhabited since Neolithic times. Its period of great wealth began in the 17C BC with the first rich burials in shaft graves. The use of tholos tombs began in the 15C BC and continued to 1300 BC. The site was burnt in 1200 BC and then abandoned around 1100 BC after another catastrophic fire. Much later, another settlement grew up but it was sacked again by Argos in 468 BC. Unlike Tiryns, where the citadel appears today as a fragment of the past isolated amidst modern surroundings, Mycenae still seems part of an ancient landscape. Approaching the site beyond the modern village, the surroundings are still visibly Mycenaean. In the valley below are the remains of a Mycenaean bridge and causeway. This carried one of the well-engineered roads that linked all the Mycenaean centres and made the use of chariots possible in such rugged terrain. In the hillsides above the modern road, numerous tholos, or beehive tombs, are to be found, together with ancient springs still in use and fragmentary remains of ancient houses. The citadel itself comes into view, brooding on the hillside, the famous Lion Gate hidden from view at this angle.

About 200M before the main car park and ticket office, the road passes close by the largest of these tholos tombs, still known today as the Treasury of Atreus. This now boasts a separate parking area and entrance, but entry is included in the tickets issued for the whole site. The identification of tholos tombs as 'Treasuries' dates from Pausanias's time, when their original function had been forgotten. By this date, the 2C AD, these massive structures had been looted of all they once contained. The Treasury of Atreus is still complete, although robbed of its decoration. It dates from 1350 BC. Positive identification of the tomb with Atreus or any other mythical king of the period is, of course, impossible. Approaching the car park, remains of Mycenaean houses lie to the right of the road, while beyond, the way turns sharp right and passes what it is now known as Grave Circle B. Found only in 1951 and of great importance, the shaft graves date from 1650 BC. There is now little to see. In the slope below the grave circle are two more tholos tombs known as the Tomb of Clytemnestra and the Tomb of Aegisthus. Again the names ascribed are fanciful. The Lion Gate comes into view at the end of a corridor formed between a section of the main wall on the left and a protruding bastion on the right. This is a famous image, with the intact gate surmounted by the massive triangular slab bearing the relief carving of the two lions, on either side of a pillar, complete apart from their heads. Immediately inside the gate, to the right, is the area unromantically named Grave Circle A.

When Mycenae was first investigated by Schliemann in 1876, he found this famous burial area with its magnificent grave goods of gold, silver and ivory almost immediately. His success was due to a simple, literal reading of Pausanias, who had seen the Lion Gate and the circuit walls in the 2C AD. He plainly stated that Agamemnon and his men were buried inside the wall, while Clytemnestra and Aegisthus were fit only to be buried outside. Schliemann had a compelling wish to bring the Homeric world of the Iliad to life and he naturally identified his finds with the tomb of Agamemnon. To this day, the best preserved of the gold death masks he found in the shaft graves inside the circle, is known as the mask of Agamemnon. These finds are now known to date from the 16C BC and are on display in Athens. It seems likely that such rich burials must belong to a royal dynasty, but where it fits into the mythical chronologies is impossible to say. However, it is now known that originally the graves lay outside the citadel, being brought within the walls in the 13C when the circuit was extended.

To the southeast of the grave circle, built between the circuit wall and the slope of the hill, are the foundations of a complex of buildings including an area known as the Cult Centre, from the clay images of idols and snakes found there.

Beyond the Lion Gate, a ramp leads up to the highest part of the hill and the palace itself. This had the features already described at Tiryns above, elaborate entrance porches, an internal court, a bathroom and the megaron with its circular hearth. In addition the palace boasted a monumental grand staircase built on its southern flank, which provided a more direct route from the lower part of the site.

To the east of the palace are some of the citadel's most conspicuous features. A massive postern gate provides another exit in the north wall. In appearance a smaller version of the Lion gate, it was built in the same period. At the very eastern end of the hill is an extension to the circuit with particularly massive walls. It was probably the last structure built by the Mycenaeans on the hill. It was designed to protect the entrance to an underground water supply. This still exists and is accessible, although a torch is necessary as it is completely unlit. From an entrance close to the wall, approximately 100 steps descend a zigzag tunnel that runs underground beneath the wall to a cistern, now dry, outside the circuit. Two sally ports also tunnel through the walls nearby, providing the means for active defence.

Midea (Midhia, Μιδέα)
Atreus and Thyestes first rule here.

Midea differs from its sister cities of Mycenae and Tiryns in two important ways. Firstly, it is unenclosed and can be visited from dawn to dusk. Secondly, apart from the occasional group of archaeology students, it is seldom explored and most visitors will have it to themselves. It lacks the more spectacular remains and mythical connections of the other Mycenaean sites, but the circuit of cyclopean walls encircling the steep hill that rises 170M above the plain is almost complete and the views are tremendous. The finds on the acropolis itself and nearby, at the important Mycenaean cemetery at Dendra, have confirmed its place within late Bronze Age palace culture. As at the other sites, it seems to have had a substantial settlement by 1600 BC. It acquired its circuit of walls in the 13C BC, but was destroyed around 1200 BC by earthquake and fire. One piece of evidence for an earthquake was the find of a young girl's skeleton beneath fallen stones near the east gate.

Midea is not totally without mythological connections. As described above, it was the first home of Atreus and Thyestes. When the myths speak of Sthenelos inviting his brothers-in-law to rule at Midea, we should perhaps think of this in terms of mediaeval feudalism, where baronies are granted to powerful junior members of a family to be held in fief to a king. Perseus was said to have raised the fortifications. It was also the site where Hippodameia, wife of king Pelops (see Chapter 7), and mother of Atreus and Thyestes, was said to have taken refuge. She had fled from Elis because of her role in the murder of Chrysippos, her husband's bastard son. Hippodameia eventually died and was buried at Midea. There was a cult shrine to her somewhere here. Eventually the Eleans brought her bones home to Olympia.

To reach Midea from Nauplio take the Argos road as far as ancient Tiryns. Turn right immediately after the citadel, signposted Ayia Triada (Αγία Τριάδα). The flat plain to the north of Tiryns is intensively farmed and covered in a network of asphalt roads. Unfortunately it is impossible to reconcile the system of roads and signposts with any map currently available. The following directions are therefore given in detail. Keep straight on through the village of Argoliko (Αργολικό) to Ayia Triada itself. Turn right in the village following signs, in Greek only, for Dendra (Δενδρά) and Midea (Μιδέα). Next, fork left signposted Midea, then right, signposted to the 'Mycenaean Citadel of Midea'. Drive through the village of Manesis (Μάνεσης), then turn right where signs again indicate 'Mycenaean citadel'. (Straight on at this junction leads after 1km to Dendra). In the modern village of Midea, turn right at a T-junction, (no signpost). The Mycenaean walls of Midea are now visible on a conical hill to the right. A final signposted right turn leads to the top of the hill where it is possible to park immediately below the walls. The road is steep but quite well surfaced.

A new information board has been erected with a good, if strangely aligned, plan of the site. A path ascends and enters the circuit through a breach in the walls. The citadel was divided into an upper and lower acropolis. The walls did not form a complete circuit, as the almost vertical slope of the hill to the south formed a sufficiently intimidating barrier. From the modern entrance, the best-preserved section of the walls climbs steeply uphill to the east gate. Straight ahead the path crosses the flank of the hill to the west gate. The two gates are the most notable structures on the hill. The foundations of several buildings have been excavated. They are grouped close to the walls. The largest lies to the left of the path near the entrance. This has been identified as the 'Megaron complex'. Other buildings abut the walls near the two gates. Evidence of a system of water collection channels and cisterns has been found on the terraces surrounding the megaron. The excavations are unfortunately difficult to decipher.

The upper acropolis is bare, but there are magnificent views over the whole of the plain of Argos. This deserted location provides an interesting contrast to the crowded hill of Mycenae.

To reach the Mycenaean cemetery at Dendra, return to the junction described above. After a short distance a signposted left turn leads to the tombs on the edge of the very small village centre. Various signs clearly indicate the location of the roofless tholos and chamber tombs. This was the site of the find, in 1960, of the complete set of Mycenaean armour now displayed in the Nauplio museum. The villages around Dendra and Midea have an isolated feel that belies their close proximity to the tourist centres of Mycenae and Nauplio.

Argive Heraion
The Sanctuary of Hera. The myth of Kkeobis and Biton

Hera was the principal goddess of the entire Argolid. After her birth (see Chapter 2 Elefsis) she was said to have been brought up by the water nymphs Euboia, Prosymna and Akraia, daughters of the local river Asterion. Their names are preserved in the countryside around the Heraion, her principal sanctuary. It lies 5km southeast of Mycenae at the foot of Mount Euboia. The slopes above the Heraion were known to Pausanias as Prosymna. As the cult centre for the whole Argolid, the site was not attached to any one town but lay between the main settlements, Mycenae to the north, Argos to the southwest and Tiryns to the south.

In myth, Hera's first priestess was Io, daughter of the river-god, Inachus, and sister of Phoroneus, the mythical founder of Argos. Unfortunately for Io, Zeus fell in love with her and seduced her. When

Hera suspected that her husband had been unfaithful again, Zeus turned Io into a white cow to protect her from Hera's wrath. Hera asked Zeus to give her the cow as a gift and when he complied, she set Argus Panoptes to guard the animal. Panoptes means all-seeing, a name given to Argus because he had one hundred eyes. Only two of his eyes slept at once. Zeus wished to set Io free and commanded Hermes to release her. Hermes managed to send all of Argus's eyes to sleep with his flute playing, and then killed him with a stone. Hera set his eyes in the tail feathers of the peacock, so that he would not be forgotten. Although Io was now free, she was still in the form of a cow. As punishment, Hera sent a gadfly to sting her continually. To escape its torment she fled from land to land, crossing the seas and eventually settling in Egypt where she regained her human form. She was said to have given her name to both the Ionian Sea and the Bosporus (Ox-crossing).

The area to the north and west of the sanctuary is covered with the fragmentary remains from Neolithic, Middle Helladic and Mycenaean settlements. There are numerous tholos and chamber tombs. Remains of the Mycenaean highway from Mycenae are still visible. Prosymna was clearly a prosperous area for several millennia. Tradition makes the Heraion the place where Agamemnon was elected leader of the forces assembled against Troy. The earliest finds from the Heraion itself, however, date from the 8C BC. There is therefore no physical evidence of continuity of cult activity at the site.

The Heraion is most easily reached from the Argos-Corinth highway by taking the road to Mycenae as above (see plan). At a crossroads immediately after the railway crossing, turn right onto a newly improved road that eventually leads to Ayia Triada. After 7km, near the village of Honikas (Χώνικας), now re-named Nea Iraio (Νέα Ηραίο), a brown sign indicates left to the Heraion. This leads directly to the site entrance. There is no entrance charge, but the site is fully enclosed. Opening hours are 08.00 – 15.00.

The sanctuary is a complex of buildings rising in a series of large terraces on the lower slopes of the hill. The centrepiece was the 'new' temple built between 420 and 410 BC. The massive foundations that remain are of a Doric temple with an external colonnade of 6 x 12 columns. It contained the gold and ivory statue of the goddess by Polykleites. The terrace on which the temple stood was surrounded by buildings, variously identified as stoas, dining rooms and the so-called telesterion. The south side of this terrace was supported by a vast, stepped retaining wall and incorporated another colonnaded stoa. To the north, an upper terrace was the site of the 'old' temple. The supporting wall between the middle and upper terraces is formed from massive boulders. Although this appears to be Mycenaean, it has been dated only to the 8C BC. The upper terrace itself is paved with massive stones, carefully levelled, like gigantic cobblestones. Built in the early 7C BC mainly of wood, the old temple is known to have been destroyed by fire in 423 BC.

The exact nature of the cult of Hera is not known. It has been speculated that it involved 'mysteries' in which initiates were perhaps shown something of the nature of death. One of the buildings of the sanctuary has been suggested as resembling the Telesterion, or hall of the mysteries, at Elefsis, on the basis of its multi-columned interior. Evidence for such a cult has also been seen in the curious legend of the brothers Kleobis and Biton. The brothers were sons of Cydippe, another priestess of Hera. During one of Hera's festivals at Argos, Cydippe had to travel from the city to the Heraion. Because the oxen that should have drawn her wagon were still in the fields, her sons volunteered to pull it themselves. The distance is perhaps 8km. They succeeded in reaching the sanctuary in time and lay down in the temple to sleep, exhausted, having received the congratulations of all the men present. In her pride at their achievement, Cydippe prayed to the goddess to grant her sons 'the best thing a man might receive'. With this prayer her sons died in their sleep. The message of this story appears to be that death was not a curse but a gift.

Argos
The location of the myths of Danaus. The myth of Melampous and Bias.

Argos is yet another city that claims to be the oldest in Greece. The mythological chronology of its kings began with the family of Phoroneus and then passed to the house of Danaus. The importance of this dynasty can be gauged by Homer's use of the name Danaans to refer to the Greeks as a whole. After the sons of Abas had split the kingship of the Argolid between them, Perseus later exchanged kingdoms with Megapenthes, who accordingly became king of Argos (see above). Megapenthes was succeeded by his son Anaxagoras. It was during his reign that Argos became a triple kingdom.

Anaxagoras had three daughters, Lysippe, Iphinoe and Iphianassa. They were afflicted with madness, either by Dionysus or Hera, because they had scorned their worship. They lost their beauty and wandered over the countryside as if they were cows plagued by flies. Eventually

171

the madness spread to the other women of Argos. Melampous, the healer and prophet, cured the women, but only after Anaxagoras had agreed to share his kingdom equally with Melampous and his brother Bias. This triple kingship was to continue for several generations. It was the descendants of Melampous and Bias who took part in the war between Oedipus's sons, the war of the Seven against Thebes (see Chapter 2). Eventually, after the Trojan War, during the reign of Orestes, son of Agamemnon, Argos again became part of a unified kingdom with Mycenae.

Today Argos is still the principal town of the plain and occupies the same site as the ancient city. For the most part the tourist buses travelling between Nauplio and Mycenae ignore the town, despite the considerable remains of its past. Argos has an undeserved reputation as an unattractive place. This, however, is simply the reflection of a local economy independent of tourism. The town is most lively on Wednesdays when there is a regular market. There are essentially three areas of archaeological interest. The first, a large fenced compound south of the town centre, bisected by the Tripolis road, contains the remains of the agora, a substantial part of the 4C BC theatre, and a Roman odeion and bathhouse. Somewhere here was the famous temple of Apollo Lykios originally supposed to have been founded by Danaus. The second area lies due north of the modern market place on the ridge that connects the Aspis, the smaller of the two acropolis hills of the ancient town, with the larger acropolis of Larissa. Here, close together, are a Mycenaean burial ground and the Sanctuary of Apollo and Athena. There are also fragmentary remains on the Aspis hill. The third main area of interest is within the magnificent mediaeval castle that crowns the Larissa hill. The Byzantine and Frankish walls are built almost entirely on ancient foundations, and incorporate material from Classical temples.

Approaching the outskirts of Argos from Nauplio, a left turn just after the railway crossings has signs for the 'Centre' (Κέντρο) and 'Archaeological Sites'. A second left turn has signs for Tripoli, Ancient Theatre and Centre. After passing a ruined mosque on the right, the road reaches a T-junction. Tripoli is left, the town centre right, and the fenced area containing the theatre and odeion is straight ahead. Opening hours are usually 08.30 – 15.00.

The theatre is comparable in size to that at Megalopolis. First built in the 4C BC, it was heavily modified by the Romans in the 2C AD. The side sections of seating, on earth banking built out from the hillside, are now missing, but the well preserved centre section, cut from the rock, still gives a very clear impression of the overall scale of construction.

Almost directly in front of the theatre are the brick and concrete ruins of the Roman baths. One section still stands to the height of the vaulting. Immediately to the south are the substantial remains of a Roman odeion. On the opposite side of the Tripolis road, the confused remains of the agora have been revealed below modern ground level. The foundations of the Bouleuterion, or meeting house, can be distinguished.

To reach the remaining two areas of interest to the north, follow the Tripolis road from the theatre north to the town centre, or from the Nauplio road, simply follow the signs for the Κέντρο and Archaeological museum. The centre of the town is formed by two linked, irregular squares. Continue north, straight through the centre, and following signs for Corinth (Κόρινθος), the road climbs the ridge between the two citadels. On the very edge of the town, opposite a sign for the monastery of the Panagia on the left, a sharp right turn leads 100M down a lane to a group of Mycenaean tholos and shaft tombs. These are cut into the rock of the hillside on the left hand side of the lane.

Just beyond this turning, brown signs point right for the Sanctuary of Apollo and Athena and left for the castle. The sanctuary lies on the ridge known as the Deiras. The temple of Apollo was therefore called Apollo Deiradiotes. Pausanias explains that Apollo had an oracle here. Prophecies were delivered by a priestess who was said to be possessed by the god after she had tasted the blood of a sacrificed ewe. Today the foundations that remain are confusing, but clearly visible is the large altar in front of the rock cut steps leading to Apollo's temple. The large cisterns are now fenced off. The clearest view of the sanctuary is from the castle above, where the benefit of height reveals the layout.

The road to the castle takes a circuitous route to the far side of the Larissa hill. The route is well marked by brown signs, until a critical left turn, which is indicated only by an extremely rusty blue sign on which the words ACROPOLIS and KASTRO can just be made out. This point can also be reached by taking the main road through Argos towards Mycenae. On the edge of town, turn left where there are brown signs for the castle, immediately before the bridge over the dry riverbed.

Approaching from a distance, the castle has the outward appearance of a Crusader fortress in Syria. In fact it is extremely difficult to date. The mediaeval walls are partly Byzantine, partly Frankish and partly Turkish, but must follow the course of the Classical fortifications as both the inner and outer circuits incorporate substantial sections of ancient walls. These date from the 5C and 6C BC and are built in a variety of styles. The road ends in a car parking area beneath the castle gate. An opening in the lower wall leads into the outer bailey. From the parapet

Figure 16 Argos: The Acropolis of Larissa

to the south there are excellent views over the town and the Sanctuary of Apollo and Athena below. However, the original entrance is directly above the car park, partly concealed by a round tower, and partly by the overgrown spoil heap left by archaeologists in the clearance of the inner bailey. A steep path leads past the remains of the outer gate and then into the upper enclosure via a restored inner gate. This area has been extensively excavated. There are fragments of temples of Zeus and Athena as well as traces of Mycenaean wall. There are substantial cisterns. Built against the north wall is a chapel incorporating much ancient material. Visitors should have this neglected site to themselves.

Nemea (Νεμέα)
The myth of Hypsipyle and Opheltes and the founding of the Nemean Games by the Seven against Thebes.

The sacred precinct of Nemea, site of the Sanctuary of Zeus and home of the Nemean Games, is one of the best-conserved Classical sites in the Peloponnese. Its museum is a model of presentation and exposition. Yet, despite its status as the site of one of the four great Panhellenic festivals, it is little visited.

Traditionally, the Games were founded in 573 BC and this date appears to be supported by the archaeological evidence. The mythical foundation of the Games forms part of the story of the Seven against

Figure 17 Nemea: The Temple of Zeus

Thebes (see Chapter 2). After the birth of his son Opheltes, the local king, Lykourgos, had consulted the Delphic oracle to establish how best to rear the child in safety. The oracle's reply was that he must not touch the ground until he could walk. His nurse, Hypsipyle, was charged with ensuring this did not happen.

Hypsipyle was the daughter of king Thoas of Lemnos. The women of Lemnos had killed all their menfolk (see Chapter 7, Lepreo), but Hypsipyle had spared her father and helped him to escape from the island. When Jason and the Argonauts landed on Lemnos, the women

175

took them as lovers. Hypsipyle, who had assumed rule in her father's place, had two sons, Euneos and Thoas by Jason. The other women subsequently discovered that Hypsipyle's father had escaped. They banished her and sold her into slavery. She became Opheltes's nurse in Nemea. When the army of the Seven, led by Adrastus, set out from Argos for Thebes, their route took them first to the valley of Nemea. While they were looking for water, they encountered Hypsipyle guarding Opheltes. She showed them the way to a spring, but foolishly set the child down on a bed of wild celery where he was bitten by a snake. When Hypsipyle and the Seven returned, the child was dead.

Amphiaraos, the seer, warned that this was an ominous sign. In an attempt to appease the gods, the Seven founded the Games in the infant's honour, renaming him Archemorus, the 'forerunner of doom'. Each of the Seven was supposed to have won an event. The Games were subsequently held every two years. The judges were said to have worn black robes of mourning for Opheltes, and the winners' victory wreaths were made of celery. Nemea, of course, was also the location of Hercules's first Labour. However, the tale that later makes him the founder of the Games after killing the Lion, is not a Greek myth but a later Roman construct.

The sanctuary lies in a small valley halfway between Argos and Corinth. Heading north from Argos on the old National road, the left turn to Nemea is just by a railway crossing beyond Dervenakia (Δερβενάκια). The site is about 4km along this road on the right, shortly before the modern village of Iraklion, now renamed Archaia Nemea. (Not the modern town of Nemea a further 6km away). A junction on the Tripolis motorway also gives easy access to this road. Opening hours are 8.30 to 15.00, closing later in summer. The stadium is about 500M to the east of the main site. A combined ticket can be bought for both areas.

Although Nemea was a sacred precinct and not a city, there is considerable evidence of settlement close by, from the Stone Age (6000-5000 BC), and again from the Bronze Age, particularly 1600 to 1200 BC. There then seems to be a break in occupation between 1100 and 700 BC. The traditional founding date of the Games was 573 BC. The Games were biennial and initially under the control of the nearby city of Kleonai. Late in the 5C BC, the Games moved to Argos and the sanctuary was destroyed. This destruction may have been by Argos itself, or it may have been the result of conflict between Sparta and Argos; the first battle of Mantinea (see Chapter 6) is dated to 418 BC. The Games returned to Nemea about 330 BC and the sanctuary was completely rebuilt. This was the period in which Macedonian control of Greece was being consolidated and the re-construction of the sanctuary may have been a political statement. The new facilities only remained in use for 70 years. In 271 BC the Games returned to Argos. The site was a ruin by Pausanias's time, but in the 5C AD a new agricultural community, possibly monastic, grew up. During this period a large three aisled, Christian basilica was built in the ruins of the old sanctuary. This settlement was destroyed by Slav invaders in the 6C AD.

Entrance to the site is through the excellent museum and it is worth taking the time to explore this thoroughly. It is a model of elucidation with models, plans, photographs and cross sectional drawings of the excavations designed to enhance the visitors' understanding of the physical remains of the site.

Like a smaller version of Olympia, the temple of Zeus stands within a sacred precinct, along with a sacred grove of cypress trees, nine treasuries or pavilions, a Xenon or hostel, a bath-house, and a Hero shrine. From the museum, a path crosses an open area reaching first the foundations of a row of 4C BC houses. Next is the long narrow building of the Xenon, again dating to the late 4C BC. It contained a number of two room apartments, each with a separate entrance to the south, and was perhaps used to house the athletes or the judges. The early Christian basilica was built on the foundations of the centre section of the Xenon using blocks scavenged from the temple. A Baptistry was added later to the north. It had a circular font, still visible. The nine Oikoi, the word simply means houses, are arranged in a line parallel to the Xenon, facing the temple. They may have been meeting halls, storerooms or treasuries, similar to those at Olympia. They were all built in early 5C BC. The open area between the row of Oikoi and the temple was the site of the sacred grove. Twenty three of the planting pits used for the cypresses of the grove have been found. According to Pausanias, Opheltes was killed by the snake here.

The first temple of Zeus on the site was constructed shortly after the foundation of the Games in 573 BC and destroyed in the late 5C. The second temple was built in same position around 330 BC. It had an external colonnade of 6 x 12 Doric columns. Their unusual, slender proportions, gave the temple a very elegant appearance. The cella was supported by a Corinthian colonnade with Ionic columns above. At the rear of the cella was a sunken crypt, possibly the site of an oracle. Virtually all the column drums of the temple lie around the foundations. Until recently, all that remained standing was one column from the external colonnade and two from the pronaos. Two more have now been re-erected and there are plans for further work.

Figure 18 Nemea: The Stadium

To the east of the temple is the exceptionally long altar of Zeus. Its length may have been designed for many simultaneous sacrifices or different sections may have been used for different deities. Remains of kilns have been found between the Oikoi and the Xenon. These date from the late 4C BC and seem to have been used to make the roof tiles for the new sanctuary on site. Beneath a modern tiled roof, which does not look out of place among the ruins, are the remains of the bathhouse with its extremely well preserved washing troughs still in situ. The baths were filled from a reservoir system that received its water via an aqueduct from the Adrasteia spring, named after Adrastus, 800M away. To the west of the stream that runs along the edge of the archaeological site, lay the Heröon, or Hero shrine, to the baby Opheltes. This originally dates from the early 6C BC. The visible foundations are of a 3C BC structure. Inside the enclosure were altars and the tomb of Opheltes.

The stadium lies about 500M from the sanctuary. Follow the road back towards Argos and fork left, signposted to Kleiones (Κλεωνές). The entrance is just to the right of the road. Initially the stadium is hidden from view. Visitors still enter the stadium by the original route taken by the competitors. The path from the ticket office leads to the excavated remains of a colonnaded building arranged around three sides

178

of a small courtyard. Here the competitors prepared before the competitions. The surviving columns have been re-erected. Through the colonnade is the long vaulted tunnel that leads under the seating embankment to the track. This is one of the earliest examples of the use of vaulting in Greece. Graffiti carved in the tunnel walls by the competitors can still be seen. During the excavation of the tunnel, remains were found of a man thought to have been sheltering from Slav invaders in the 5C AD. He had taken up residence in the partly filled in tunnel. His skeleton was found along with cooking utensils. His skull showed evidence of a healed wound from previous fighting.

The stadium was constructed about 330 BC with the rebuilding of the sanctuary. The southern, rounded end is built into a hollow in the hills. The northern end is built out over the plain. The starting lines and the water channel around the circuit are still in position. The starting gate system is illustrated in the museum. Finds of coins in the stadium seem to indicate that spectators from the different cities congregated together in set areas, Argos behind the judges seats on the east side and Corinth on the west.

Lerna – The House of Tiles
Site of the entrance to the Underworld use by Hades and Dionysus.

Lerna, on the site now occupied by the modern village of Mili (Μύλοι) at the western end of Nauplio Bay, now seems an innocuous spot. Yet it is both the location of one of the most important pre-Mycenaean archaeological sites in southern Greece and an ancient sacred area with many mythical links.

The coast road west around the Bay from Nauplio meets the main road from Argos in the centre of Mili. On the edge of the village, about 300M south on the Tripolis road, a sign points seawards to the archaeological site, identifiable by the ugly concrete roof protecting the centre of the excavations. A short, but very narrow track, leads to a car park. The site is enclosed and opens daily from 08.30 to 15.00.

The modern road through Mili passes between the marshy seashore and the Pontinos hill. Springs flow from the foot of the hill and once turned watermills. The village's name, Mili, simply means mills. These are the springs revealed to Amymone by Poseidon. This area has always been marshy, and lagoons or ponds easily form. In antiquity there was a lake called Alkyonia here. It was thought to be bottomless and an entry into the underworld. This is the spot where Hades dragged Demeter's daughter Persephone down into his kingdom. Pausanias describes a sacred wood of plane trees that stretched from the edge of the hill to the sea, where there were statues of Demeter, Dionysus and Aphrodite. Here, as at Elefsis (see Chapter 2), mysteries were celebrated in honour of Demeter. Dionysus had used the same entrance to the underworld when he descended to bring back his mother, Semele, who had been killed by Zeus when he appeared to her in the form of thunder and lightning. Annual nocturnal rites to Dionysus were performed by the lake.

The swamps around Lerna were the home of the famous Hydra. This serpent had nine heads, one of them immortal, and the ability to sprout new heads if one was severed. Its very breath was poisonous. Hercules drove it from its lair by, the spring of Amymone, with fire. As he cut off its heads, Iolaos cauterised each severed neck with a burning brand, preventing a new head from growing. Finally, Hercules was able to cut off the immortal head and bury it.

Today Lerna is better known for the important archaeological site known as the House of Tiles. This building is the centrepiece of a fortified settlement dating from the early Bronze Age. Excavation has revealed that the site was occupied for perhaps 2000 years of the Neolithic period from about 5500 BC. It was re-occupied c. 2500 BC. The surviving remains date from this period. The settlement was surrounded by substantial fortifications and a long section of wall with towers is preserved to the south. The largest of the buildings within the walls is known as the House of Tiles after the large number of clay roof-tiles found during excavation. This two-storey 'palace' had mud-brick walls and was destroyed, along with the rest of the settlement, about 2200 BC. It was subsequently covered by a round tumulus, or mound, surrounded by a circle of stones, perhaps marking it as a sacred area. This burial contributed to the survival of the remains into the modern era. Smaller buildings were erected nearby and the settlement continued until c. 1700 BC. During the Mycenaean period the site was mainly used as a cemetery and two shaft graves were cut into the tumulus. It was finally abandoned entirely about 1250 BC.

West and south from Nauplio

The routes west from Nauplio towards Olympia are described in Chapter 6. Lakonia and Messenia to the south are described in Chapter 9. All routes west and south are reached most quickly via Argos and the connecting link road to the motorway at the Sterna junction. However, if time permits, the old road to Tripoli from the coast at Mili (Μύλοι, see above), offers a drive through an empty landscape of barren grandeur. From the coast, the road climbs the mountain in a series of switchback curves. Before the opening of the motorway, this was the main route south and heavily used. Now, almost completely deserted, it makes a pleasant drive. Occasionally it will be necessary to avoid fallen debris where the road passes through cuttings. Tripoli is reached in an hour and a quarter. The road crosses the motorway just outside the town. Turning north on the motorway for 10km to the Nestani junction, gives access to Olympia via Langathia. Sparta and Megalopolis lie to the south.

9

Messenia and Laconia

This route follows the coastal road from Olympia to the southwest corner of the Peloponnese. Here, near Pylos, is the best preserved of all the Mycenaean palatial centres. Known as the palace of Nestor, it was the centre of a kingdom which, by the 14C BC, encompassed most of Messenia. Pylos is an attractive town that makes an ideal base for exploring the area.

In the heartland of Messenia, stand the ruins of ancient Messene, the city founded beneath Mount Ithome in the 4C BC when the Messenians recovered their autonomy after centuries of Spartan domination. It lies 20km north of the modern town of the same name. It is still being actively investigated and restored. Despite its extensive remains, it is almost completely neglected by modern tourism.

Laconia is reached via the dramatic Langadha pass across the Taiyetos mountains. Although Messenia and Laconia are separated by this great mountain ridge, their post-Mycenaean histories are both dominated by rise and fall of Sparta.

South from Olympia

South of Pyrgos, the main road has been improved as far as Kiparissia (Κυπαρισσία) and is a pleasant drive. Six kilometres after the Krestena junction it passes close to the sea between an area of pine covered sand dunes and the ancient lagoon of Lake Kaiafas. A left turn, just before the lake, leads to hot sulphur springs that emerge from caves at the base of the cliff. They were believed to cure leprosy in ancient times and one is still in use as a bathing establishment. The smell makes them impossible to miss. A second, much larger spa complex lies on an island in the lake, accessed from the main road. The left turn for Lepreo and Phigalea (see Chapter 7) is reached 15km beyond Kaiafas. The road then crosses the river Neda into Messenia. At Kalo Nero (Καλό Νερό), 10km further on, the main road to Megalopolis branches left.

Although Kiparissia is a harbour town, the old mediaeval settlement lies almost 1km from the sea, beneath the walls of the imposing castle on its hill. The modern town is laid out on a grid pattern on the gentler slopes below. From the north, the main road reaches the commercial centre at a T-junction with a long avenue that runs in a straight line between the old town, uphill to the left, and the harbour to the right. A branch of the Peloponnese railway terminates here.

Whilst there is a brief reference in the Iliad to a Mycenaean settlement in Messenia called Kiparissia, its precise location is unknown. The town traces its history back to the 4C BC when it was founded by Epaminondas as a port to serve his new city of Messene. The castle walls are now a confusing mixture of Byzantine, Frankish and Turkish work. They include much ancient material and this must have been the site of the ancient acropolis. There are good views from the castle, but it is more impressive from below than within.

Ancient Pylos
The Palace of Nestor.

South of Kiparissia, the road is narrow and follows a wandering route away from the coast. Nestor's palace lies on a low ridge, just to the right of the main road, about 4km after the village of Hora (Χώρα). Although it lacks the imposing walls and dramatic situation of Mycenae or Tiryns, it should not be missed. The site was only re-discovered in 1939 when trial trenches were dug by the American archaeologist, Carl Blegen. His initial excavation revealed the first Linear B tablets to be found on the Greek mainland. The preservation of so many of these clay records was due to the intense heat generated when the palace was burnt. They subsequently provided a huge amount of information about the nature of Mycenaean society and confirmed that the name of the place in antiquity was indeed Pylos. Serious excavation did not begin until 1952. The wealth of information revealed was the result of the great care taken by the archaeologists.

The palace is named after King Nestor, famous for his role in the Trojan War. Although an old man by the time of the war, he was respected for his wisdom and past deeds. With his sons, he led the second largest contingent of ships to Troy. After the war had ended, he was the only one of the Greek leaders able to return to his homeland without mishap and live peaceably again. His was not the first dynasty to rule in Messenia. The foundation myths of the area start many generations earlier and are linked to the other important kingdoms of Bronze Age Greece. The founder of the kingdom of Messenia was Polykaon, son of Lelex, the first ruler of Laconia. When Lelex died, he was succeeded by his eldest son, Myles, and there was no role for Polycaon, the younger son (see Sparta below). Polycaon was married to Messene, daughter of Triopas, king of Argos. She was extremely ambitious, wanting her husband to establish a kingdom for himself. She persuaded him to raise an army. With forces from Argos and Laconia, they invaded the southwest corner of the Peloponnese.

Polycaon named the territory Messenia after his wife. Pausanias tells us that their capital was at Andania in the upper Messenian plain. Polykaon's line lasted for five generations, although the names of his descendants are unknown. With the end of this lineage, the kingdom was seized by Perieres, a son of Aiolos, ruler of Thessaly. Perieres married Gorgophone, Perseus's daughter, and their son, Aphareus succeeded his father. During Aphareus's reign, his cousin, Neleus, was expelled from Iolkos in Thessaly by his twin brother. He came to Messenia to seek refuge. Aphareus granted him the land along the coast by Pylos and here he built his palace.

Aphareus had two sons, Idas and Lynceus. It was Idas who journeyed to Aitolia and carried off king Evinus's daughter, Marpessa, with the aid of a winged chariot given to him by Poseidon (see Chapter 4). However, the two brothers were most famous for their rivalry with Castor and Polydeuces of Sparta. This rivalry was to end in the death of all four (see Sparta below). With Perieres's line at an end, Neleus, now well established at Pylos, became king of all Messenia. Neleus's reign ended with Hercules's attack on Pylos (see Chapter 7). The city was sacked and Neleus and almost all his family perished. Of his twelve sons, only Nestor survived. He was said to have ruled over three generations of men but nothing is recorded about his death. According to Pausanias, the Neleid dynasty lingered on for two generations more, but essentially the mythical history of the Bronze Age comes to an end with king Nestor.

Excavation has shown that around 1200 BC Nestor's palace was destroyed by fire. Other major palace sites were destroyed across the Mycenaean world at approximately the same time. The archaeological evidence points to the collapse of Bronze Age society as a whole. The reasons for this collapse are still the subject of debate. Theories range from the catastrophic effects of severe earthquakes, the collapse of the

centralised palace economies due to climate change, or simply destruction by barbarian invaders. The Greeks of the Classical era, however,
had a straightforward mythical explanation, an invasion known as the
return of the children of Hercules.

After Hercules died, Eurystheus expelled his sons, who were known
as the Heraclidae. They fled to Doris, an area of central Greece around
the southern Pindos mountains. Three generations after their expulsion,
the children of Hercules invaded the Peloponnese with the Dorians to
reclaim their inheritance. The real events of the Greek Dark Ages are
little understood. What is certain is that after the Mycenaean collapse,
Greeks lived in much smaller communities until the emergence of the
city-state around 800 BC. The Dorian invasion is now thought to have
been more of an infiltration of Greek speakers from the north, re-
occupying abandoned sites, than a military expedition. However the
Classical Greeks believed in a specific invasion. Pausanias gives detailed lists of the sons of Hercules who took over the cities of the
Peloponnese.

The three main leaders of this mythical invasion were Aristodemos,
Kresphontes and Temenos, great, great grandchildren of Hercules. On
the eve of the invading army's departure, Aristodemos was killed at
Nafpaktos by a bolt of lightning. His sons, Procles and Eurysthenes,
took his place. The invaders defeated both the great ruling houses of the
Peloponnese. Tisamenus, son of Orestes (see Chapter 8) was expelled
from Argos and Nestor's descendants were defeated in Messenia. Temenos took possession of Argos, but it was decided that the distribution
of the other territories of the Peloponnese would be decided by lot, the
winner having first choice. Kresphontes particularly wanted Messenia.
He persuaded Temenos to assist him by trickery. The lots were clay tablets and were to be drawn from a water-filled jar. But the tablet for
Kresphontes was fire-baked, while the one for Procles and Eurysthenes
was merely dried in the sun. This, of course, disintegrated in the water.
Kresphontes drew the winning lot and claimed Messenia. The two
brothers took Sparta and founded the curious double kingship that was
to survive for centuries (see below). The trickery with the lots was later
one of the reasons advanced by the Spartans for their war against
Messenia and its subsequent subjugation.

Kresphontes moved the capital of Messenia to Stenykleros, thought
to be in the upper Messenian plain. Pylos remained abandoned and its
very location was forgotten.

The Archaeological Site

Pylos is the least visited of the major Mycenaean palace sites and its opening hours are more restricted. In summer it is open from 8.30 to 15.00 every day, but it closes at 14.30 in the winter. The main road runs downhill to the site from the north and the imposing position of the palace is not immediately obvious. Once within the precinct, however, the fine situation on the edge of the ridge becomes apparent. To the south, the palace overlooks the gently sloping olive-covered plain and the view encompass the entire Bay of Navarino with the island of Sphakteria beyond.

The buildings are in three groups. The main palace block is now covered by a corrugated iron roof. Although often described as ugly, the sense of enclosure makes it easier to visualise the remains as buildings. Beneath the roof, the fragile walls stand to a height of one metre. They provide a clearer impression of a Mycenaean palace layout than at any other mainland site. The first buildings on the ridge are thought to have been constructed around 1400 BC. They were followed by a succession of palaces. Originally there were fortifications here and traces of a complete circuit wall have been revealed, both by excavation and geophysical survey. As the society centred on Pylos extended its influence throughout Messenia, it is probable that the need for fortification disappeared and the wall was dismantled.

As at Mycenae, the hills around Pylos contain many tholos tombs. The most important lies just to the northeast of the car park. This must have been of great religious significance to the Mycenaeans. When it was first built, the tomb, the massive gate in the original circuit wall and the entrance to the earliest palace, were all in direct alignment. However, the later palaces were built to a different orientation, with the main entrance to the southeast. The visitor today enters by the same route. It is conceivable that the succession of palaces reflects the mythical events described above.

The principal rooms of the main block are arranged on a simple axis. The outer entrance, or Propylon, is flanked on the left by two rooms where the first discovery of Linear B tablets was made. When deciphered, the tablets were found to record tax assessments and palace inventories. These rooms must have either been the palace archives or the tax collector's office. The Propylon leads into an open inner court. On the opposite side another entrance porch supported by two columns leads through an intervening vestibule to the central megaron. Its centrepiece was the great circular hearth of plastered clay, 4M in diameter.

The bases of the four pillars that supported an upper storey or balcony are still in position. On the right hand side is the base for a throne. The megaron was probably as much a place of religion as a throne room. Mycenaean society may have resembled the Egyptian world where religious and political leadership were combined. Excavation revealed that the entire room was decorated, with the image of an octopus on the floor and lions and griffons on the wall behind the throne.

Off to the right of the inner court is the famous bathroom with its terracotta tub still in place. Storerooms lined each side of the megaron. Behind are the rooms used to store olive oil in huge jars built into permanent positions along the walls. More of these jars, or pithoi, stored wine in a separate building to the northeast. Also on the eastern side of the site was a range of buildings identified as workshops and an armoury. To the southwest is another megaron complex. It may represent the remains of an earlier palace and may have functioned as the residence of a second in command in the royal hierarchy.

Modern Pylos (Πύλος)

Modern Pylos, 17km south of Nestor's palace, is the ideal centre for exploring this corner of the Peloponnese. It lies at the southern end of Navarino Bay, the great natural harbour between the mainland and the island of Sphakteria. This area of Greece is now a low-key holiday destination in summer but is little visited at other times.

From the edge of the town, the road from the north loops down the hillside and leads to the quayside and the main square. Its name, the Plateia of the Three Admirals, commemorates the commanders of the combined fleets of the Russian, British and French navies that sank the greater part of the Ottoman fleet in the Bay in 1827. The Battle of Navarino as it came to be called, was one of the defining events of the Greek War of Independence. It led to the complete Ottoman withdrawal from the Peloponnese. Shaded by trees and surrounded by arcaded buildings the square is the centre of Pylos in every sense.

Pylos has the look and feel of an old town but was founded only in 1829 by the French. It has simply appropriated the ancient name. Before 1829, the only settlement here was the large Turko-Venetian artillery fort covering the entire hill to the south. First built in 1529 to command the southern entrance to the Bay, it is now known as Neokastro and is invisible from the town. Access is from the road to Methoni. The opening hours are 8.30 to 15.00, closed on Mondays.

187

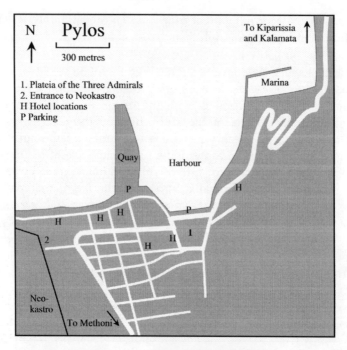

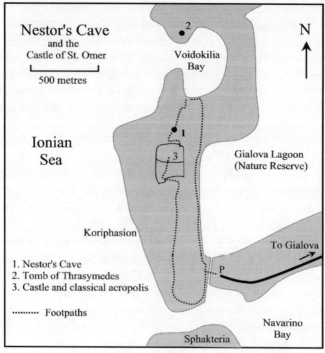

Nestor's Cave
The myths of Hermes and Apollo

The lower slopes of the prominent hill of Koriphasion at the northern end of Navarino Bay are thought to be the most likely site for the Mycenaean harbour town associated with Nestor's palace. The harbour itself may have been at the very north of the Bay in the area now occupied by the Gialova lagoon, or in the beautiful half-moon Bay of Voidokilia on the seaward side of the peninsula. However, recent surveys have also found evidence of an artificial harbour basin cut through the sand dunes about 2km to the north. In the cliff overlooking Voidokilia Bay, below the Classical acropolis and mediaeval castle on the heights, is the large cave known as Nestor's Grotto. It was said to be the place where Neleus and Nestor kept their animals, and where the infant Hermes hid the cattle he stole from Apollo.

Hermes was an ancient Arcadian god originally having many of the roles subsequently taken over by Pan as protector of the flocks and homes. It was common for Greeks to place a stylised statue of Hermes by the doors of their houses. These took the form of a square pillar with male genitals and a head of Hermes on top of the pillar. When Hermes assumed the role of protector of travellers these images were set up at crossroads. He was the son of Zeus and Maia, the eldest of the Pleiades (see below), and was born in a cave on Mount Kyllini. In the Homeric hymn to Hermes he is called a robber, a cattle driver, a bringer of dreams, a watcher by night, a thief at the gates. The hymn recounts the tradition that Hermes was such a precocious child that, born in the morning, by midday he had invented the lyre, and, by the evening, he had stolen Apollo's cattle.

In this myth, he escaped from his cradle and travelled to Pieria, the narrow coastal plain near Mount Olympus. There, Apollo was grazing his cattle. Hermes separated fifty beasts from the herd and drove them off, contriving to make them move backwards over a sandy spot to disguise the direction he had taken. He drove them to Pylos and hid them in the cave. After he prepared fire and sacrificed two of the animals he returned to Kyllini. Apollo, possessing the gift of prophecy, was able to divine the identity of the thief. He made his way to Kyllini to confront Hermes and demand the restoration of his cattle. Hermes denied all knowledge of the crime until Apollo carried him to his father, Zeus, who compelled him to reveal the truth. Zeus commanded that the two gods should make their way to Pylos and Hermes should restore Apollo's property. When they reached the cave, Apollo saw the hides of

189

the sacrificed animals spread out on the rocks. He was astonished that the infant Hermes could have dispatched such large beasts. Hermes carried with him the lyre he had made by stretching strings of sheep-gut across a tortoise shell. When Apollo heard the music of the lyre he was so charmed that he agreed to exchange the instrument for the cattle. Apollo and Hermes became close friends. Zeus appointed Hermes as his messenger. He appears in numerous myths as Zeus's agent.

To reach Nestor's cave, take the main road north from Pylos for 6km. Towards the northern end of the Bay the road runs close to the shore then makes an abrupt turn to the right in the village of Gialova (Γιάλοβα). About 200M further on, a left turn, with difficult to spot brown signs but with a conspicuous sign to "Camping Erodios", leads after 4km to the northern tip of the Bay directly below the southern end of Koriphasion. The last part of the road is gravel. At the time of writing, it was possible to drive right up to the rock, but the area of the lagoon is an important nature reserve and it may soon be necessary to walk the final section. At the end of the track, a footbridge crosses the creek that connects the lagoon to the sea. An information board provides a good map of the nature reserve and surrounding area. Paths fork left and right. Signs for the castle point left along a footpath that follows the rocky shore of the narrow northern entrance to the Bay. This leads to the gentler slopes on the seaward side of Koriphasion and an obvious track, recently cleared, leads up to the main gate of the castle. This track provides a less strenuous route to the summit than that described below.

To the right, the path to the cave runs beneath the cliffs along the edge of the lagoon to an area of sand dunes between the lagoon and Voidokilia Bay. The cave lies in the hillside above the dunes. The easiest way to find it is to walk through the dunes to Voidokilia beach and, from the seaward end of the curve of sand, climb the dunes where they abut the rocky promontory. Above the dunes, which are surprisingly high, is a footpath that leads through a meadow to the cave now visible at the base of a cliff. The interior of the cave is enormous and a dim light is cast from a hole in the roof. The stalactites inside were thought to represent animal hides hanging from the roof. Pottery has provided evidence of occupation from Mycenaean times.

On the opposite side of Voidokilia Bay is a very early tholos tomb, contemporary with the shaft graves of Grave Circle A at Mycenae. It is known as the tomb of Thrasymedes, a son of Nestor, but if mythical chronologies are at all accurate, this must be fanciful. However, evidence of votive offerings from the Classical period onwards shows that a cult developed here and the tomb was clearly believed to have housed an important mythical figure.

On the summit above the cave is the Frankish castle of St. Omer, erected in 1278, on foundations, still visible, of the Classical acropolis. A very steep path, requiring some scrambling, leads from the cave to the north wall. Access to the interior is through a breach in a collapsed round tower. The castle has been recently cleared of vegetation and it is now possible to explore the remains with less risk of falling into the large cisterns that provided the inhabitants with water. The views are superb. The walls include Classical, Byzantine, Frankish, Venetian and Turkish work. It is easiest to return by walking through the castle's two baileys to the main gate and following the path described above. Access is possible at all times.

Pylos to Kalamata

From Pylos, it is possible to loop south around the coast to visit the great Venetian fortresses at Methoni (Μεθώνη) and Koroni (Κορώνη). Both are pleasant seaside towns with accommodation. The direct route to Kalamata (Καλαμάτα) leads through rolling countryside across the broad peninsula of southern Messenia to the Gulf of Messene. The modern town of Messene is 40km from Pylos in the centre of the Pamisos valley. Kalamata is a further 10km.

The main road skirts the southern edge of Messene. On the eastern side of the town a well signposted road on the left leads north up the western side of the Pamisos valley towards the superb site of ancient Messene (Αρχαια Μεσσηνη), also sometimes referred to as Ithome. The quickest way to the site is to follow this road north for 14km through the villages of Triodos (Τρίοδος), Eva (Εύα) and Lambena (Λάμβαινα). Just north of Lambena, take a left turn with signs for the ancient site and for Mavromati (Μαυρομάτη).

Ancient Messene
Substantial remains of the 4C BC city. Sanctuary of Asklepios.

The road from Lambena climbs over the southern ridge of Mount Ithome. After approximately 7km, it crosses the line of ancient Messene's walls and enters Mavromati. The village centre is still marked by the spring of Klepsydra, literally 'stolen water'. Fed by an aqueduct from Ithome, water flows into a huge draw basin on the right

191

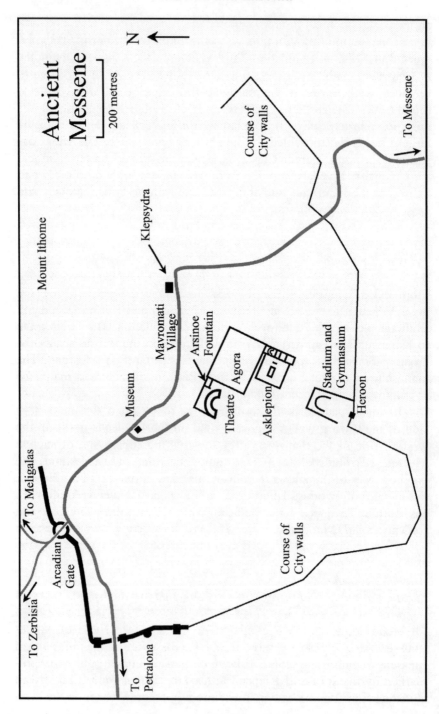

N

Ancient
Messene

200 metres

Mount Ithome

Course of
City walls

To Messene

Klepsydra

Mavromati
Village

Museum

Arsinoe
Fountain

Agora

Theatre

Asklepion

Stadium and
Gymnasium

Heroon

To Meligalas

Arcadian
Gate

To Zerbisia

To
Petralona

Course of
City walls

hand side of the road. This was one of two springs or fountains providing water for the ancient city. Mount Ithome is still crowned by the ruins of the Monastery of Voukano, but it was originally the site of the Sanctuary of Zeus Ithomatas, founded by Messene herself. Pausanias remarks that it would be impossible to number all the claims made for the location of Zeus's birth. The Messenians' version has the nymphs, Neda and Ithome, bathing the infant Zeus in the mountain's springs. After the founding of the sanctuary and altar on the summit, water was carried every day from the spring in commemoration of Zeus's birth.

Tradition placed the original capital of Messenia at the northern end of the Pamisos valley, both before the founding of Nestor's palace and again, when Kresphontes established it at Stenykleros. However, although a Sanctuary of Zeus existed on the peak of Mount Ithome from a very early period, no settlement is known in the broad valley to the west of the mountain before 369 BC. After the coming of the Dorians, whenever this actually occurred, the existing population is thought to have lived alongside the newcomers. This period of peace was violently disturbed when the Spartans crossed the Taiyetos in the 8C BC intent on annexing Messenia. Their eventual subjugation of the Messenians was to last for 350 years but was only achieved by the transformation of Spartan society into a permanent armed camp (see Sparta below). The Messenian response to their predicament was to revolt whenever the opportunity arose, or to emigrate and establish colonies abroad. Somehow they maintained their culture over the centuries.

When Epaminondas of Thebes defeated Sparta and invaded the Peloponnese, he helped the Messenians to found a new city of Messene as part of a strategy to prevent a resurgence of Spartan power. He achieved this by developing a ring of strong states around Lakonia; Mantinea to the north, Megalopolis to the northwest and Messene west across the mountains. The result was both a powerfully fortified city, with sections of walls still impressive to this day, and a showpiece of Messenian culture. The city continued to be embellished throughout the Hellenistic period and was still important in the Roman period.

The modern village stands in the centre of the vast area enclosed by Messene's walls. The principal remains lie below the road but are almost invisible from above. The site is unenclosed and accessible from dawn to dusk but site guards ensure that the area is cleared as darkness falls. Access is from the northern edge of the village where a dirt road on the left, by the museum (permanently closed), runs down to a parking area by the village cemetery. This is the starting point for a visit to the theatre, agora, Asklepion and stadium. The Arcadian gate, the best-preserved element of the fortifications, is 1km north of the village. The modern road still runs through this monumental structure, which stands to a height of 5M. It consists of a double inner gate, a large circular court and an outer gate protected by two flanking towers. Pausanias describes a protective statue of Hermes, in the square style described above, standing within this gate. It probably occupied the niche that still exists in the east wall of the circular court. To the east and west the walls and towers are still in excellent condition. Overall, the circuit was 9km long. Another well-preserved section with a semi-circular tower can be seen by following the road that turns left in front of the Arcadian gate for a further ½km.

The remains of the city's civic buildings lie below the car park by the cemetery. The area is laid out on a series of level terraces. New information boards have been erected at various points and have excellent site plans. The path first leads past the theatre. The cavea is partly cut into the slope of the hill and partly supported by massive retaining walls. Pointed doorways pierce these walls with steps leading to the rear of the auditorium. The construction is a step in the transition from the original Greek form of theatre, cut into the hillside, to the completely self supporting style built up with retaining walls. Unfortunately, the interior is a ruin with the finely carved seating blocks now merely a jumbled mass. Beyond the theatre is the huge square of the agora. The visible remains are scanty apart from a Roman stoa on its northern side. At the west end of this stoa, close to the theatre, are the massive foundations of the Arsinoe fountain. This was fed by water piped from Klepsydra and is named after Arsinoe, the daughter of Leukippos, a younger son of Perieres (see above). The Messenians held her in great regard as the mother of Asklepios. They were thus able to claim Asklepios as a Messenian citizen. This myth is in direct contradiction to the Epidavrian version.

The Hellenistic Sanctuary of Asklepios or Askleopion to the south of the agora is Messene's glorious centrepiece. Linked directly to the agora, it formed the religious, political and civic centre of the city, combining all these functions in one complex building. Until the 1960s, the area was largely buried and only a rough square shaped outline was visible. This was thought to be the agora itself. Careful excavation over many years culminated in the discovery of the temple and altar of Asklepios in the centre of a courtyard, surrounded by colonnaded stoas. Excavation has revealed inscriptions and sculptural fragments that have confirmed the identification of each element of the complex, previously known only from Pausanias's detailed description of the city. As is so

Figure 19 Messene: The re-erected colonnades of the Gymnasium

Figure 20 Messene: the Stadium complex

often the case, his description has proved to be completely accurate. The sanctuary entrance is on the east side through a monumental Propylaea. To the north of the entrance is a well-preserved small theatre, originally roofed. To the south was the Bouleuterion or Council House. Facing the entrance is the massive altar of Asklepios with the temple beyond. Behind the stoa, on the west side of the courtyard, is a row of cult rooms or small temples. These contained statues and dedications to the gods Artemis, Tykhe (Fortune), and the Muses. Here too, according to Pausanias, was an iron statue of the Messenians' great hero, Epaminondas, and another representing the city of Thebes itself. The large number of deities represented in the sanctuary's temples and cult rooms is a vivid example of the polytheistic nature of Greek religion. The size of the central temple and altar is testament to the importance of Asklepios to the Messenians. Unlike the Asklepia found elsewhere on the Peloponnese, there does not appear to have been a healing centre here. Perhaps no other site on mainland Greece better illustrates the complete integration of the secular and religious aspects of Greek society.

About 200M south of the Asklepion is Messene's final surprise. Concealed from view in a natural depression, is the stadium, surrounded by the stoas of the gymnasium. These were designed as a single architectural unit. The re-erection of many of the columns of the stoas has made this the most spectacular part of the site. The scale of the complex once again emphasises the importance of games in Greek culture. The columns of the entrance to the west stoa have been recently restored. Facing the entrance was a statue of the hero, Theseus. Behind the statue was a cult room dedicated to Hercules and Hermes. The stadium is curved at its northern end and surrounded by elaborate stone seating. The straight southern end ran right up to the city walls. Facing the stadium, on a massive podium astride the walls, was an Heröon, or sanctuary of Messenian heroes. This, too, is slowly being restored.

Messene may well be the best preserved city on the Greek mainland. On weekdays, outside the summer season, you may well have it to yourself.

Messenia to Lakonia via the Langadha pass.

From modern Messene the road passes the airport, now used for charter flights, and crosses the Pamisos plain. At a T-junction with the Megalopolis – Kalamata road turn right. This quickly leads through the scruffy and surprisingly extensive commercial suburbs of Kalamata, the second city of the Peloponnese. A well signposted left turn leads to the town centre and eventually to the broad artery of Othos Artemidos. This road runs the length of the town from north to south, along the course of the river Nethonas, although in places the river has been culverted and is invisible. Sparta (Sparti, Σπάρτη) is signposted left. The port of Kalamata, and the extensive sea front, are 2km south (right).

Turning left for Sparta, the broad thoroughfare passes, or rather seems to go through, the bus station. The castle is on a low hill visible to the right. Beyond the bus bays, a sign points right, across the river, onto the narrow Sparta road. Kalamata is quickly left behind and the road begins to climb. Potential hazards include minor landslips, fallen rocks and herds of goats lying in the road in the shade of a tree. After 8km, the road begins to drop down into the dramatic gorge of the river Nethonas and the austere landscape gradually softens as it becomes more wooded. Seventeen kilometres from Kalamata it begins to climb again, reaching the mountain village of Artemisia (Αρτεμισία) after a further 6km. Roadside stalls sell honey and herbs produced on the local hillsides. After a total of 34km, the road reaches the summit of the pass where there is an hotel and taverna. The views are of snow capped peaks well into May.

Descending through a landscape recovering well from the ravages of fire in previous years, the road crosses the border into Lakonia and enters the gorge of the Langadha. In places this is so narrow that the road is carried on overhung ledges cut into the cliff wall. Emerging from the mountains at the village of Tripi (Τρύπη), there is a choice of routes. Straight on leads directly to Sparta. A minor road on the right leads to Sparta via the ruined late Byzantine city of Mistra, the outstanding mediaeval archaeological site of the area. After a kilometre the distinctive conical hill of the city appears in the distance, ringed by the walls and towers of the upper town and surmounted by the Frankish castle built by William de Villehardouin in 1249. The red tiled roof of the newly restored Palace of the Despots is prominent on the hillside. This was the main settlement of the area from the second half of the 13C AD onwards, completely replacing Sparta. It knew real importance for two hundred years as a one of the last bastions of the Byzantine Empire. It still contains numerous churches with wall paintings and frescoes in various states of repair. The town was effectively abandoned in 1834 when the modern city of Sparta was founded.

After 2km, a side road leads right to the upper entrance to the mediaeval city. Straight on, the road passes below the walls to the lower entrance. The site has the standard opening times 08.30 to 15.00 daily, with longer hours in summer. The modern village of Mistras is 1km beyond the lower gate and has modest tourist facilities. Sparta is a further 5km and is clearly signposted.

Sparta (Sparti, Σπάρτη)
The city of Menelaus, Helen, Castor and Polydeuces

There have been two great foundations known as Sparta, three if we count the modern city that was laid out only in 1834. The Sparta of Greek mythology is the Bronze Age city, steeped in the myths of Leda, Hyakinthos, Helen and her brothers, the Dioscuri. Although the site of this Sparta has not yet been identified with certainty, it probably lies at Therapne, east of the Evrotas river, near the site of the Menelaion, the later shrine to Menelaus and Helen (see below).

The second Sparta is the warrior state that developed in the 9C and 8C BC, subdued Messenia, defeated Athens in the Peloponnesian War and gave us the very idea of a Spartan way of life. Located on a new site to the west of the river Evrotas, this was a society characterised by self-sacrifice and austerity, where every Spartan adult male was a soldier. The ideals of this later Sparta have become a myth that has endured into modern times. The names of few other Greek cities are as well known.

Although Mycenaean 'mansions' have been excavated at Therapne, no great palace-fortress resembling those of the Argolid or Pylos has been located. Similarly, Classical Sparta was, virtually uniquely among Greek city-states, never more than a collection of villages or townships, with few of the grand public monuments possessed by every other Greek settlement calling itself a city. It is the myths of Sparta that have survived rather than the physical remains.

Bronze Age Sparta
Evrotas, Sparta and Lacedaimon

Sparta has a complicated series of foundation myths. They provide explanations for the naming of the principal cities and the natural features of the territory. They also gave the early rulers of Lakonia genealogical links to the gods, as well as the other Mycenaean royal houses. Hercules is given a role legitimising the lineage of the kings. Finally, the myths describe the lives of Sparta's most famous heroes, Castor and Polydeuces, and of Helen, the woman at the centre of the Trojan War.

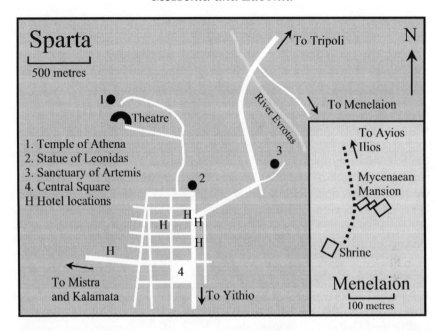

Sparta's earliest myth is of Lelex, the first ruler of the Leleges, mythical inhabitants of Laconia, rather like the Pelasgians. His son, Myles, succeeded him. He was said to have invented the mill and accordingly was known as the Miller. He was succeeded in turn by his son, Evrotas, who drained the marshy plain by cutting a river south to the sea. Thereafter the river was known as the Evrotas, as it still is today. Evrotas's daughter was named Sparta. She married Lacedaimon, supposedly a son of Zeus and Taiyeta, daughter of Atlas and Pleione. Taiyeta and her sisters were known as the Pleiades, virgin companions of Artemis. They were placed among the stars when they prayed to the gods for rescue from the hunter Orion. Taiyeta also gave her name to the mountains to the west of the Lakonian plain that form such a dramatic backdrop to the modern town. Evrotas died without a male heir so left the throne to his son-in-law. Lacedaimon renamed the land Lakedaimonia and founded a city that he named Sparta, after his wife. In turn their son, Amyklas, founded the city of Amyklai. Their daughter, Euridice, married Akrisius of Argos. Euridice's daughter, Danae, became the mother of Perseus (see Chapter 8). Amyklas's son, Hyakinthos, had an affair with Apollo, and, after he died in an accident, a famous shrine was established at Amyklai in his honour (see below).

After Amyklas, the kingship passed to his sons and then to Oebalus, his grandson. Oebalus had two sons. Tyndareus, the eldest, was his child by Gorgophone, who he had married after her first husband Perieres had died (see Messene above). Pausanaias tells us that she was the first woman to remarry instead of remaining a widow. Hippocoon, the younger son, was Tyndareus's half-brother, born of the nymph Bateia. Tyndareus succeeded his father on his death. Hippocoon had twelve sons and with their help he was able to depose his brother and drive him into exile. Tyndareus fled to the court of king Thestius in Aitolia. There, he fell in love with and married Leda, Thestius's daughter. Leda's sister, Althaea, was the wife of king Oeneus of Kalydon. Tyndareus met Hercules at Oeneus's court (see Chapter 4 for Hercules and Deianeira, Oeneus's daughter). Hercules agreed to assist Tyndareus in recovering the throne of Sparta. He raised an army and, with the assistance of Cepheus of Tegea, he defeated Hippocoon and his sons. Tyndareus and Leda returned to Sparta.

Leda's children were the result of her famous liaison with Zeus when he came to her disguised as a swan (see Chapter 2, Rhamnous). Although all born at the same time, Helen and Polydeuces, known to the Romans as Pollox, were thought to be the children of Zeus, while Castor and Clytemnestra were the children of Tyndareus. This curious arrangement meant that although Castor and Polydeuces were generally spoken of as twins, one was mortal and the other immortal. The brothers were known as the Dioscuri, that is, the sons of Zeus. Usually the myths involving brothers are tales of rivalry. Castor and Polydeuces however, were renowned for their devotion to each other and they always acted together in their heroic exploits. Castor was famed for his skills with horses and Polydeuces was a renowned boxer.

Although Helen is famous for being carried off to Troy by Paris, this was not the first time she had been abducted. When she only twelve, Theseus, with the help of his friend Pirithous, king of the Lapiths, led an army into Lakedaimonia and captured Helen. He took her to Aphidnae, a village near Athens, to be cared for by his mother Aethra, until she grew older. Following the deaths of their wives, Pirithous and Theseus had decided that they would both marry daughters of Zeus. After their success with Helen's abduction, Pirithous resolved to be even more ambitious and carry off Persephone, during the third of the year that she spent in the Underworld. Theseus believed this was a foolish enterprise, but was bound to assist his friend. His misgivings proved justified when they were both captured and imprisoned by Hades. After four years of imprisonment, Theseus was finally released by Hercules when he came to the Underworld on his last Labour.

During Theseus's long absence from Athens, Castor and Polydeuces raised an army and invaded Attica. They rescued Helen and brought her back to Sparta along with Aethra, who became her handmaid. The Dioscuri set Menestheus on the Athenian throne. After his escape from the underworld, Theseus was unable to recover his kingdom and died in exile. Castor and Polydeuces took part in the Kalydonian boar hunt and sailed with Jason and the Argonauts. Their rivalry with Idas and Lynceus, the sons of Aphareus, king of Messene, was to end with the death of all four.

Some time before the events of the Trojan War, they were drawn into battle in a dispute over cattle. Idas killed Castor, Polydeuces killed Lynceus, and Zeus, coming to the aid of his son, killed Idas with a thunderbolt. Polydeuces did not want to outlive his brother so refused his gift of immortality. Zeus allowed the two brothers to share each other's fate. They lived alternate days in the Underworld and in the heavens with the gods. Their images were set among the stars as Gemini, the twins. The Dioscuri became important divinities for the later Spartans. Their cult eventually spread through the rest of Greece. Shrines for their worship were common. Poseidon was thought to have given them power over wind and waves and they were regarded as protectors of sailors. They were also gods of horsemanship. Statues often represented them on horseback.

Agamemnon and Menelaus came to Tyndareus's court at Sparta after they had been exiled from Mycenae (see Chapter 8). Agamemnon married Clytemnestra. Helen, however, was besieged by suitors. Many of them were powerful princes. Tyndareus feared that whichever husband his daughter chose, the other suitors would become his enemies. Accordingly, he took Odysseus's advice and made all the suitors swear that, whoever Helen chose, the others would accept her choice and protect her and her husband. This was the crucial oath that was to bind the leaders of the Greek world together when Helen was carried off to Troy. Eventually she chose Menelaus as her husband and Tyndareus bequeathed his throne to his new son-in-law.

The subsequent events of Helen's elopement or abduction by Paris and the ten-year Trojan War would require an entire book to recount. Eventually, Menelaus and Helen did return to Sparta and lived out their lives in peace. There are various legends of their deaths. In one version, they are brought by the gods to Elysium, a land far to the west that provided an afterlife for favoured heroes. There they lived as immortals. In other versions they both died and were buried at Therapne.

After Orestes had regained power in Mycenae, he succeeded to the throne of Sparta on the death of Menelaus, as he was the son of Tyndareus's daughter Clytemnestra. For a brief period virtually the entire Peloponnese was united in one kingdom. Orestes was succeeded by his son, Tisamenus. This is the point at which the mythical history of the Mycenaean kings comes to end, coinciding with the archaeological evidence for the collapse of Bronze Age society as a whole.

Archaic and Classical Sparta

The Spartans of the Classical age believed that their line of kings began with the return of the Heraclidae and the invasion of the Dorians (see above). They traced the royal lineage back to Aristodemos, the great-great-grandson of Hercules. There is no doubt that the founders of Sparta were Dorians. Their Greek dialect was Doric, and most of their religious festivals were dedicated to Apollo, the Dorians most favoured god. A key element of Sparta's unique political constitution, its dual kingship, began with the twin sons of Aristodemos, Eurysthenes and Procles. This arrangement, which persisted until the latter part of the 3C BC, may have originally been devised to avoid a dynastic struggle between two families. Agis, son of Eurysthenes, gave his name to the senior royal house, the Agiads. The Eurypontid line took its name from Eurypon, the grandson of Procles. It is with this pair of kings that the ancestry of Sparta's rulers ceases to be purely mythological and acquires an historical dimension.

By the 8C BC, the initial foundation of small villages, Pitane, Mesoa, Limnai and Konosura, had become organized into a single entity known as Sparta. During the first half of the 8C this small state expanded southwards until it controlled the entire Evrotas valley and the coast to the south. Sometime around 725 BC, the Spartans sought to expand into the other great fertile plain of the southern Peloponnese, that of Messenia, to the west of the Taiyetos mountains. Traditionally the first Messenian War lasted 20 years, although it probably took the form of annual raids into Messenian territory. Eventually the Spartans completely subdued the Messenians, despite the natural barrier of the Taiyetos Mountains between the two plains.

They introduced a form of serfdom, in which the Messenians continued to farm what had been their own land, but with a large proportion of the produce going to their new masters. The Messenians bore this burden until the first half of the 7C BC when they revolted. The traditional date for the second Messenian War is 685 to 668 BC. At the end of it, the Messenians were once again subjugated. The surviving rebels were exiled to Sicily, where there is a city called Messene to this day.

202

The effort of this second war seriously weakened the Spartans. They were vastly outnumbered by their subject, Helot, populations, not just in Messenia but also in the lower Evrotas valley. Their response to this predicament was to formalise their constitution and create the first military state. Thereafter, they were able to keep the Messenians effectively enslaved for another 300 years.

The mechanics of Spartan government were traditionally devised by Lycurgus, a shadowy figure who may have lived at any time between the 9C and 7C BC. The later Spartans worshipped him as a god, but he may be a completely mythical character. The laws and constitution that bear his name established both a complex system of checks and balances in the government of the state, as well as a set of social institutions designed to maintain and enhance Spartan military prowess. The core of this system was the compulsory military education called the Agoge, the raising, that every male child of the ruling class had to undergo. This system created soldiers with a level of discipline and courage previously unknown in Greece.

Spartan government had four divisions that combined elements of monarchy, oligarchy and democracy. Executive power was in the hands of the five ephors. Although they were the most powerful element of the system, their power was constrained by annual elections. Legislation and foreign policy were in the hands of a council of elders, the Gerousia. This consisted of the two kings and 28 citizens, elected for life, who had reached 60, the age of retirement from military service. A general assembly of all Spartiates, males over 30, had the power of veto over council proposals. The power of the kings was restricted to command of the army when at war.

Spartan society consisted of three distinct castes. The most numerous were the lowest caste, the Helots, the conquered peoples of Lakonia and Messenia, whose land now formed the estates of absentee Spartiates. They lived a subsistence existence as serfs, cultivating the land to provide produce for their rulers. The middle caste, known as the Perioikoi, literally "dwellers around", were the merchants and traders of Spartan society. They lived in their own towns and villages and had local autonomy within those communities. They had no status as Spartan citizens, their sole obligation to the state being military service in time of war. It was the Perioikoi who effectively ran the non-agricultural part of the Spartan economy. Spartan citizens, or Spartiates, were the ruling class, presumably the descendants of the original Dorian invaders. Citizenship, as elsewhere in Greece, was restricted to men, but women had a much stronger role in Sparta than was typical in most Greek societies.

Male Spartans were raised for a life as a soldier so that the state could continually maintain a standing army.

The role of the state, or more accurately, the community, to avoid the modern notions of state control, began at birth. The community first decided whether a child was fit to live. Weak infants of both sexes were exposed on the mountains to die, although this was not exclusively a Spartan practice. Male children lived with their mothers until the age of seven when their life of military and athletic training began. From the age of seven to twenty, they lived in training camps where the regime was designed to teach discipline, military skills and endurance of pain. No doubt this was also intended to replace family ties with loyalty to the state. A fundamental part of a child's education was the role of a young adult soldier as mentor, teacher and lover. Homoerotic bonds between teacher and pupil were regarded by all Greeks as normal and a positive aid in education. In Sparta, homosexual love between a young adolescent and a soldier in his twenties was thought neither unusual nor incompatible with later heterosexual marriage. Homosexual relationships between soldiers were considered a distinct advantage, producing exceptional bravery in battle. This was taken to its logical conclusion by Thebes in the 4C BC with their elite troops, the Sacred Band, which consisted of 150 pairs of lovers. These were the forces that decisively defeated Sparta in 371 BC.

At the age of twenty, male Spartiates joined the army. They continued to live in barracks and were barred from any form of trade or business other than that of professional soldier. In fact, these strictures extended to a prohibition on holding wealth as gold or silver coin. Spartans measured their wealth in terms of land and its productivity. Membership of a communal dining mess was a compulsory requirement for each soldier. He was required to provide his share of the food. This came from two sources. Firstly, the allotment of land that the state granted to each citizen. This was, of course, actually farmed by the Helots. The second source was hunting, an activity conducted on foot. It was a practical method of providing food beyond the agricultural staples of grain, olives and grapes, and also a ritual of manhood.

Despite continuing to live communally, Spartan men were encouraged to marry. Those who did apparently continued to sleep in barracks, visiting their wives briefly at night, virtually in secret. The maintenance of an adequate adult population was a continual problem for Sparta. The total number of Spartiates that made up the state probably never exceeded 10000. By the 4C BC, it had fallen to perhaps 1500. Only when a soldier reached the age of thirty did he acquire full citizenship. At that point he could finally live with his family in his own house. However his military service continued until 60, or his death.

Spartan girls, uniquely among Greeks, also received a state education. Again the emphasis was on physical skills, running, wrestling, throwing the discus and javelin. The Spartans believed that strong women would become the mothers of strong soldiers. If women were in charge of their sons until the age of seven, it was also essential that they were brought up to share the ideals of an austere military society. As Spartan men were full time soldiers, women managed domestic affairs. However they were spared the drudgery of a normal domestic role, as the Helots did all physical tasks. Another unique feature of Spartan society was the freedom that women had to hold and manage their own land. Among Greeks, only Spartan women could inherit in their own right and were not merely intermediaries to the next male heir. Women also had a curious freedom in sexual matters. Sparta had no adultery laws. As the important thing to society was the production of more fighting males, procreative sex outside marriage was not unknown when a husband proved incapable of fathering children.

By the time of the Persian Wars, Sparta was, in military terms, the strongest of all the city states. This was recognised throughout Greece and Sparta was given the command of both the land and sea forces assembled against the Persians (see Chapter 2). Sparta had spent much of the 6C BC subduing her northern neighbours and forcing them into an alliance that came to be called the Peloponnesian League. This was the coalition that spent 27 years fighting Athens in the latter part of the 5C BC in the conflict conventionally called the Peloponnesian War. It ended in 404 BC with Spartan victory and, for a brief period, Sparta was the most powerful state in Greece.

This situation lasted a mere 33 years. The rapid growth of the military power of Thebes in this period culminated in the decisive Spartan defeat at Leuktra in 371 BC. The subsequent campaigns in the Spartan homelands led by the Theban general, Epaminondas, the liberation of the Messenians and the construction of the fortified cities of Messene, Mantinea and Megalopolis, ended Spartan power forever. After 338 BC and the battle of Chaironia (see Chapter 3), Sparta's domination by Macedonia was inevitable. It was absorbed into the Achaian League by force. After the Roman defeat of the League in 148 BC (see Corinth Chapter 5), Sparta along with the whole of Greece became a Roman protectorate.

Modern Sparta and the Archaeological Sites

The modern town, founded in 1834, was developed in a grid pattern of broad streets. The prosperous main avenue of Palaiologou runs north to south and is lined with impressive palm trees. The road from Mistra enters the town from the west along Othos Lycourgou, meeting the main avenue by the principal square. Approaching from the north, the Tripolis road crosses the Evrotas river on the edge of the town, bears right by signs on the left for the temple of Artemis Orthia and then meets the main avenue at a crossroads. Left at this junction leads down to the main square. Right leads to the remains of ancient Sparta on the low acropolis hill. Few tourists visit Sparta's scattered archaeological sites, but the proximity of Mistra means that it has many hotels catering for overnight visitors

Acropolis

There are numerous brown signs for the acropolis, but they are hardly necessary. Standing in front of the archaeological area at the top of Palaiologou, where it changes its name to Stadhiou, is the prominent modern statue to Leonidas, almost double life size. This striking landmark in bronze represents a 5C BC Spartan warrior. It is based on a marble head and torso found nearby in 1925. Although nothing was found to indicate the identity of the figure, the hero represented could well have been Leonidas. The image is surely how he ought to have looked. Inscribed on the base of the statue is the reply Leonidas was said to have given the Persians when they demanded that the Spartans should lay down their arms: "Μολών λαβέ", come and take them.

Most of the remains visible today date from well after the great period of Spartan power. The Spartans always boasted that the strength of their army meant that they had no need of city walls. Only during the long slow period of decline, from the end of the 4C BC onwards, were walls constructed. These encircled the whole area occupied by the original four settlements. Although they were rebuilt and strengthened many times, nothing is now visible, although their course has been identified. The acropolis itself was only fortified for the first time in the 3C AD. It is effectively an unenclosed site, hardly meriting the name acropolis, consisting only of a low wooded hill, now landscaped to form a park and covered with olive trees. The entrance is just to the west of the statue. The remains are principally of Roman Sparta, particularly the period of renewed prosperity in the 2C AD. A modern cobbled road enters through the site of the south gate. Fragments of half buried masonry represent sections of Byzantine wall. Concrete and brick structures are from a large Roman portico.

The theatre, which dates from the 2C BC, is built into southern flank of the hill. A sign indicates a track to the left, which skirts the base of the hill and leads to the orchestra. Although the greater part of the theatre's stone seating has disappeared, there are still substantial remains of the stage and the finely built retaining walls. The wall to the east is engraved with long lists of magistrates' names from the 2C AD. The paved road continues on to the summit of the hill passing the foundations of a large Byzantine basilica dating from the 7C to the 10C AD. Directly above the theatre stood the famous temple of Athena Chalkioikos, Bronzehouse Athena, so-called because its interior was lined with bronze sheets. This is one of the few buildings known to have existed from the early history of Sparta, with pottery evidence dating to the 7C BC. Athena was Sparta's patron goddess. The position of the temple has been determined, but there is little to see.

Sanctuary of Artemis Orthia (Standing Artemis)

The site of the famous initiation rites that young Spartans endured as part of the Agoge lies to the northeast of the town. This is the only spot where substantive remains from Archaic and Classical Sparta can be seen today. To reach the sanctuary, leave the town centre on the Tripolis road. Where it makes a right-angled turn to the left, a brown sign points straight on down a track. The fenced site lies 200M further on. Although it is enclosed, the gate is generally open and, in any case, the remains are visible from the lane. The sanctuary is named after the cult statue of Artemis supposedly brought back from Tauris by Orestes and Iphigenia. The Lakonians believed that Orestes brought the statue to Sparta when he assumed the kingship. The Athenians, of course, maintained that the statue had remained at Braurona (see Chapter 2). The sanctuary dates back as far as the 10C BC when it consisted of a simple open-air altar. A temple was first erected in the 8C BC with rebuilding in the 6C and 2C BC. The initiation rites took the form of ritual flogging that was said to be severe enough to leave blood on the altar in lieu of a sacrifice. Roman admiration for the austere traditions of Classical Sparta led to a late revival of these rites, but with overtones of a spectacle laid on for tourists. In a final Roman restoration in the 3C AD, tiered seating, in effect a theatre, was built around the edge of the sanctuary, with the altar as the focus. These are the remains that survive today.

Menelaion (Therapne)

The site of the Menelaion, the shrine of Menelaus and Helen, is the best candidate for the location of Mycenaean Sparta. It is also the spot from which to appreciate the view of Sparta, the Evrotas plain and the magnificent backdrop of the mountain wall of the Taiyetos to the west.

Leaving the town north on the Tripoli road, turn right, immediately after crossing the river, onto a road signposted to Skoura (Σκούρα). After about 3km, a sign points left to the Menelaion down a rough concrete road. It is possible to drive as far as the church of Ayios Ilias where there is room to park. The track continues beyond the church but quickly becomes unsuitable for vehicles. The unenclosed site is a pleasant 15min away on foot.

The shrine stands in a commanding position on a small hill high above the river. The rather formless ruins, dating from the 5C BC, stand on a large stepped platform. This replaced earlier structures that first appeared in the 8C BC. Below, the river flows through wide gravel banks. The view encompasses the modern town scattered over the plain, perhaps much as Classical Sparta must have done. The great peaks of the mountains are covered in snow well into May. There is no doubt that this is the shrine of Helen and Menelaus, as inscribed dedications have been found that include both names. Pausanias says specifically that Helen and Menelaus were buried here and that it was called Therapne after Lelex's daughter. It must originally have been a prominent landmark when viewed from the town.

Only 100M away, on the eastern side of the hill, are the remains of an important Mycenaean site, probably the best candidate in the area for the palace of Menelaus and Helen. The location of the Menelaion must itself be seen as strong evidence for this identification. Excavations have revealed occupation from the Middle Bronze Age. By the 15C BC, a complex 'mansion' had been built, so called, because it conforms, on a smaller scale, to the palace layout known from the other Mycenaean centres. At its core was the megaron, basically a rectangular hall with walls projecting from one end to form a porch. On either side were long corridors that led to rows of further rooms. The building was probably of two storeys. Three separate phases of building have been identified, but the site was finally destroyed about 1200 BC. Evidence of further buildings on the two small hills to the north and south indicates a considerable settlement. Unlike the great Mycenaean sites of the Argolid, there were no defensive walls. Perhaps the Spartans' disdain of city walls unconsciously imitated their Mycenaean heroes.

Amyklai
Sanctuary of Hyakinthos

Amyklai, 6km south of Sparta, was an important Mycenaean settlement and has been considered another candidate for the location of Menelaus's capital. It became part of the urban area of Sparta early in the 8C BC when the Spartans expanded their territory into the rest of the Evrotas valley. The site became their most important religious sanctuary. They took over the earlier cult of Hyakinthos and linked his worship with Apollo. The festival known as the Hyakinthia became their greatest religious event. Here Apollo took precedence over Athena, the city's patron deity.

Hyakinthos was the son of Amyklas, the founder of Amyklai and the son of Lacedaimon. The myth linking him to Apollo was based on his legendary youthful beauty. His love affair with the poet, Thamyris, was thought to be the first recorded homosexual relationship. The beauty of Hyakinthos next attracted the attention of Apollo, who fell in love with him. The two became constant companions. Zephyrus, the west wind, also fell for Hyakinthos's charms. His jealousy of Apollo was so intense that one day when the two lovers were practising with the discus, he deflected the spinning disc in mid-air so that it struck Hyakinthos on the head. The blow was so severe that even Apollo's healing powers could not save the boy. He was buried at Amyklai. Violet flowers grew where his blood fell to the earth. Thereafter they were called hyacinths. The annual festival of the Hyakinthia was said to have been founded on Apollo's orders.

At the Menelaion there is break in the archaeological record between the 12C and the 8C BC. At Amyklai, however, there is evidence of continuous occupation from perhaps 2000 BC. Hyakinthos seems to have been worshipped from the Bronze Age. Possibly he was a pre-Greek god of vegetation before his cult as a hero developed. The myth linking him to Apollo may be then be a deliberate absorption of the earlier cult by the Dorian Spartans.

To reach Amyklai, take the main road south from the centre of Sparta towards Githeo (Yithio, Γύθειο). Approaching the modern village of Amykles (Αμύκλες), a large blue sign in English indicates a left turn for the sanctuary. The site is 2km from the main road. After 100m bear left at an unsigned fork, then right at the next junction where there is a battered blue sign. The road leads more or less straight to the sanctuary with brown signs at intervals. A paved tree lined avenue ends at the church of Ayia Kiriaki, which stands in the centre of the sanctuary.

The site is unenclosed. As is often the case with sites of great archaeological importance, there is actually little to see. The sanctuary was probably built around an earth mound that formed the tomb of Hyakinthos. In the 6C BC, the so-called throne of Apollo was erected. This large altar was covered by stone-carved mythological scenes, described in detail by Pausanias. It supported an earlier statue of Apollo, in the curious form of a cylinder with a helmeted head and vestigial limbs holding a bow and spear.

Today only sections of retaining walls and fragmentary foundations remain. Again there are good views of the mountains across the plain.

Tegea
The bones of Orestes

The route north from Sparta towards Tripoli passes close by the site of ancient Tegea, once a large and important city. It is now known principally for the 4C BC temple of Athena Alea, on the site of the ancient cult centre of the region. This was the largest temple in the Peloponnese after that of Zeus at Olympia. It is still impressive today, although reduced to ruins.

The Tegeans traced their history back to the Bronze Age. Along with other contingents from Arcadia, they joined the forces that set out for Troy using sixty ships provided by Agamemnon. They played a major part in repulsing the first generation of the Heraclidae when they attempted to return to the Peloponnese. Echemus, the Tegean king, had led his forces north to the Isthmus of Corinth to engage the invaders. Hyllus, son of Hercules and Deianeira, suggested that instead of the mass slaughter of an all out battle, the claims of the Heraclidae should settled by single combat between himself and a champion chosen from the Peloponnesian forces. Echemus himself offered to meet the challenge and was accepted. He slew Hyllus and the Heraclidae withdrew. They did not return for two generations (see above).

Tegea ultimately lost its independence to Sparta, its powerful neighbour to the south. The story of the Spartan conquest is a complicated tale that mixes myth and historical fact. After the Spartans had subdued Messenia, they looked north to Arcadia for further conquests. Seeking religious legitimacy for their claim, they consulted the oracle at Delphi. She told them that Arcadia was beyond their reach but that she would give them Tegea to measure out. Taking this to mean that they would succeed in a war, the Spartans marched north in total confidence

of victory, taking with them chains with which to enslave their antici-
pated victims. However, the result was a victory for the Tegeans. The
captured Spartans found themselves fettered with their own chains.
They were forced to labour in Tegea's fields. It was in this sense that
they 'measured the land'. The Spartans, like so many before them, had
failed to understand the ambiguity of a Delphic prophecy.

After this setback, Sparta continued to wage war on the Tegeans suffering nothing but further defeats. Eventually, the oracle was consulted
again. This time the question was more specific; to which gods should
they sacrifice in order to overcome their foe? The answer was to find
the bones of the Bronze Age king and hero, Orestes, and re-bury them
in Sparta. Orestes, son of Agamemnon and Clytemnestra (see Chapter
8), had, towards the end of his reign, ruled a wide territory including
Mycenae, Argos, the greater part of Arcadia and Sparta. By retrieving
the remains of one of the last, great figures of the heroic age, the
Spartans of the 6C BC would have a mythical foundation for their goal
of political domination of the Peloponnese.

However the search for the bones was fruitless. Yet another visit to
the oracle produced a further enigmatic reply; the bones lay in the
ground beneath the Tegean plain, where 'two winds are forever blowing, where counter-stroke answers stroke and where evil lies upon evil'.
This prophecy seemed to offer no practical guidance, until one day a
Spartan named Lichas, who was in Tegea during a period of truce, happened to fall into conversation with a blacksmith in his forge. The smith
told him that while digging a well, he had come across a huge coffin
containing the bones of a giant of a man. Lichas realised that this must
be Orestes for the smithy matched the prophecy. Here two bellows were
perpetually blowing, the hammer and anvil provided stroke and coun-
terstroke and the forging of iron weapons was the evil. The bones were
re-buried in Sparta, in the agora, according to Pausanias. When the
Spartans and Tegeans fought again, Sparta at last triumphed. Tegea became a subordinate state but there was no attempt to enslave its people.
It was subject only to political control, as part of the Spartan led Peloponnesian League.

At a crossroads, about 10km south of Tripoli, a blue sign points right
to ancient Tegea and the village of Alea (Αλέα). The temple is in the
centre of this quiet village on the left of the road opposite the church.
The massive foundations lie below modern street level. The site is
fenced but unlocked. The temple dates from the 4C BC. It replaced an
earlier version destroyed by fire. Tegea was the birthplace of Atalanta,
the famous Arcadian heroine. Here in the temple were displayed the

211

trophies from the hunt for the Kalydonian boar (see Chapter 4). Originally both the tusks and the hide of the boar were displayed. Pausanias wrote in the 2C AD that he saw the hide 'rotted by age and completely without bristles'. By then the tusks, along with the image of Athena Alea itself had gone. They had been carried off to Rome by Augustus shortly after the battle of Actium (see Chapter 4). Here too hung the famous fetters brought by the Spartans. Both Pausanias and Herodotus, writing six centuries earlier, claimed to have seen them.

Like Sparta, Tegea grew from a collection of small villages scattered over the plain and was without walls for much of its early history. The city was extensive. It flourished well into the Roman period, was destroyed by the Goths, but was later reborn as the Byzantine city of Nikli. It was even the centre of a Frankish barony in the 13C AD. Glimpses of this later history, as well as the Classical theatre and agora, can be seen at Palaia Episkopi, about 1km to the north and well signposted from the temple. The continuity of occupation here could not be more graphically presented. A late 19C church is built on the remains of the Byzantine basilica of Nikli, which in turn is built on top of the ancient theatre, known to have been rebuilt in the 2C BC. The supporting wall for the auditorium can be seen encircling the church. An information board by the church identifies the scattered remains of the agora as well as other Roman and Byzantine work. The area is now the site of the annual Peloponnesian exhibition.

10

Athens

Although this book is primarily an exploration of the myths and landscapes of rural Greece, it would be incomplete without some mention of the mythology of Athens, its most important city. A brief description of the monuments connected to the myths follows. The numerous guidebooks to Athens provide all the practical information a visitor might require and it is unnecessary to repeat it here.

The Athenians of the Classical era believed that their ancestors had always lived in the territory of Attica. They referred to them as 'autochthonous', sons of the soil. Their great bronze-age hero was Theseus, most famous for his encounter with the Minotaur in the Labyrinth of Knossos. The myths of Theseus and his father Aegeus are related in Chapter 8. However the foundation myths of the city start many generations earlier. The first ruler of Attica was said to be Acteus, who named the area Actaea after himself. Acteus had a daughter, Agraulos, but no sons. On his death his throne passed to his son-in-law Kekrops, who is generally described as the founder of the city. His family's history is interwoven with that of Erichthonios, the other great figure from the earliest myths of Athens (see below).

As a son of the soil, Kekrops was said to be a son of Gaia, Mother Earth. Myth describes him as being half man and half serpent. He is supposed to have brought some of the first elements of order to society. He introduced marriage and the substitution of sweet cakes as offerings to the gods in place of live sacrifice. He was the first to acknowledge Zeus as the father of the gods. Kekrops was king during the famous dispute between Athena and Poseidon for the patronage of the land. An area on the Acropolis, now occupied by the complex shrine known as the Erechtheion, was the spot where the two gods made their claims and demonstrated their powers. Poseidon struck the ground with his trident and created a well of sea-water. Athena caused an olive tree to grow

213

from the bare rock. Zeus appointed the Olympian gods as arbiters in the dispute. They decided in favour of Athena who named the city after herself. When Kekrops died he left no male heirs and the kingship passed to Cranaus simply because he was the most powerful man in Athens. He named the territory of Athens, Attica, after his daughter Atthis. He was deposed by his son-in-law Amphictyon, who reigned for only twelve years, before being deposed in turn by Erichthonios.

Erichthonios was born during Kekrops's reign. The story of his birth is particularly strange. Athena had come to Hephaistos's smithy to ask him to make her a set of armour. Hephaistos was the god of fire and of metalworking. He was famed for his artistry and skill. He had fallen in love with Athena but she refused his advances. When he attempted to embrace her, she repulsed him, and he ejaculated against her thigh. Athena was revolted. She wiped his semen from her leg with wool and threw it to the ground. There his seed impregnated Gaia. Erichthonios was the result. Like Kekrops he was born of the earth.

Athena became his foster-mother and brought him up in secret in her precinct on the Acropolis. To conceal the child she hid him in a chest that she entrusted to Pandrosos, a daughter of Kekrops. Pandrosos was strictly forbidden to open the chest, but her two sisters, Herse and Agraulos, could not restrain their curiosity. They looked inside the chest and saw the infant with a snake coiled about him. The serpent had been placed there by Athena to protect the child. Other versions of the myth make the child himself part serpent. In her anger at the sisters' actions, Athena drove them mad and they threw themselves from the Acropolis.

When he grew to manhood Erichthonios deposed Amphictyon and assumed the kingship. He was believed to have founded the Athenians' most important religious festival, the Panathenaia, and to have erected the famous olive-wood statue of Athena on the Acropolis. He is supposed to have taught the Athenians how to smelt silver, yoke horses and the use of the plough. Erichthonios was succeeded by his son, Pandion, who himself had two sons, Erechtheus and Boutes. When Pandion died, his sons divided his legacy between them. Erechtheus assumed the temporal element, the kingship, while Boutes received the priesthood of Athena and Poseidon. His family were to provide priests on the Acropolis thereafter.

Erechtheus was succeeded by his eldest son, another Kekrops. He in turn was followed by his son, Pandion, the father of Aegeus and grandfather to Theseus. The recurrence of the names of Kekrops and Pandion, and the similarity between those of Erichthonios and Erechtheus suggest that generations may have been invented to provide a continuous genealogy from the first Kekrops to Aegeus and Theseus. Nevertheless the key figures in these stories, Kekrops, Pandrosos, Hephaistos, Erichthonios-Erechtheus and Boutes, were all represented in the cult centres established on the Acropolis.

The dramatic outline of the Athenian Acropolis, surmounted by the ruin of the Parthenon, is the defining image of modern Greece. Although Athens is now a vast urban sprawl, home to almost half of Greece's population, the Acropolis remains, as it always has been, at the core of the city. It is also the centre of the relatively compact archaeological area and the best place from which to understand the layout of the classical city. The majority of the major historical sites are visible from the Acropolis walls.

Built into the southern slopes of the Acropolis are two theatres. To the west is the 2C BC Roman Odeion of Herod of Attica. This well preserved structure was originally roofed and its restored seating is used for modern performances. To the east is the sanctuary and theatre of Dionysus. Here was held the festival of the Great Dionysia. The myths of Dionysus's birth and the introduction of his worship to Athens from Eleutherai are described in Chapter 2. Between the theatres are the remains of an Asklepion. This sanctuary of Asklepios was created after a great plague in 429 BC. As at Epidavros, the sanctuary was a healing centre. The birth myths and cult of Asklepios are described in Chapters 6 and 8. To the north of the Acropolis lie substantial remains from Roman Athens: the market with its monumental Doric-columned entrance; the ruins of Hadrian's library and the Tower of the Winds, a combined sundial, water clock and wind indicator. The classical agora lies to the west of its Roman counterpart. Archaeological work began in the 1930's and the area has now been cleared to its original levels. On the east side of the agora is the Stoa of Attalos, reconstructed in 1956. This two-storey building now houses the agora museum. The original was completed around 150 BC. Its accurate reconstruction provides a unique view of a form of building so characteristic of a Greek city. Further west again stands the striking Doric temple of Hephaistos. This temple, built in the 5C BC, is also called the Theseion, although it is now known to have no connection with Theseus. It was used as a Christian church for thirteen centuries. As a result, externally at least, it is virtually complete.

According to Homer, Hephaistos was the son of Zeus and Hera, although Hesiod claimed that Hephaistos had no father, and that Hera bore him independently. However he was born lame and weak. Hera

215

was ashamed of him and threw down from Olympus so that he fell into the sea. There he was rescued by the sea goddesses, Thetis and Eurynome. He lived with them for nine years in a cave beneath Oceanus, the waters that the Greeks believed surrounded the earth. Although he was a smith and is often depicted in his workshop with its giant anvil and the bellows that worked for him of their own accord, he was also a great artist. During his time with Thetis he created large amounts of beautiful jewellery. Although a goddess, Thetis had been forced by Zeus to marry a mortal, Peleus, and had borne him a son. This was Achilles, the great hero of the Trojan War. After Hephaistos had returned to Olympus, Thetis came to him to ask that he make a suit of armour for Achilles. Homer describes in great detail the marvellous inlaid shield that Hephaistos forged. The temple of Hephaistos stood in an area of the city devoted to metalworking. His importance to the Athenians was as the father of Erichthonios. Today the temple stands as the best-preserved example of the Doric style in existence.

The whole area of the agora between the Stoa of Attalos and the Hephaistion is a mass of excavated foundations and now appears surprisingly rural. Through the agora ran the Sacred Way, the route of the Panathenaic procession to the Acropolis. This procession began at the Sacred Gate, a little to the northwest, in the area known as the Kerameikos. Here are the remains of the most substantial portion of the ancient city walls still visible. The procession carrying the sacred objects to Elefsis passed through the Sacred Gate (see Chapter 2), as did the procession that began the festival of the Great Dionysia (see also Chapter 2). Connected to the west slopes of the Acropolis is the low hill of the Areopagus where justice was dispensed by councils of the city's elders. Although first used for this purpose in the 7C BC, myth describes the trial of Ares for murder here. Hallirhothios, a son of Poseidon, attempted to rape Alcippe, Ares's daughter by Agraulos. Ares slew him in her defence. At his trial by the other Olympian gods he was acquitted and the hill was named after him. Orestes was also supposedly tried here for the murder of his mother Clytemnestra (see Chapter 8). A cave on the northeastern flanks of the hill is thought to be a sanctuary of the Furies and the site of the tomb of Oedipus.

To the east of the Acropolis are the remains of the monumental temple of Zeus completed in 130 AD in the reign of Hadrian. Further east again, between two low hills lies the stadium. Originally built for the games of the Panathenaic Festival, it was restored with marble seating in 144 AD by Herod of Attica. Following its excavation at the close of the 19C, its reconstruction in marble was completed in 1906. With the exception of the modern running track, it must appear now much as it did in 130 AD.

The Acropolis was the site of the city's original settlement and has been occupied since Neolithic times. It became a fortified palace settlement in the Mycenaean period and was reputed to have been untouched by the Dorian invasions. However by the beginning of the classical era the settlement had outgrown its origins on the rock and the Acropolis acquired a purely religious function in the centre of a vastly enlarged city. The principal visible monuments of the Acropolis itself comprise the monumental gateway of the Propylaia, the small temple of Athena Nike, the Erechtheion and the Parthenon. The Parthenon was completed in 438 BC. It was conceived primarily as a work of art and also housed the state treasury. Although it is the largest and best-known structure on the Acropolis, it was not the religious centre despite its status as the temple of Athena the virgin. This distinction belonged to the area occupied by the Erechtheion, a complex building not completed until 406 BC but designed to incorporate the original Mycenaean cult sites.

All of the elements of the foundation myths described above had a physical counterpart within the Erechtheion. Today only the bare shell of the building, much reconstructed, remains. Although Pausanias described all of the cult objects to be found there, their exact locations are still the subject of much debate. The best-known element of this complicated structure is now the Porch of the Caryatids, named after the six stone maidens that support the porch's entablature. It stands at the southwest corner of the building. The foundations at this point are believed to incorporate the original Tomb of Kekrops. On the opposite side of the building, the North Porch has in the rock beneath its floor three marks said to represent either the blow from Poseidon's trident, or a thunderbolt from Zeus. An opening in the roof above was left to symbolize the path of the trident. Immediately to the east of the Erechtheion was the Sanctuary of Pandrosos. Within its precinct stood the olive tree that Athena had brought forth from the bare rock. Herodotus describes how the tree was burnt down during the Persian sack of Athens but produced a new shoot four feet long the following day. The tree to be seen now was planted in 1917. Between the two porches stands the central structure of the Erechtheion, in plan a simple rectangle but built to incorporate a dramatic change in ground level from north to south. Within stood the shrine to Athena of the city, Athena Polias, with its olive-wood statue of the goddess. Here too was a wooden statue of Hermes, said to have been dedicated by Kekrops. Pausanias lists the other altars

217

that stood here, to Poseidon, Hephaistos and Boutes. At the altar to Poseidon sacrifices were also made to Erechtheus. He also describes Poseidon's sea-water well inside the building and notes how the sound of waves could be heard when a southerly wind blew.

The procession of the Great Panathenaia ended at the Erechtheion. The festival was held every four years. Traditionally founded by Erichthonios it was renewed by Theseus. By the 6C BC it had expanded to include Panhellenic games. A smaller scale version of the festival, known as the Lesser Panathenaia, was held in the intervening years. The purpose of the procession was to bring to the wooden statue of Athena a new peplos, a dress or robe. For the first part of the procession, from the Sacred Gate through the agora to the foot of the Acropolis, the robe was carried on a wheeled boat, before being carried by hand up the steep approach. This is the procession represented by Pheidias on the Parthenon frieze.

Chronology

5500 BC	First settlement at Lerna
2500	Lerna re-occupied
2300	Lerna destroyed
1800-1700	First settlement at Elefsis
1650	Shaft graves at Mycenae
1350	Treasury of Atreus constructed
1300	Mycenaean drainage project at Gla
1200	Gla abandoned
1184	Traditional date of the Trojan War
1200-1100	Collapse of Mycenaean civilisation
1100	Sanctuary of Pelops appears at Olympia
900	Beginning of Geometric period
776	Traditional date of the first Olympiad
750-720	Composition of the Iliad
720	End of first Messenian War. Subjugation of Messenians by Sparta
700	Possible date of Hesiod's Theogeny
700	Beginning of Archaic period
685-668	Second Messenian War
648	Horse racing introduced at Olympia
630	Temple of Apollo erected at Thermo
625	War between Argos and Sparta
600	Temple of Hera built at Olympia
595-586	First Sacred War for control of Delphi
584-582	Founding of Isthmian Games
573	Founding of Nemean Games
490	Beginning of Classical period
490	Persians defeated at Marathon
486	Death of Darius
480	Destruction of Plataia by Persians

Chronology

480-479	Persians defeated at Salamis and Plataia
465	New temple built at Isthmia
464-455	Third Messenian War
460-446	First Peloponnesian War
455	Nafpaktos taken by Athens and given to Messsenians
455	Oiniadai besieged by Messenians of Nafpaktos
447-438	Parthenon built
443-429	Age of Pericles
431-404	Second Peloponnesian War
427	Destruction of Plataia by Spartans
420	Temple of Apollo at Bassai erected
420-410	'New' temple built at the Argive Heraion
418	First battle of Mantinea. Sparta defeats Athens and allies
410	Chariot races introduced at Olympia
404	Triumph of Sparta
403-377	Period of Spartan power
395-386	Corinthian War
385	Spartans destroy Mantinea
373	Thebans destroy Plataia
371	Spartans defeated at battle of Leuctra by Thebans
371-362	Period of Theban ascendancy
371-369	Construction of Megalopolis
369	Messene built and Messenians liberated
364	Orchomenos destroyed by Thebes
362	Sparta defeated by Thebes at Second Battle of Mantinea. Death of Epaminondas
357-355	Social War and Sacred War
349	Orchomenos again destroyed by Thebes
339	Amphissa destroyed by Philip II
338	Macedonian victory at battle of Chaironia
337	Philip II founds Corinthian League
336	Assassination of Philip II
335	Revolt and destruction of Thebes
330	Stadium and second Temple built at Nemea
323	Death of Alexander the Great in Babylon
323	Beginning of Hellenistic period
323	Athens and Aetolia in revolt against Macedon. War of Lamia.Thermo sacked by Antipater.
316	Thebes restored by Kassander
314	Stratos falls to Kassander

303	Sikyon destroyed by Demetrios Poliorketes and immediately refounded
279	Gauls invade Macedon and Greece
277	Defeat of Gauls. Domination of Aetolian League
263	Partition of Akarnania
242	Aratos of Sikyon takes Corinth
239	War between Macedon and the Achaian and Aetolian leagues
234	Pleuron destroyed by Demetrios II
218&206	War of the Leagues. Thermo sacked by Philip V
197	Defeat of Philip V by Romans
167	Romans sack Dodona
146	Corinth razed to the ground by Roman General Mummius
44	Romans re-found Corinth
44	Julius Caesar assassinated
31	Octavian defeats Anthony at Battle of Actium. Founding of Nikopolis
30	Antony and Cleopatra commit suicide
18-23 BC	Strabo - Geography
130 AD	Temple of Zeus in Athens completed by Hadrian
180	Approximate date of Pausanias's Guide to Greece
324	Foundation of Constantinople
380	Christianity becomes official religion of the Roman Empire
395	Vandals plunder Nikopolis
410	Alaric – Vandals sack Rome
527-565	Reign of Justinian
1204	Fall of Constantinople to 4th Crusade
1453	Fall of Constantinople to Ottoman Turks
1571	Battle of Lepanto
1825	Byron dies at Mesolonghi
1827	Battle of Navarino
1828-34	Nauplion first capital of Greece
1834	Athens becomes capital of modern Greece

Bibliography

Classical Sources

Although almost all the works listed below continue to be published in Penguin, Everyman, the Loeb Classical Library and other editions, the full texts are now also available online. References below are to these freely available sources:

P - Perseus Digital Library, www.perseus.tufts.edu
C - Internet Classics Archive, http://classics.mit.edu
G - Project Gutenberg , www.gutenberg.org
M – Online Mediaeval and Classical Library, http://omacl.org

Aeschylus, (525-456 BC), Agamemnon, Eumenides, Libation-Bearers, Prometheus Bound, Seven Against Thebes, Suppliant Women, *P, C.*

Apollodorus, (c. 140 BC), Library, *P.*

Euripides, (480-406 BC), Bacchae, Cyclops, Electra, Heraclidae, Heracles, Hippolytus, Iphigenia in Aulis, Iphigenia in Tauris, Medea, Orestes, The Phoenician Women, Suppliants, *P, C.*

Herodotus, (484-430 BC), The Histories, *P, C, G.*

Hesiod, (c. 700 BC), Shield of Heracles, Theogony, Works and Days, *P, G, M.*

Homer, (750-720 BC), Iliad, Odyssey, *P, C, G.*

The Homeric Hymns including the Hymn to Demeter, *P, G, M.*

Ovid, (43 BC–18 AD), Metamorphoses, *P, C.*

Pausanias, (c. 180 AD), Description of Greece, *P, C.*

Pindar, (522-442 BC), Odes, *P, G.*

Polybius, (200–118 BC), The Rise of the Roman Empire, http://penelope.uchicago.edu/Thayer/E/Roman/Texts/Polybius/

Sophocles, (495-406 BC), Antigone, Electra, Oedipus at Colonus, Trachinae, *P, C, G.*

Strabo, (64 BC–25 AD), Geography, *P.*

Bibliography

Thucydides, (460–400 BC), History of the Peloponnesian War, *P, C, G.*
Xenophon, (c.420–350 BC), Hellenica or A History of My Times, *P, G.*

Modern Sources

Carl Kerenyi, Eleusis: Archetypal Image of Mother and Daughter, Princeton University Press, Bollingen series.
Deborah Lyons, Heroines in Ancient Greek Myth and Cult, Online text: http://pup.princeton.edu/books/lyons.
R.E. Wycherley, How the Greeks Built Cities, W.W. Norton and Co.
Jon D. Mikalson, Ancient Greek Religion, Blackwell publishing.

General summaries of the myths

Robert Graves, The Greek Myths, Penguin.
Rex Warner, The Stories of the Greeks, Farrar, Straus and Giroux.

Guidebooks

The Blue Guide to Greece, Somerset Books.
Rough Guide to Greece.

Index

224